T0283248

Only
in America

Only
in America

AL JOLSON
AND
THE JAZZ SINGER

Richard Bernstein

Alfred A. Knopf   New York

THIS IS A BORZOI BOOK
PUBLISHED BY ALFRED A. KNOPF

www.aaknopf.com

Knopf, Borzoi Books, and the colophon are registered trademarks
of Penguin Random House LLC.

Library of Congress Cataloging-in-Publication Data
Name: Bernstein, Richard, [date] author.
Title: Only in America : Al Jolson and the jazz singer / Richard Bernstein.
Description: First edition. | New York : Alfred A. Knopf, 2024. | Includes index.
Identifiers: LCCN 2023006774 (print). | LCCN 2023006775 (ebook). |
ISBN 9780805243673 (hardcover). | ISBN 9780805243680 (ebook).
Subjects: LCSH: Jolson, Al, 1886–1950. | Jazz singer (Motion picture : 1927). |
Singers—United States—Biography. | Entertainers—United States—Biography. |
Jewish singers—United States—Biography. | Jewish entertainers—United
States—Biography.
Classification: LCC ML420.J74 B47 2024 (print) | LCC ML420.J74 (ebook) |
DDC 782.0092 B—dc23/eng/20230522
LC record available at https://lccn.loc.gov/2023006774
LC ebook record available at https://lccn.loc.gov/2023006775

Jacket photograph by Scotty Welbourne / Photofest
Jacket design by Rex Bonomelli

Manufactured in Canada

First Edition

To Herbert Bernstein, in loving memory,
and Elias Bernstein

Of life immense in passion, pulse, and power,
Cheerful, for freest action form'd under the laws divine,
The Modern Man I sing.

—Walt Whitman, *Leaves of Grass*

I too believe you are entirely blameless in the matter of our
estrangement. But I am equally entirely blameless. If I could get
you to acknowledge this, then what would be possible is—not,
I think, a new life, we are both much too old for that—but still
a kind of peace; no cessation, but still, a diminution of your
unceasing reproaches.

—Franz Kafka, *Letter to the Father*

Contents

Preface   xi

1. The Risky Dreams of the Fathers   3

2. The Fraught Triumphs of the Sons   16

3. Street Singers   25

4. A Power Beyond Himself   39

5. The Good Story   61

6. Different and the Same   73

7. From Lithuania to "Alabammy"   92

8. Warner Bros. Takes a Chance   120

9. "A highly unlikely prospect for immortality"   131

10. "The cry of my race"   145

11. It Played in Paducah   158

12. Stars Crossing   175

13. The Final Decade   189

14. The Afterlife   202

    Epilogue   217

Acknowledgments   221
Notes   225
Index   241

Preface

Only in America—it's the idea that things, mostly good ones, happen in the United States that don't and didn't happen in any other country, at least not on the American scale. It's the idea that only two conditions need be met for limitless, extravagant riches and fame—talent and the freedom to exercise it. It's not who you know but what you are, the content of your character, that counts.

I use Al Jolson as an example. He has faded considerably from the public consciousness in the seventy-two years since his death in 1950, his style outmoded, some features of it retrograde, cringe-worthy. I speak of his appearance in blackface, a fraught topic to be addressed in due course. But in his heyday, from roughly 1912 to 1934, there was nobody who dominated the public space more than did this slim, rather ordinary-looking man of colossal energy, ambition, and ability. In baseball there was Babe Ruth, Charlie Chaplin in silent movies, Houdini as a magician, Enrico Caruso in opera—and Al Jolson in popular song. "There was nobody as good as Jolson," the comedian George Burns once said. "When he got through, you forgot there had been anybody on before him."

"To call him the biggest hunk in entertainment was an under-statement," his friend and rival Eddie Cantor, also a star of stage and screen, said at his funeral. "He was the only entertainer who was his own lighting and his own scenery."

Where does "only in America" come into this? Jolson's story is the American immigration story at its best, the escape from a place where a rise to fame and fortune like his would have been impossible to a place where such a rise defined what the country considered special about itself. Jolson was born in a small, mostly Jewish town in Lithuania, then part of the vast, Jew-hating Russian Empire. He came to America in the last years of the nineteenth century, when he was nine years old. His name then was Asa Yoelson. His language was Yiddish. He lost his mother in the first year of his American life, struggled against a strict father immured in the ways of the Old Country, and then, within about fifteen years, had become the most famous and highly paid popular entertainer in America. He was the biggest star of musical theater, on Broadway and in the dozens and dozens of other places he played across the country. In 1927, he starred in a movie about Jews, *The Jazz Singer,* made by the Jews who created Hollywood but who rarely made movies about Jews, that became a national sensation. Its main themes, drawn from Jolson's own life, were generational difference, the conflict between father and son, tradition and modernity, freedom and obligation, and it struck a chord. It was a "Jewish movie," complete with authentic-looking synagogue scenes and the chanting of Hebrew prayers, and though it played in an America that still stoked many of the ancient hatreds (Henry Ford's antisemitic newspaper, *The Dearborn Independent,* for example, had the second-highest daily circulation in the country), it crossed over to all races and creeds. Gentiles of all varieties saw something poignantly, universally meaningful in its main themes. And it made Jolson, the poor boy from Lithuania, even richer and more famous.

Is there any other country where that could have happened? Perhaps on an individual level. There were fortunes made by Jews in England, Germany, and France, celebrities like Sarah Bernhardt, writers like Marcel Proust, bankers like the Baron de Rothschild, medical scientists like Sigmund Freud, political leaders like Léon Blum and Walter Rathenau, and, to go back to an earlier generation, Benjamin Disraeli. But what a figure like Jolson and a movie like *The Jazz Singer* represented is the mass nature of this kind of occurrence. Asa Yoelson/Al Jolson was part of a cohort of entertainers whose roots were in the Russian Empire and who came nearly to dominate American popular culture, remaking themselves and remaking the country in the process. It's hard to imagine anything like that happening any place but in these United States of America.

Perhaps a personal note, the only one you'll find in this book, would be apt here. Like Asa Yoelson, my father, Herschel Bernstein, aka Herb, was born in the Pale of Settlement, that zone of territory, much of which is no longer part of Russia, where Jews were once allowed to live in the Russian Empire, even as they were persecuted, excluded from the universities and the liberal professions, and subject to the all-too-common spasms of murder, pillage, and vandalism known as pogroms. Herschel escaped under a pile of hay in a wagon that crossed the border into Poland in 1920. He arrived in New York in 1922 and lived in Corona, Queens, at the very end of the mass immigration of huddling masses from eastern Europe. My father fought bitterly with his father, a deeply Orthodox man whom I imagine to be something like Al Jolson's father and many other fathers who came to America to preserve the traditional Jewish way of life and were disappointed in sons who wanted to forge something new and different. The fights between my father and his father became so violent that my father

XIV   PREFACE

was sent away to a Jewish farm school in Pennsylvania so that, as my grandmother used to tell me, the two wouldn't kill each other in their mutual fury and disillusionment.

Then my grandfather died, leaving my father, about twenty years old, liberated in a way, but also burdened with guilt over his refusal to live up to his father's expectations, which was his enactment of Jolson's anguish in *The Jazz Singer*. He was also now responsible for the economic survival of his mother and his younger brother and sister. He didn't become a jazz singer but, after serving as a heavy artillery gunner in the United States Army in World War II, he bought a modest poultry farm in rural Connecticut, where we had everything we needed. My mother, Clare Brown, was born in Kishvarda, a town in Hungary near the Ukrainian border, where her grandfather and great-grandfather were bakers. She came to America by coincidence in the same year as my father. Within a year, she had lost her father—and her three sisters—to pneumonia. She lived with what was left of her family above a hardware store in Astoria, also in Queens. Like my father, higher education for her was out of the question, though her brother and her two half brothers went to college. There was no inclination to pay for a girl's college education.

I belong to the next generation, the made-it-in-America generation. I have the incredible good fortune to be able to write articles and books for a living. Like many of you, dear readers, I am an American at the time in world history when more Jews (and many others) live in conditions of freedom, security, and prosperity than at any other time since the era of the Second Temple in Jerusalem two thousand years ago.

In writing these words, I don't think I'm naive, or afflicted with Panglossian optimism, or with maudlin sentimentality, or that I'm unaware of the ongoing critique of American life in the liberal circles in which I live. I'm well aware that there's still antisemitism, which, at the time of this writing, December 2022, has been on the rise, with some prominent figures reiterating the age-old calumnies. More broadly, there's racism, poverty, and inequality, the heritage of our original sin of slavery, as well as gun violence, political discord, and shocking misbehavior, especially by a certain former president and his followers. I'm also aware, when it comes to Jolson, that his entry into the cultural pantheon rested on a sentimentalized portrayal of blackness that, like the burnt cork he used to mask his Jewish face, masked the racist history of the country. Jews like Jolson illustrate the "only in America" theme of the book, but it worked for them in part because they didn't have the burden of Black skin.

There's plenty of darkness to remember, in other words, and plenty to worry about—and I do worry—but I also know that I'm lucky, and I'm grateful. I think that "only in America" applies to me. That's one of the reasons I wanted to write this book, not about me, but about another person, illustrative of his generation, which was collectively the first in the great Jewish migration from Russia to whom the only-in-America idea was real. The other reason was my wonder at the fact that refugees from the Pale of Settlement glowed so brightly in the American culture. What a difference between them and the ones who stayed behind.

Only
in America

1

The Risky Dreams of the Fathers

Asa Yoelson was born in 1886 in Seredzius, an insignificant village, a shtetl, now in independent Lithuania but at the time just a speck in the sprawling, autocratic Russian Empire. Seredzius in Lithuanian, Srednik in Yiddish, Sredniki in Russian. It wasn't a terrible place as those kinds of places went during the time when Jews in the Russian Empire were restricted to the Pale of Settlement, much of which is in current-day Ukraine, Belarus, Lithuania, and Poland. The Jews lived under the twin and related curses of poverty and the "normal" antisemitism of Russia, the contempt and suspicions of Jews ordinary at that time and in that place, the Jews as the despised murderers of Christ who needed the blood of Christian children to accomplish their secret dark rituals. It's not by accident that the word "pogrom" is the Russian word for devastation.

There were no recorded pogroms in Seredzius, which lay on the north bank of the Niemen River as it flows westward to the Baltic Sea about a hundred miles away. There was a single meandering, unpaved, often mud-choked street parallel to the river that was lined with cottages of thatched roofs and earthen floors, about a hundred of them. There were a few shops, an orthodox church, a common well, and, reflecting the large Jewish population, two synagogues built of wood, one for everyday use and the other for feast days and holidays. Seredzius was an owned village, meaning that it was the property of a Russian nobleman who lived in a nearby manor and who, when he rode by in his horse-drawn carriage, would arouse the excitement of Asa and his older brother, Hirsch.

According to Hirsch, the gentiles of Seredzius were "gentle and tolerant folk." There was no "violent persecution." Still, there's that rabbinical blessing in *Fiddler on the Roof,* which takes place in a fictitious shtetl for which Seredzius could have been the model, "May the Lord bless and keep the Czar"—a pause here—"far away from us." The Jews of Seredzius may have been spared pogroms, but surely they knew of those that had taken place elsewhere, in Kiev, Kishinev, Kropyvnytskyi, Odessa, and dozens of other places in the Pale following the assassination of Czar Alexander II in 1881, an act falsely and maliciously blamed on Jews and that ended the brief period of relative liberalism toward them that Alexander had fostered. But even if the Jews of Seredzius were not the victims of mob violence, their shops vandalized, their homes set on fire, the corpses of their children laid out for mass burial as happened elsewhere, they were aware of Jewish vulnerability in Jew-hating Russia. And their lives were constricted and precarious in other ways besides the threat of violence against them.

The very name Yoelson stems from that fact. During the reigns of Alexander II and his antisemitic successor, Alexander III, young men starting at the age of twenty had to serve for five years in the army, except for one boy in each family. This was already an improvement on the conscription of earlier times in Russia, when boys were conscripted at the age of twelve and made to serve for as much as twenty-five years, if they survived that long. Those five years were still an unwelcome intrusion into the lives of poor families, though the hardship was mitigated by a kind of corrupt black market in fake documents identifying a boy as the only boy in his family and thereby exempt from military service.

Asa's grandfather, Meyer Hesselman, a shoe merchant from a village in what is now Latvia, had five sons. He was well enough off to purchase certificates for at least two of them, falsely identifying them as the sole sons of fictitious families. One of these sons was Asa's father, Moshe Reuben Hesselman, who took the name Yoelson. Two of the other Hesselman brothers, Asa's uncles, fled to America before they were twenty. There, one shortened his name to Hessel, the other, a rabbi in Chicago, to Hess.

Moshe, the newly minted Yoelson, dreamed as a young man of being an opera singer, which is something of a paradox given that all his later life, even after Asa became Al Jolson, the celebrated American star of vaudeville, Broadway, and movies, he was outspoken in his contempt of the theater, which he viewed as lower-class, mediocre, unkosher. Paradoxical or not, there's something veritably oracular about this dream of Moshe, which, if carried out, would have brought him into the secular, non-Jewish world that was the stuff of both nightmares and fantasies in the Russian Empire, the place of glamour and near unattainable ambition where Jewishness was destroyed. The Yiddish literary archive contains a nineteenth-century legend of one Yoel-David Levinshteyn-Strashunsky, famous from the age of eleven as a cantor in Vilna, who ruined his life by running off to Vienna with a Polish singer. A play based on the legend, *Der Vilner Balebesl,* by Mark Arnshteyn, first performed in 1902, became a staple of the Yiddish theater in the 1920s. In it, the cantor forsakes the synagogue to become an opera singer in Warsaw, where he falls in love with a non-Jewish Polish woman, leading to his repudiation by his father and the Jewish community. As J. Hoberman, a chronicler of the Yiddish theater and cinema, has written, the play "embodies the paradox of the Jewish artist, torn between traditional imperatives and a desire to participate in the culture of the West." Not entirely by coincidence, Hoberman notes that "the

archetypal Yiddish stage performer is a cantor's son or daughter,"
this phenomenon being a product of the blurring of the bound-
aries in Jewish immigrant America between the celebrity hazan,
cantor, and the theater.

We don't know how strong Moshe's operatic dreams were. We
do know that he learned to sing the Hebrew liturgy and went to
live with an uncle in the Kedainiai District, a railroad junction
(and the birthplace of the Nobel laureate Czesław Miłosz) not far
from Seredzius. There, he sang in synagogue services to earn the
money that he hoped to use to further his operatic education.
The quality of his voice and his scholarly appearance attracted
the attention of a prosperous village notable named Asa Cantor,
who invited him to his house for Shabbos dinner, and with that
Moshe's life took a decisive turn.

At the dinner, he met Reb Asa's daughter, Naomi. In two
weeks, they were married, "with elaborate ceremony and great
feasting," according to Hirsch. While still living under the village
notable's roof a year later, the couple had their first child, Rose.
Now blessed and burdened with a wife and family, Moshe gave up
his operatic ambition and studied to become a rabbi instead. His
father-in-law, in part by making a donation to the community
bathhouse, helped get him a position as the cantor of the Jewish
community of Seredzius.

More children came along, a girl named Etta, Hirsch, and,
after a third daughter died in infancy, Asa, born around May 25,
1886—the exact date is unknown—and named for his grandfather. "With such a lusty voice, I'm sure he'll be a great cantor,"
Moshe said of him.

Moshe's modest salary meant that the Yoelson family lived
a spare life, though probably somewhat less spare than many of
the other Jews of Seredzius. When Asa was born, they crowded
into a three-room house with a thatch roof and an earthen floor,

which was sprinkled with sand and hemlock needles on Shabbos, to provide adornments of cleanliness and fragrance on the day of rest. After a while, they were able to move to the unoccupied half of a larger house, owned by a well-off, kindly lumber merchant with a heavy black beard and long hair named Haym Yossi, a house whose rare luxury was its wooden floor. There was no public school in Seredzius, so every day a tutor came to the house and taught Hirsch and Asa secular subjects, such as Russian grammar—most important—and some German and English. Expecting both of his sons to grow up to be cantors, Moshe trained them in voice, thereby unwittingly preparing them to be Hoberman's archetypal Yiddish stage performers, except, from Moshe's standpoint, even worse: archetypal Jewish musical comedy entertainers in America. The lessons were serious. Moshe put matchsticks, clipped of their phosphorus tips, just behind the boys' front teeth to force them to open their mouths wide, "so our vocal tones could issue unrestricted through wide-open spaces," Hirsch said later.

Jews had lived for hundreds of years in the territories between the Baltic and the Black Seas where internally, according to the literary and social critic Irving Howe, they were a "ragged kingdom of the spirit" that comprised "a society, impoverished and imperiled." The main distinction among them—Howe again—was between "the poor and the hopelessly poor," but they valued two things above all: one, the rituals by which they preserved their identity as a people separate from those trying to force them to give up that identity, and two, learning, which meant Jewish learning, the study of the ancient texts. Seredzius wasn't big or rich enough to house a yeshiva, an actual Jewish school, and this was in its way fortunate for Hirsch and Asa. Despite their strictly Orthodox father and his yearning for his sons to devote themselves to Jewish life, there was no chance for them to be among

those pale and sickly boys in larger cities like Kovno and Vilna
who spent their days bent over books in some yeshiva presided
over by a rigid and reactionary melamed, or teacher. Hirsch and
Asa were ritually observant, Yiddish-speaking, and thoroughly
schooled in the Hebrew liturgy, so much so that even decades
later, when they warmed up their voices, they sang the Hebrew
Sabbath prayers. Yet they were not deprived of the exhilarating
physicality of boyhood, even as they lived lives whose every detail,
as Hirsch remembered, "was governed by the Law," meaning the
Mosaic law imposed by their father.

They went to the synagogue for prayers three times a day;
they had one hour a day of heder, a Jewish primary school, smaller,
more basic, and for children younger than those at a yeshiva, where
they would have studied Hebrew and some Torah. Moshe threatened them with beatings if they forgot to put on tzitzit, fringes
on the four corners of an undergarment, to remind them of the
613 commandments a Jew is supposed to observe, including the
wearing of tzitzit. Whenever they entered the house, their fingers
grazed the mezuzah, the small, decorated wooden or silver box
containing a sacred inscription that was nailed to the doorposts of
all Jewish homes. They said the Shema every night before going to
bed—"Hear, O Israel, the Lord our God, the Lord, is One." On
Shabbos there was no cooking, no touching of money, no sewing or tearing of paper or cloth, no riding a horse or carriage, no
lighting a fire even in the coldest of winter. But there were those
hemlock needles on the floor, the glow of candles, the rich Friday
night dinner, the music of the blessings, and the weekly reading
of the Torah in shul. On Passover, other families, including some
gentiles, would stop in front of the windows of the Yoelson house,
kept open intentionally, so they could hear Moses and the boys
perform the seder prayers and rituals, a premonition of the crowds
that would fill theaters to hear Asa sing popular songs in America.

As the youngest child, he chanted the traditional four questions. He was, no doubt, very good.

To supplement his modest income, Moshe served as village shohet, or ritual slaughterer, the work consisting largely of following the strict procedures outlined in the Jewish law for the killing mostly of chickens and geese brought to him for the purpose. The custom of the time was for the woman of the house who brought the fowl for slaughter to give a chicken or goose leg to the shohet, which meant that a stew of bird legs was common fare for the Yoelson family. Once, in a well-intentioned gesture, a woman cut off the leg of a goose to give to Moshe before the ceremonial killing was complete, which meant that it was no longer kosher. "It was a serious loss for the poor woman," Hirsch recalled, since the woman and her family could no longer eat the bird, "but the law is inexorable."

There were charms to the lives of young boys in Seredzius. Not all was Torah study and the strictness of the law. Hirsch wrote of the snow in winter when "droshkies and sleighs sped through the village street accompanied by the merry music of bells." Water for drinking and washing came every day from the village well, brought by a man and a woman with their buckets suspended from a yoke—two kopeks a bucket. In winter, when the Niemen froze over, Hirsch and Asa went out on wooden skates and watched as men cut out blocks of ice to be stored in straw for the summer. In the spring, when the ice on the river broke into large floating blocks, they tried to leap from one to the other, often falling into the ice-cold water and having to be brought home for a warm blanket and a scolding. In the spring, they picked wild strawberries, abundant in the meadows near the village; in summer they picked cherries. Steamboats, impressive sights, went up the river to Kovno, but the 50-kopeck fare (35 cents) made going there impossible, except for one memorable time when a price war between steamboat companies drove the price to 5 kopecks, allowing the only excursion outside Seredzius that the family ever made in the nine years that Asa lived there.

Despite his favorable portrait of the "gentle and tolerant folk" of Seredzius and the absence of "actual suffering from want," Hirsch allows that the Jews endured many "annoyances and humiliations from officials and army officers." Most notably, a "terrorizing official" would show up every year to tell each family how many soldiers would be billeted in their home during an annual training encampment that took place in the village, marking the number in chalk on the door. For a few weeks, there would be the music of a military band and the sound of soldiers marching in the town square and firing their weapons in practice drills.

Hirsch doesn't give a very rich portrait of his kid brother, Asa, in these early years, but what does come across in his minimal description is Asa's scrappiness, and the description is believable given that even in America Al at times settled quarrels and grievances with his fists. As children, the two boys fought ferociously but always defended each other "from the attacks of outsiders." Their aggression turned Asa into "a little demon, tearing into [another boy] with fist, tooth, and claw." Prefiguring the chronically restless man of later years, he says that Asa "would drop a thing half finished in order to take up another." He could never have been "satisfied with a career that called for order, persistence, and faithfulness to a given task."

The Jews of Lithuania, who numbered something under a million at the end of the nineteenth century, were by no means a homogeneous group. In fact, the last half of the century was a period of ferment and division for the Jews. Notions of Haskalah, the Jewish Enlightenment, were spreading through the larger cities of the Pale—places like Kovno, Vilnius, Minsk, Odessa,

and Warsaw—a repudiation of the medieval Dark Ages of insular
Jewish life. Jews needed to become modern citizens of the world,
their collective nose no longer buried in the ancient texts of an
Iron Age tribe. The movement, somewhat paradoxically, revived
biblical Hebrew as the preferred literary language of the Jews, and
at the same time encouraged modern, secular learning so they
would be equipped for success in the non-Jewish world that surrounded them. At the other end of the East European spectrum
was Hasidism, the movement of religious ecstasy that originated
in Poland and Ukraine in the eighteenth century but made few
inroads into Lithuania. The main resistance to Haskalah there
came from traditional rabbinical Judaism with its centers of Tal-
mudic learning in the main cities. In Kovno alone, just upriver
from Seredzius, there were sixty-three Talmud-Torah institutions
with more than three thousand students. Despite the oppression
they endured, the Jews of the Russian Empire were able to publish
some newspapers in Yiddish or Hebrew. They wrote books; they
created an enduring literature; the nationalism that led to Zionism was in the air.

Perhaps there were Jews in Seredzius who were affected by
all of this, who knew of Haskalah, who read the Yiddish publications, studied the revitalized Hebrew, had even encountered
here or there a wandering maskil, an activist ready to denounce
the arid scholasticism of Talmud study. It's possible that Moshe
Yoelson was among them, though the brief portrait drawn by his
elder son makes no mention of it. Whether or not he followed
the heated debates that took place among Lithuania's Jews, or
whether the family talked about them during Shabbos dinner or
with other Jews, Moshe hewed to the traditional rabbinic side
of things. In this sense, while Asa and Hirsch were schooled in
the liturgy and the traditions, they seem to have been unaffected
by "the Jewish questions" that swirled in imperial Russia, as well

as among the Jews of Germany and of the Austro-Hungarian Empire. They didn't dream of a Jewish homeland, or yearn for the revival of Hebrew, or read Moses Mendelssohn, the German-Jewish founder of Haskalah, or think about the new ways being proposed by which the Jews might break out of the constrained and impoverished lives they'd led for centuries. Not studying Torah, feeling no strong attachment to their Jewishness or to Jewish observance, certainly not allowing it to define them or to limit their very non-Jewish ambitions, may well account for their readiness to plunge headlong into the risky, bohemian American demimonde so disfavored by their father.

* * *

One thing that united the Yoelsons with other Jews of Russia was their dream of going to America. Two and a half million Jews from the Russian Empire, about a third of the population, did exactly that between 1880 and 1924. That was their direct, individual way of escaping their poverty and their unchanging status as second-class citizens. What affected the Jews, as Howe puts it, "was the explosive mixture of mounting wretchedness and increasing hope," the hope nourished by a new and extraordinary fact of world historical importance, "that for the first time they could suppose there was someplace else to go, a new world perceived as radically different from the one in which they lived." The assassination of Alexander II and his replacement by the far harsher Alexander III helped fuel the exodus.

The lure of America was strong, but getting there wasn't easy. Emigration from Russia was mostly forbidden, so escape was the main means to begin the journey, which was long and expensive. But even if they were able to cross the border to some nearby territory, few men had the ready cash to buy steamship tickets for all their family members, so this often meant that the father or an older brother would venture forth first, leaving the others to fend for themselves, usually for years before they could follow him. The great Jewish emigration was marked by many scenes of departure, when such a father or son would embark on the great adventure of a journey to America, leaving behind him no certainties as to the future, not even that he would ever be seen again. Given these difficulties, combined with the absence of overt violent persecution in places like Seredzius, taking into account that life was bearable, even sometimes pleasurable, the Yoelsons might have opted just to stay where they were, like many others, to try to make the most of the life they knew rather than risk an unknown one.

But the Yoelsons did leave. Hirsch, who recounts their departure, doesn't explain what exactly prompted them to do so, but presumably it had to do with their willingness to take a chance, to the fact that others in their extended family had gone before them, and to the occasion presenting itself. The Yoelsons' landlord, the lumberman Haym Yossi, used to serve as a foreman on the rafts that floated shipments of timber down the Niemen River to East Prussia, now Russian territory but part of Germany in those days, and he was willing, even eager, to help those who wanted to cross that border. First to go was Naomi's younger brother, Charlie, smuggled by Yossi down the river into Germany. Very likely, Charlie's successful escape inspired Moshe to follow in his footsteps.

And so, one day in 1889, Yossi smeared axle grease on Moshe's face, had him dress in ordinary workman's clothes so that he'd fit in with the rest of the lumbermen, and announced in his booming voice, "Off you go to America." Moshe kissed his wife and children good-bye, shouldered a bundle that contained better clothes, and stepped gingerly onto a log raft, low in the water because of the weight of the uncut lumber tied onto its deck. As Yossi had instructed him, Moshe took a position at one of the oars. A member of the crew untied the raft. It drifted from the dock out into the current. Hirsch and Asa, Rose, Etta, and Naomi watched the large, rectangular craft drift on the river, pick up speed in the current, and then disappear around a bend.

After fifty miles or so the river became the border between Russia and East Prussia, where the raft was steered to the bank on the German side. A frontier guard registered the names of the raft's crew and collected a fee of 40 kopecks from each of them. The German border guards were generally pretty casual when it came to escaping Russians—one less man for the armies of the Czar, they felt—and so the border wasn't an insurmountable barrier for those who could reach it. Farther downriver, Yossi's raft tied up at Tilsit, where there was a sawmill. Moshe put on his good clothes, no doubt scrubbed the grease off his face, and departed, probably for Königsberg—current-day Kaliningrad— where he got on a Baltic steamer for points west.

After unloading their cargo, Yossi's crew rowed against the current back to Russia. If questioned about the missing crewman, Yossi would simply have told the Russian border guards that maybe he'd gotten drunk and fallen overboard, maybe he'd escaped to America; he didn't know.

* * *

Hirsch doesn't say much about the life of the family during the four years of Moshe's absence. No doubt it was a difficult time, especially for Naomi, but very likely for the two boys it was also liberating in its way, probably somewhat explanatory of the defiant adventurousness of the lives they embraced once they too got to America. Asa was five when Moshe left, taking his strictness and authoritativeness with him, his demands, his threats of beatings for failing to put on tzitzit or studying Torah, not to mention his insistence that Asa and Hirsch both follow in his footsteps as cantorial guardians of Jewish orthodoxy. Where the money for food and rent came from is not clear; very likely from remittances sent by Moshe, meager as they must have been. Naomi likely got some help from her father, or from other members of the Hesselman clan. In any case, they didn't starve or go homeless.

And then, four years after Moshe floated away on Yossi Haym's raft, a letter from America arrived in Seredzius "with the magic word, 'Come!'" It contained money that Moshe had managed to save in America, enabling Naomi, the two girls, and the two boys to book passage on a steamship to New York. What a day that must have been, marking the end of one life and the beginning of a new one. They rode on a wagon all night to Kovno, covered by straw for warmth. From there they took the first train rides of their lives to the Baltic coast; then, "after thrilling rides and several changing of trains," they took a steamer to Liverpool, where they boarded the S.S. *Umbria,* "a terrible ship," Jolson said later, steerage class, for America.

2

The Fraught Triumphs of the Sons

There they were, Jewish titans of American show business, gathered at the Hillcrest Country Club in Los Angeles, itself an emblem of their success. The club was started in 1920 so Jews, who were barred from L.A.'s other clubs, would have one of their own, which is what Jews tended to do when they ran into the social antisemitism of America in the first half of the twentieth century. Within a few years, most of the Jews who made Hollywood were members—including Jack Warner, Samuel Goldwyn, Adolph Zucker, and Louis B. Mayer—even if they didn't play golf.

George Jessel, the actor who played the lead role in the stage version of *The Jazz Singer* in 1926, went to the Hillcrest for the food and the company, both of which could be enjoyed at a large oak table, known as the Round Table, set in a corner of the dining room. That's where the Jews who had made it big as singers, actors, and comedians gathered to eat, drink, smoke, and kibitz. Al Jolson was prominent among them. His friends George Burns and Groucho Marx were regulars. So were Eddie Cantor, Danny Kaye, Jack Benny, and Jessel himself, all of them huge stars of Broadway, the movies, and, later, television. Burns and Marx wrangled over who was funnier. It seems likely that these men, in the privacy of their minds or perhaps out loud to each other, engaged in some amazed self-congratulation over how low they had started and how high they had risen. Certainly, one of the things that bound them together was an awareness of having achieved a degree of wealth and fame unimaginable to their immigrant parents, not to mention the families in the Pale of Settlement they'd left behind.

They had all risen in similar fashion from similar origins along similar paths. Most of the Round Table regulars—Danny Kaye being the sole exception—were born in the last decade and a half of the nineteenth century, Jolson of course in eastern Europe, the rest in America, though just a few years after their parents' immigration, so they could all speak Yiddish and were familiar with the ways of their ancestors. Except for Marx and Jessel, none of them were known by the family names they'd been born with. George Burns, whose 272 episodes of *The George Burns and Gracie Allen Show,* first on radio, then on television, lasting from 1934 to 1958, made him one of the most beloved personalities in America, started out as Nathan Birnbaum, son of Eliezer Birnbaum and Hadassah Bluth, from a Polish shtetl called Kolbuszawa, then in the Austro-Hungarian Empire. Eddie Cantor was born Isidore Itzkowitz in 1892; his parents were also Russian immigrants, both dead by the time Cantor, raised by a beloved grandmother, was two years old. Jack Benny, the son of Meyer Kubelsky and Emma Sachs from Poland and Lithuania, was named Benjamin Kubelsky at his birth in 1894. The youngster of the group, Danny Kaye, born in 1911, was formerly David Daniel Kaminsky, his parents from Dnipropetrovsk, then part of the Russian Empire, now in Ukraine, who emigrated to Brooklyn two years before he, their third son, arrived on the scene.

They also knew the poverty, or certainly the very modest circumstances, of Jewish immigration, and of American immigration in general, and of the people, especially African Americans, who were already here. These were the *Ostjuden,* the eastern

Jews, poorer, coarser, less educated, more desperate than the mostly German Jews who'd arrived a generation before them, and their itineraries were rougher and more dangerous. The German Jews had no experience of the shtetl either in Europe or in the transplanted ghetto that was the Lower East Side in New York, where the *Ostjuden* were concentrated. The point for the German Jews was to continue climbing the ladder of American success, to eliminate the blatant antisemitism that, for example, limited their enrollment in the Ivy League (some did go there).

The *Ostjuden* sought to escape the grim urban quarters where most of the Jewish immigrants from eastern Europe landed. If escape wasn't immediately possible, simple survival was the temporary goal, and there were many ways of achieving that, some of them unsavory. There were pimps and prostitutes among the Lower East Side Jews plying their trade on Allen Street, "with its dark and smelly houses and its rattling elevated train." There were socialist journalists and more radical revolutionaries; Abraham Cahan, the founder and editor of the Yiddish *Forverts,* in the former category, the firebrand Emma Goldman in the latter. The immigrant Jews were less inclined to outright criminality than some other immigrant groups, but there were plenty of petty thieves, pickpockets, fences, and bookies, and a few big-time gangsters, most notably Meyer Lansky and Bugsy Siegel, both of whom started their careers as thieves and pushcart extortionists on the Lower East Side, before they moved on to gangland murder in conjunction with Lucky Luciano and the mob.

Show business was an escape from the soul-destroying weariness of the metal workshops, shirtwaist sweatshops, cigar sheds, pushcarts, and small retail establishments where most of the first generation of immigrants eked out their daily bread. That was where the Round Table stalwarts came from, the subculture of street performance, vaudeville, and burlesque, the saloons and

restaurants and beer parlors with their singing waiters and wait-
resses, the street corners where they busked for nickels and dimes,
the flophouses or park benches where they sometimes spent the
night, dreaming of making it big, which, needless to say, most of
them didn't. Those who did make it, like the fellows of the Hillcrest Round Table, were the talented few, finding success because
of the rise of what the German critic Theodor Adorno called the
culture industry, the distracting popular entertainments of the
urban working class, with their simple themes, sentimentality,
spoof, and slapstick. This culture gave birth to music halls, nick-
elodeons, the vaudeville and burlesque houses, then radio, the
movies, and finally television. The knights of the Hillcrest Round
Table were lucky to be in a country that, having taken in millions
of huddling masses from eastern and southern Europe, was ready
for mass amusement and didn't care much about who provided it,
or where they came from, or even, at least to some nascent extent,
what their color was.

Sophie Tucker, born Sofiya Kalish in Russia in 1886, sang for
tips at the restaurant her parents owned in Hartford, Connecticut. "I would stand in the narrow space by the door and sing with
all the drama I could put into it," she said later. "At the end of
the last chorus, between me and the onions, there wasn't a dry
eye in the place." She eloped with a beer cart driver named Louis
Tuck, went with him to New York, and by 1909 was singing at
the famed Ziegfeld Follies, where she was discovered by William
Morris, the founder of the William Morris talent agency (born
Zelman Moses in 1873 of German Jewish parents who immi-
grated in 1882).

Sophie Tucker was "the last of the Red-Hot mamas." She
was fat, which she turned to her advantage with hit songs like
"Nobody Loves a Fat Girl but Oh How a Fat Girl Can Love."
Fanny Brice, who inspired the musical and movie *Funny Girl,* was

Fania Borach at her birth in New York in 1891; she dropped out of school to work in a burlesque review, and, like Sophie Tucker, ended up for a few years at the Ziegfeld Follies.

Dropping out of school was a common element in these biographies, as was singing for small change at ages so young as to be shocking by today's standards. When he was just seven years old, Nathan Birnbaum worked making syrup in a Lower East Side candy store, where he used to practice harmony with fellow child workers. This led to something called the PeeWee Quartet, which performed on ferries and in neighborhood talent shows. "We'd put hats down for donations," Birnbaum, a.k.a. George Burns, said years later when he was one of the country's most recognizable television comedians. "Sometimes the customers threw something in the hats. Sometimes they took something out of the hats. Sometimes they took the hats."

Julius "Groucho" Marx, whose parents were German Jewish immigrants, lived above a butcher shop on East Seventy-eighth Street in New York. At a very early age he had decided he wanted to become a doctor, but there was no money to send him to medical school. Instead, with the encouragement of his mother, he became a boy singer when he was twelve. When he was fifteen, he performed in a theater in the municipal amusement park of Grand Rapids, Michigan.

Cantor, the orphan, was perhaps the most closely acquainted with dire poverty among the later Hillcrest crowd. He was raised in a cramped, miserable basement flat on the Lower East Side by his grandmother, who had come to New York when she was already sixty, understanding not a word of English, eking out a precarious living as a shadchen, a matchmaker. "We had to laugh to keep from crying, there was such poverty, such misery and disease," Cantor would write years later. "All the things that weren't good, we had."

"Our neighborhood produced one boy who became the greatest song writer in the world, Irving Berlin, and another boy, Lefty Louie, who was electrocuted for the Rosenthal murder," he continued. The reference was to the gangland-style killing in 1912 of underground bookie and gambler Herman Rosenthal, a sensational crime orchestrated by a corrupt policeman, for which five men were arrested, tried, and executed.

* * *

It's certainly a possibility that had Asa grown up on the Lower East Side where Lansky, Siegel, and Arnold Rothstein (the man who fixed the 1919 World Series) were building their criminal enterprises, he would have ended up in organized crime. He had the scrappy readiness for it. And, as we'll see, Asa Yoelson was ready to take risks. But when the Yoelsons' ship arrived in New York on April 9, 1894, a man they didn't recognize was there to meet it. The children watched as their mother ran into Moshe's embrace, after which their father took them straight to the train station and to Washington, D.C.

Moshe had spent what must have been an austere and lonely four years separated from his family in Seredzius. In fact, we don't know much about him during that time, only that he served for a while as a rabbi in Newburgh, New York. Russian immigration was rapidly enlarging the Jewish population, not only in New York but in other American cities, and there was a demand for rabbis and cantors, especially Yiddish-speaking Orthodox rabbis and cantors who embodied the culture and mores of the Old Country. Following the Civil War there were about fifteen hundred Jews in Washington, largely second-generation Americans with origins in Germany, many of them merchants downtown on Seventh Street and Pennsylvania Avenue, N.W., some of them government clerks, a few of them lawyers, doctors, and other professionals. By the turn of the century, the great *Ostjuden* migration swelled the Jewish numbers in Washington to about ten thousand. Most of the newcomers were like the Yoelsons, poor Yiddish speakers from various points in the Russian Empire. The established German Jewish community was divided among Orthodox, Conservative, and Reform congregations. The Russians were all Orthodox. They lived above their shoe stores, hat stores, groceries, haberdasheries, tailor shops, hardware stores, dry goods stores, furniture stores, and other stores that they managed to establish in various neighborhoods, and they set up small synagogues close enough to walk to on Shabbos.

In 1887, a group of twenty-eight families, most if not all of them recent arrivals from Russia, were living in the southwest district of the city. At first, they met for a daily minyan in Isaac Levy's clothing store, known as Levy's Busy Corner, on 4½ Street S.W., but after a few years they were able to build a small wooden sanctuary at 467 E Street S.W., and Moshe served there as cantor, ritual slaughterer, and mohel, the performer of circumcisions. He lived in a cold-water flat above a store on 4½ Street not far from Levy's, and that's where the rest of the family first experienced American life.

The street, since renamed Fourth Street, was broad as an avenue. It had cobblestones, rows of elm trees, and two-story brick or wooden buildings with shops at street level and living quarters upstairs. Very soon, Naomi and Moshe had restored the old Seredzius way of life, the strict Jewish observance, the Shabbos candles on Fridays at sunset, the chanting of the Hebrew liturgy, the smell of fresh challah and hemlock needles on the day of rest with everybody in their best clothes.

Hirsch and Asa went to public school during the day, Hebrew school afterward. Moshe resumed singing lessons to prepare his sons for the careers he had marked out for them as cantors in the growing Jewish world of America, though the boys now began the rebellion that would lead them to stray far from their father's path. Once, on the street, Hirsch and Asa ran into some boys belonging to a neighborhood gang. The leader of the gang, calling them "greenhorns," asked them their names, and Asa said, "This is Harry and my name is Al," inventing their new names. That didn't stop them from getting into a fistfight. From then on, while they remained Hirsch and Asa at home, they were Harry and Al outside.

Harry makes no mention of the fight in his autobiography, so it's possible that that story, told by Al, is apocryphal, but there's no question that both boys were moving away from their father's orbit, forming new kinds of lives in their adopted country. They soon spoke English much better than Moshe did, and, as Hirsch put it, "the spirit of freedom and unrest had entered our blood, and we soon wandered far from the orthodox beliefs of our fathers."

This may have been easier, more natural for them than it was for the majority of Jewish immigrants, concentrated as they were in New York's Lower East Side. Washington wasn't easy, but it didn't have the oppressive feel of New York's insalubrious ghetto, with what Jacob Riis, the muckraking chronicler of New York's poor, called its "crazy old buildings, crowded rear tenements in filthy yards, dark, damp basements, leaking garrets, shops, outhouses and stables, converted into dwellings, though scarcely fit to shelter brutes." The Lower East Side, in Riis's words, "enslaved [the Jews] in bondage worse than that from which they fled." The Yoelsons may not have known enough to make the comparison between that and the life they led in Washington, but they benefited from the absence of the worst of the normal horrors of Jewish immigrant life.

Tragedy struck nonetheless. After being in Washington for

barely a year, with Hirsch preparing for his Bar Mitzvah, Naomi fell ill. One day they heard terrible screaming from her room. Summoned there, they saw a doctor standing solemnly at the foot of the bed where Naomi lay, her eyes closed, her hands unusually still.

The graveside funeral was held the next day. Snow swirled around the small group of mourners. Stockings were pulled over Asa's hands because he had no mittens, and he used them in a futile effort to dry his eyes. For the next year, no matter what else the boys were up to, and they were soon beginning their careers as street performers, they never forgot to say the Kaddish, the Hebrew prayer for the dead—"Magnified and sanctified be God's great name"—three times a day.

Although Asa—Al—didn't talk much about it, he never recovered from Naomi's death. Here was a ten-year-old boy recently arrived in a new country, now stranded with a stern, uncompromising father who, having been absent from his life for four years, was a veritable stranger, and an old-fashioned, authoritarian stranger at that. From the moment of his mother's death, Asa Yoelson, later the celebrated singer of what were called "mammy songs"—nostalgic, sometimes maudlin ballads sung by Black boys, or by white boys pretending to be Black, remembering their mothers, not in Lithuania but in the American South—spent his life in a sometimes desperate, essentially futile effort to fill a hole in his heart that couldn't be filled.

3

Street Singers

One of the greatest careers in the history of American popular culture started on the sidewalk in front of the Raleigh Hotel in Washington, D.C. On the corner of Twelfth Street and Pennsylvania Avenue, between Congress and the White House, the Raleigh was one of the two most fashionable hotels in the American capital, an ornate, Empire-style, seven-story building topped by a mansard roof and endowed with a restaurant where congressmen, senators, and government bureaucrats would go for lunch and dinner. In the warm weather, they would often sit on the ground floor veranda adjacent to Pennsylvania Avenue, where they would enjoy long cool drinks and cigars. That's where Harry and Al went to sing, on the sidewalk in front of the veranda, earning nickels, dimes, and even the occasional quarter. They sang popular songs like "Sweet Marie," "Daisy Bell," and "Who Threw the Overalls in Mrs. Murphy's Chowder," and Stephen Foster favorites, among them "Listen to the Mocking Bird" and "When You and I Were Young." The very fact that they had turned their cantorial training into music like this was a sign of the speed of the Americanization of these two immigrant boys, and their distance from the Orthodox Jewish world of their father.

Though Harry joined Al in duets, Al must have been the star in front of the Raleigh, with his clear boy's voice. There must have been something special about his presence too, a boyish charisma, energy, enthusiasm, a desire to perform, that would make him very famous later. The two boys used the money they earned to buy tickets to a local theater, another step away from the world of their father. The theater, possibly the very grand Bijou on Ninth Street and Louisiana Avenue, not far from the Yoelson home, displayed a billboard that must have been fascinating to Harry and Al, with its images of chorus girls, dancing bears, knife throwers, and acrobats. Whatever theater it was, it was surely a vaudeville house, one of the thousands of venues in every city and town in America where ordinary people enjoyed the inexpensive, accessible variety shows that were the most popular entertainment in the last decades of the nineteenth century and the first of the twentieth, before the movies replaced them. Almost everybody who became anybody in show business in that era got their start in vaudeville, or in the related burlesque, with its emphasis on parody and farce. Vaudeville was a great job market for the itinerant, bohemian masses of comedians, singers, jugglers, magicians, bicycle acrobats, escape artists, and others who roamed the theater districts of America, where they could scrape together a meager living and perhaps get noticed for something better.

Even at thirteen and ten, Harry and Al were beginning to live by their wits much in the way that all the later denizens of the Hillcrest Country Club did when they were children, growing up quickly. For most of their teen years, they lived lives that, certainly by today's standards, seem reckless and dangerous, not to mention illegal. Except for a few brief interludes here and there, Al stopped going to school after his twelfth birthday. By the time he was thirteen, he was experienced in the ways of the world, a veteran of "riding the rods," as jumping a freight train was called, "busking around," and even "carrying the banner"—slang for sleeping on a park bench. At fourteen or fifteen he smoked, had been to horse races and prizefights (he continued to frequent them all his life). In those early days in Washington, he and Harry sang whenever they could, not just in front of the Raleigh veranda but on Potomac cruise ships as well. They also sold newspapers on street corners and bought watermelons wholesale at the wharf, three for five cents, transported them downtown on a battered wagon, and sold them for a nickel apiece to customers who they attracted with a song—"Waaaaatamelons / Red to the rind."

Their older sister, Rose, was trying to play the motherly role left vacant by Naomi's death, but she didn't have the authority or the gravity or the sense of humor for it. Moshe did his best to stop his sons' drift toward what he saw as truancy, to the point of searching them out on the street every so often and hauling them back home, one boy in each hand, as their friends looked on. He persisted in the boys' singing lessons and tried to maintain the routines of an Orthodox Jewish life, but he also spent more and more time at his synagogue, which was growing larger thanks to the continuing immigrant flow. A decent interval after Naomi's death, he wrote to a cousin of hers in Seredzius asking if the cousin's daughter, Hessi, would come to America and be his wife. A correspondence of a few months ensued, and then Hessi arrived. Rose and Etta were cooperative, Harry and Al resentful, angry, and often absent.

And then they truly broke free of the trammels of traditional family life that Moshe was trying ineffectually to preserve. One day, Harry was pulling the watermelon wagon down a street of darkened houses and red lights, where the women who worked there were good customers. He saw a man emerge from one of the houses, unsteady on his feet, who Harry recognized as a congressman often seen on the terrace of the Raleigh Hotel. The man asked Harry to fetch him a cab, which Harry did. The congressman told Harry not to tell anyone what he'd witnessed, and, as

he got into the cab, pressed a coin into Harry's palm—a $10 gold
coin, a fortune.

Harry felt he'd been miraculously staked to an independent
life. The next night, he "rode the rods" all the way to the freight
yards in Jersey City, New Jersey. He took the ferry across the Hud-
son River to Manhattan, and there he embarked on the life of an
adolescent vagabond, not so unusual a thing in those days when
thousands of children roamed the streets. He sang for tips, sold
newspapers, carried luggage, worked for a while for a team of men
who he thought were hawking knives, until he discovered that
they were actually professional pickpockets. He slept in doorways
and at the Newsboys' Lodging House on Duane Street, a place
whose very existence in New York and other cities testified to the
number of boys who were on their own in America. The one on
Duane Street was run by the Children's Aid Society, founded in
1853 by one Rev. Charles L. Brace. Along with the New York Society for the Prevention of Cruelty to Children, a.k.a. the Gerry
Society (named after Elbridge Thomas Gerry, who founded it in
1874), it was the main charitable organization created to tend to
New York's mass of abandoned, homeless, or runaway kids, the
ones Jacob Riis called "the rough young savages familiar from the
street." The Newsboys' Lodging House was cheap, and the boys
who lived and ate there took classes and played cards and domi-
noes. After Harry ran up an unpaid bill, he was too embarrassed
to go there anymore.

Harry said that he then sent a postcard home, which prompted
Al to "ride the rods" to New York. According to Al, he'd decided to
seek his fortune in show business, for which purpose he jumped a
freight to New York. Al found Harry, on the Bowery, New York's
famous bums' row. The two boys slept in a produce wagon near
the docks their first night together, and when they woke up, they
discovered that someone had stolen Al's shoes while they were

sleeping, forcing them to spend the next day roaming secondhand shops begging for a new pair. They tried singing in a saloon, but "were quickly shown the way out through the swinging doors." Al, almost destitute, went back to Washington. His trip to New York had been brief and surely miserable. Most boys in his position would have learned their lesson and opted for a more conventional, respectable path—home, school, perhaps even more lessons in the Jewish liturgical music so he could become a cantor. Not Al, who even then seems to have known that he had a talent that set him apart and was determined to use that talent doing something more exciting, more adventurous, than singing in his father's shul. Within a week of his return, he was singing for a vaudeville troupe called Rich & Hoppe's Big Company of Fun Makers. It was 1898. Al was twelve years old.

For the next few years, Al and Harry doggedly pursued careers in what was called the theatrical trade. They picked up change singing in saloons. Al especially was able to find gigs as a boy singer with various traveling burlesque or vaudeville troupes, and by the time he was fourteen or fifteen, he had passed through a lot of cities and towns. At one point in 1898, he got on a train with the intention of rejoining Harry in New York, but instead he fell in with a group of Spanish-American War volunteers on their way to a military training camp in Pennsylvania. There he got picked up by Walter L. Main's traveling circus, his salary $5 a month for two months. When that gig ended, he took a train to Baltimore, where for a while he earned money as a singing waiter in a beer parlor. But the saloon was raided by the Gerry Society, one of whose admirable, but to Al unwelcome, purposes was to enforce the laws forbidding children under the age of sixteen from working in music halls. Al refused to give his name or home address to the police, who brought him to St. Mary's Industrial School for Boys, which housed truants and runaways. He tried,

unsuccessfully, to escape, earning him a stint in solitary confine-
ment, a horrid punishment since Al hated being alone. Babe Ruth
went to St. Mary's four years after Al was there, though there were
erroneous news reports that they were there together.

It was a terrible time. Al got into fights, kept trying to escape,
refused to work or to study. Only when he got so ill that his life
was at risk did he tell his warders who he was and provided a home
address, whereupon Moshe was contacted and asked to retrieve
him. One can only imagine how vexing it must have been for an
Orthodox rabbi and cantor to find one of his sons in a Catholic
home for wayward boys. Indeed, one recounting of the incident
has Moshe arriving just in time to hear Al singing hymns in a
children's choir, which must have led him to wonder what it was
about his two sons that drove them to perilous vagabondage when
they could have been safely home studying to become cantors.
Moshe had no sense of the urgency of his boys' need to escape the
drab cultural and religious fate that he and Hessi, Al and Harry's
stepmother, must have represented to the boys.

In fact Moshe wasn't a hard or intransigent man, and the
Yoelsons, father and son, never repudiated each other, as other
Jewish fathers and sons sometimes did in the titanic battles waged
between tradition and Americanization. There's a photograph of
Moshe and Hessi, standing side by side, not touching each other,
in front of a wooden fence, looking like a kind of Jewish American Gothic, their posed stiffness mirroring the stiffness of the
upright boards behind them. They are both on the stout side,
Cantor Yoelson dressed in dark formality complete with bow
tie, Hessi looking a bit frumpy, as if she'd been rushed straight
from cooking dinner to pose with her husband for a professional
portrait photographer. As the Yiddish writer Sholem Aleichem
put it, the cantor, the hazan, is "a messenger of the congregation,
an advocate, a representative, and consequently, the congrega-

tion demands of him that he is a person of impeccable virtue, a respectable Jew," and Moshe Yoelson seems to be striving to meet that expectation as he poses in front of the camera—dignified, self-possessed, traditional. That requirement of sedate respectability is also what made it impossible for him fully to be reconciled with, much less to admire, Al's choice of a career in vaudeville, which was loose, racy, spiritually untethered, at the opposite end of the spectrum from the orderly sanctimony of the synagogue. Old-fashioned and Orthodox as he was, however, there is nothing forbidding or angry about Moshe in the photograph, and there is a kind of shy gentility on Hessi's round, bespectacled, careworn face.

* * *

Ironically, in escaping the conventional life that Moshe and Hessi wanted for them, Harry and Al were doing what turned out to be a very Jewish thing. One scholarly estimate is that in the early years of the twentieth century, about half of the people working in entertainment in New York were Jewish. It was an avenue open to them at a time when their large-scale arrival in New York and the emergence of what Riis called "Jewtown" was prompting a wave of antisemitism. On the one hand the very impoverished condition of Lower East Side Jews gave rise to fears that they were a kind of bacterial infection, that they were "utter strangers to soap and water and on social terms with parasitic vermin," as the *New York Herald* indelicately put it. The accusation that they were filthy coexisted with the age-old stereotype of the Jews as transfixed by money; they were greedy, conspiratorial, cunning, in secret control of the world of finance. "The journalism of those years betrays a nervous anticipation that the immigrant Jews, despite their momentary wretchedness, will yet come to exercise powers of the uncanny," Irving Howe writes in *World of Our Fathers.*

And so, poor, suspected of being both too poor and too rich, parasite-infected and bloodsucking bankers, the Jews went into domains enabling them to claw their way out of the ghetto, and in flocking into the theatrical trade they created another sort of ghetto, one far better than the ghetto they escaped, and one where Jews striving for a way in faced no antisemitism. In 1896, six theater managers and owners, all Jews, started the Theatrical Syndicate, which enjoyed a near monopoly on which performers could play what roles in what theaters. The only serious competition to the Syndicate was the Shubert Organization, created late in the century by three brothers from Syracuse, New York, Sam, Lee, and J.J. On the talent agency side, William Morris, Vaudeville Agent—now the powerful Hollywood-based Endeavor Talent Agency—was founded in 1898 by William Morris, born Zelman Moses, later William Morris, as noted earlier. After his death, the agency was taken over by his son, William, Jr., but it was his partnership with another Jewish immigrant, Abraham Lastfogel, that turned it into the most powerful such organization in the country, its clients including Charlie Chaplin, the Marx Brothers, George Burns, and Al Jolson, later Milton Berle, Elvis Presley, and many others. In 1905, Simon J. Silverman, known as Sime, born in 1873 in a middle-class Jewish family, started *Variety,* which immediately provided a weekly, opinionated chronicle of vaudeville goings-on across the country and even in London. *Variety* from the outset was friendly to Jews and African Americans.

In its very first issue, *Variety* identified the lure of "the theater trade" for Americans. It quotes a publisher in London amazed that in England a "moderately successful" song might sell 200,000 copies; in the United States hit songs sold 800,000 to a million copies, and it wasn't all that unusual for a songwriter to make

$25,000 a year in royalties alone—around $400,000 in today's value. The paper identified top vaudeville actors earning salaries of $1,000 a week, a hallucinatory sum for a person whose relatives slaved over Singer sewing machines for pennies an hour in tenements and sweatshops.

When Harry and Al "rode the rods" to New York, they joined a veritable army of other boys and a smaller number of girls powerfully drawn to the theatrical trade. What was unusual about them was the talent, especially Al's, though it took a few tough years for that to break through.

* * *

After Al's misadventure at St. Mary's, both boys lived at home in Washington for a while. Harry got a job selling peanuts and popcorn at the Bijou Theatre, where he sometimes sneaked Al into the balcony. Onstage was the Victoria Burlesquers, whose main attraction was a supposedly French chanteuse named Aggie Beeler (sometimes called Agnes Behler). One evening Al started singing with her from his seat upstairs, and that led Beeler to invite him to join the company as her "stooge," a member of the cast planted in the theater who would get things going when the actor onstage asked the audience to join in. It's significant that the company manager, William Eversole, took the trouble to ask Moshe for permission for Al to accept Beeler's invitation, and Moshe, perhaps knowing that resistance was futile, gave his consent.

Al then traveled with Beeler to Providence, Rhode Island, Queens, Brooklyn, Montreal, Pittsfield, Massachusetts, and other places. One might think that he was living his dream: He had his father's acquiescence in his chosen way of life, and there's no doubt that his greatest pleasure even at that early age was to sing in front of an audience. But Al was only fifteen, a beardless boy whose voice hadn't yet changed. What if it did, and he couldn't work? It was a time when children of twelve were sent out as itinerant peddlers of soap and brushes, pots and pans, when they rode trains selling newspapers and cigarettes, sat at sewing machines in urban sweatshops, ran numbers for local gangsters. Al's saddest moment came when he fell for one of his fellow troupers, a certain Grace Celeste, who laughingly dismissed him as the boy he was. That Christmas of 1901, alone in his room in a third-class hotel in Chicago, he felt, as he later put it, "thoroughly miserable and unhappy. I can see myself—a kid singer warbling questionable songs for a meager living, and dreaming of footlight fame." He expressed "a peculiar dread of loneliness."

For two years, ending when he was a scrawny sixteen, Al toured with a veteran vaudevillian named Fred E. Moore, a stout Irishman singing the popular ballads of the day. When that came to an end, Al's voice had indeed changed, and he didn't know if he had a future as a singer. He was no longer a soprano, and it was his soprano voice that had sustained him. For a while he went back to the two-room cold-water flat above the store.

While he was there, Harry came home dressed in a snazzy suit and straw boater, enthused by the success he'd had as a singing waiter in New York. At his urging, the two brothers worked up a comedy routine they called "The Joelson Brothers" in "The Hebrew and the Cadet." Harry would be the Hebrew, with a big hat, a beard, and a Lower East Side accent; Al would wear the uniform of an army or police trainee.

"One time I hit a jackass with my fist and killed him," Al says in one skit. Harry says he hopes he won't hit him, and Al assures him that he won't, for two reasons.

"And vat are dem two reasons?"

"Well, the first is that I like you."

"Dat is fine. Vat is the second reason?"

"The second reason is that I promised never to hit another jackass."

In going for ethnic parody, Harry and Al were following a well-worn pathway. In the world of entertainment, the era of mass immigration was an era of raw ethnic caricature. In turn-of-the-century America, there were no rules regarding ethnic sensitivities, no requirement of ethnic politesse; everybody, at least everybody who wasn't a WASP, was fair game and nobody was expected to take offense.

The most common ethnic comedy categories were "Dutch" (meaning German, a derivative of *Deutsch*), Irish, and "Hebrew." Long before Harry and Al created "The Hebrew and the Cadet," just about every traveling burlesque and vaudeville troupe had its Yiddish dialect comedian, "a grotesque figure" with "a hang-dog look, unkempt hair and whiskers, false nose, oversize shoes, a black derby hat pulled over his ears, and a dark coat drooping to his ankles," as one scholar has put it.

This caricature of a Jew was often portrayed by non-Jewish actors, some of whom had long, successful careers in the role. When he was eighteen years old and just starting out, Charlie Chaplin tried playing a character called "Sam Cohen, Jewish comedian" because, as he put it in his autobiography, "Jewish comedians were all the rage"—that is, Jewish comedians played by non-Jews. But Jews too, like Harry and Al, performed Hebrew caricatures. Among the most famous of them was Julian Rose, born Julius Rosenzweig in New York in 1868 to a family from Crakow, Poland, who discovered his talent for mimicry when he was an accountant for the New York & Philadelphia Telephone and Telegraph Company and often entertained his fellow employees with Yiddish impersonations. Rose went into vaudeville portraying a character called Levinsky that he then played for more than thirty years, in New York, London, even Sydney, Australia, earning $550 a week at his height.

The Jews who did these acts, wearing false hooked noses and heavy beards and speaking with their exaggerated accents—"Oy, vey I gedt troubles"—were, of course, getting laughs, appealing to audiences for whom ethnic humor was a release from the tension of spare economic lives. They were also making fun of their parents, parents like Moshe and Hessi, with their old-fashioned ways and giveaway accents. For Harry and Al it was part mockery and part affection, but most of all it was an attempt to cash in on a fad that enabled people to make a living in "the theatrical trade." It was all in good fun, and fun was in short supply in turn-of-the-century America.

But that, of course, made Jewish dialect comedy a competitive field, in which Harry and Al's success was modest, though they were just starting out. New York's vaudeville houses were around Union Square and along Fourteenth Street, a broad thoroughfare that cuts east and west across Manhattan. In Union Square Park itself were the benches where actors and actresses hung out, traded stories, and sometimes slept. Around Twenty-eighth Street were the music publishers, songwriters, and theatrical agents, the original Tin Pan Alley where Irving Berlin and the young George Gershwin sold their first songs.

But if the smell of success drew a lot of Jews from the Lower East Side up to Fourteenth Street, Tin Pan Alley, and, a bit farther uptown, to Broadway, when it came to their artistic careers most performers had to leave their Jewishness behind. Berlin, after all, wrote "White Christmas" and "God Bless America"; Gershwin composed "An American in Paris," "Rhapsody in Blue," and "Porgy and Bess"; Jolson sang "Mammie," "Swanee," and "Camptown Races," in blackface. But that came later. When they were just starting out in 1900, the Jolson boys rented a space in a

Twenty-eighth Street studio to get attention for their "Hebrew and the Cadet" routine. According to Harry, they were noticed by the songwriter Harry Von Tilzer, who introduced them to an agent working for the recently created William Morris Agency, and they got a few bookings for "Hebrew" in music halls in Rockaway, Queens, Coney Island, Brooklyn, and even an out-of-town show in Baltimore (though when they asked directions to the theater there, a policeman told them that it had burned down that morning).

Soon after, Harry and Al traveled a vaudeville circuit playing a burlesque skit called "A Little of Everything" with a wheelchair-bound Yiddish dialect comedian named Joe Palmer. Palmer, who wrote the scripts, played a kvetchy hospital patient; Harry was his doctor; and Al was a wisecracking orderly. This is important not only because it shows that parodies of immigrant Jews played to non-Jewish audiences in America. It's also important in an account of Al Jolson's life because it marked the beginning of his career in blackface.

Jolson himself told how this came about in an interview in 1928 with *The Washington Tribune,* a Black newspaper in Washington, D.C. "Al Jolson's Negro Valet Made Him a Success; Suggested that Comedian Use Burnt Cork," the headline ran. "I was not creating the riotous enthusiasm I wanted to create," Jolson told the paper, remembering "A Little of Everything."

> Finally the solution came from an unexpected source. I was living in Washington, D.C. in the midst of Negroes. I had often imitated their dialect. At the time I was playing an engagement in Brooklyn and had an aged Negro assist me in dressing. "Boss," said he one night, "Why don't you put some black on yo' face? Why don't you sing yo' songs all blacked up that a way. That always makes 'em laugh." I

got some burnt cork and put on a rehearsal for the benefit of the old man. In his opinion I was an unparalleled success. "Mistah Jolson," he beamed, "you just as funny as me." With his encouragement, I tried out the experiment on a theater audience, and the change was so well received, that I have clung to the characterization ever since.

Harry tells a similar story, but with one important difference. He, Al, and Palmer were doing "A Little of Everything" at the Keeney Theatre in Brooklyn, where Al's portrayal of the hospital orderly, which he did in a southern accent, wasn't getting the "riotous enthusiasm" he wanted. But it wasn't an "aged Negro" who suggested that he "black up"; it was James Francis Dooley, a white comedian who played in blackface. In any event, it worked. "The nervous, monotoned, self-conscious kid of just two weeks before was gone, his place taken by an impudent and joyous harlequin," Jolson's principal biographer, Herbert G. Goldman, has written. The device gave Al a mask. It enabled him to be somebody else.

Or that's just an excuse for an unforgivable act of racial appropriation and insult. We'll come back to this fraught topic. For now, it should be noted that given how common blackface was, including by Black minstrel entertainers, Jolson wasn't so much losing his inhibitions as he was copying everybody else. Blackface was unremarkable at the time, unexceptional, entirely noncontroversial for a seventeen-year-old just starting out and experimenting with his theatrical persona, to give it a try. He did it because everybody did it, because it led to success.

4

A Power Beyond Himself

Starting in the first years of the new century, when Al Jolson was in his late teens and early twenties, the local newspapers in the cities and towns where he toured with his vaudeville or minstrel troupes began to note his special talent. Not that he didn't struggle and suffer as he acquired a reputation. The cheerful, buoyant stage persona that Jolson adopted and that was soon to become familiar to the world was always a mask, something like the burnt cork he used to cover his face. Later, he had the compensations of riches and fame, but in the early years there were "heartaches," as Jolson put it in an interview. He experienced "months and months of the bitterest disappointment," remembered only by him, he said, but actually not only by him. His lifelong friend, Harry Akst, songwriter and pianist, recalled the bitter days at the turn of the century,

> when the aroma of beans and coffee at Max's Busy Bee on the Bowery would assail [Jolson's] quivering nostrils and the sign said: "Coffee—2¢ a cup, but COFFEE"— and he didn't even have the price of a smell; the nights when he slept on park benches; Horatio Alger Jolson; the tuxedos he hired at 50 cents for a night so he could play a $5 benefit in formals, and the endless walking down Four-

teenth Street, Luchow's restaurant beckoning on one side, and Tony Pastor's vaudeville house on the other. The billboards had names up like Honeyboy Evans, Eddie Leonard, McIntyre & Heath—names that taunted Al because they didn't spell Jolson. He'd mutter, "Someday. I'll show em."

But he started to be recognized, if mostly locally at first. He became known as a singing comedian, or, in the terms of the day, an "eccentric" rather than just a songster. His "Hebrew" and other skits had taught him that he had a gift for talking to audiences, and he was, or so they said, very funny. "Everything he touches turns to fun," a critic in *The New York Evening World* wrote. "He calls forth spontaneous laughter." The press used the word "aura" to account for his stage presence. There was a kind of crackling in the air as soon as he walked on the stage. He's "immensely clever, a laugh producer of the first class," the *Oakland Tribune* said in 1906, "one of the best comedians ever to have appeared on a stage." He "entertained theater-goers as they've never been entertained before," a review in Reading, Pennsylvania, said that same year. Jolson regularly received standing ovations long before they became commonplace. He was a great whistler, had been since his days as a boy street performer with Harry in Washington, whistling with the fingers of one hand between his lips, the fingers of the other hand tapping his knuckles as if he were playing a wind instrument, a flute or a piccolo. The billboards sometimes described his upcoming performances as "comedy, singing, and whistling." He had an easy complicity with the audience, and a knack for roping them into a joint enterprise, as when he'd poke his head through the curtains before the show had begun and say, "I'll be with you in a minute" or ask them what songs they wanted him to sing.

Jolson's emergence as a minor star and then, after a few years, as a super-famous entertainment luminary, took place as the protean figures of American popular entertainment, also immigrants themselves or born into eastern European Jewish immigrant families, were also soaring into the theatrical stratosphere—the Shuberts, Sime Silverman of *Variety,* and, most significantly for Jolson at this stage of his career, the Morris Agency. A few years after posting his first signboard on Fourteenth Street in Manhattan, William Morris moved to Fortieth Street and Broadway to be closer to the nascent theater district. He sent a young agent, Jesse Lasky, to open an office in Chicago. There, as the historian of the Morris Agency put it, Lasky "was wowed by a blackface singer"—Jolson. He signed him to a contract the next day. Jolson, now a client of a powerful booking agent, got performances all over the country still doing his Hebrew act, sometimes with Palmer, sometimes without. It wasn't long before *Variety,* which almost instantly became a kind of national newsletter, first for vaudeville and then for every other aspect of popular entertainment, began chronicling almost every move Jolson made, which it continued to do for nearly the next half century. Around the same time the songwriters, who would produce the material that Jolson and others would take to the stage, entered the picture—Irving Caesar, Irving Berlin, Harry Von Tilzer, George Gershwin, and many others—and Tin Pan Alley was born.

It took a few years for all these pieces to fall into place for Jolson, as well as for others of the cohort of Jewish vaudevillians and musical theater entertainment—the theaters, the producers, the agents, the celebrity press, the critics, all of them, coincidentally or not, domains of pioneering creativity for immigrant or first-generation Jews, all part of the rough-and-ready democratic meritocracy of show business in the first third of the twentieth century. Many stars emerged from this world, not just Jolson and certainly not all of them Jews. This was also a time when Black entertainers—Louis Armstrong, Ethel Waters, Ma Rainey, Bessie Smith, Eubie Blake, and others—were also reaching crossover white audiences. These Black entertainers of course were not recent immigrants or first-generation Americans, but their emergence seems like a collateral effect of the opening up of the culture that was a product of mass immigration, which, in turn, produced the raucous democracy of talent that was popular entertainment. They and the immigrants were introducing something new to America; they were shaking up the constraints and the pretensions of the Anglo-Saxon establishment, lampooning it often by lampooning their own positions in it. The result was a culture with a raw, unvarnished quality, more mocking, provocative, open to new topics and new styles, a culture disdained and even feared by the highbrow conservatives—and the masses loved it. It was huge. Every town of any size had its vaudeville theater; there were thousands and thousands of performers roving the country striving to make it.

Those who made it big broke the rules, made a wreckage of the old ways. Harry Houdini, born Erik Weisz in Hungary in 1874, among whose features was to challenge law enforcement agencies to make handcuffs that he couldn't break out of, pushed escape artistry to a new, thrilling level. The Marx Brothers, as Irving Howe put it, "split open the conventions of stage entertainment into extremes of social satire and chaotic farce." They didn't just aim to please their audience, they sought to take it "helplessly, dizzily away from standard expectations of coherence." The critic Gilbert Seldes, a member of the "high" culture who was an unabashed admirer of vaudeville, musical theater, cartoons, slapstick, and other elements of the "low" culture, singled out Jolson and Fanny Brice for their ability to give their audiences "a genuine emotional effect ranging from the thrill of the shock." Like Jolson, in Seldes's view, Brice rode "exceptional qualities of caricature and satire" to remarkable stardom. In songs like "Second Hand Rose" and "I Should Worry," Brice helped bring Yiddish dialect humor into the mainstream.

In this sense, two things are noteworthy about Jolson and Brice, according to Seldes. One is that they "bring something to America which America lacks and loves." And second, "both are racially out [not part of] of the dominant caste," meaning, though Seldes was too discreet to make this explicit, that both were Jews (as was Seldes), and that is what "accounts for their fine carelessness about our superstitions of politeness and gentility." Was he talking about one of Brice's most famous gestures, when she emerged on the stage and declared, in her Yiddish accent, "I may be a bad voman, but I'm dem good company"? The Jews were outsiders deeply knowledgeable about the insider's ways, which gave them the capacity to defy the conventions and invent something new. It may seem odd—and George Jessel teased Jolson publicly about it—that Jolson, the son of an Orthodox Jewish woman who spent all but one year of her life in a Lithuanian shtetl, would wax nostalgic in his songs about "My mammy from Alabammy." But that was the oddity, which today might be called cultural appropriation. But it was a less aware time when it came to ethnic sensitivities. Everything was possible, or almost everything. Jolson singing passionately, "demonically," about Swanee and Dixie was the immigrant becoming America and America accepting the immigrant in the process.

By being "racially out of the dominant caste," the Jewish performers, along with their Black counterparts, whose music they imitated and adapted, mounted an assault on what Seldes called "solemnity." Most of the Jews adopted the ways and manners of the celebrity class—the Hillcrest Country Club; their Cadillacs and Rolls-Royces; their houses in Santa Monica and Scarsdale; being seen at the Friars Club, the Stork Club, or Delmonico's; or disembarking amid popping flashbulbs like members of some royal family from transatlantic ocean liners; making big bets at the racetrack or at the prizefights; occupying box seats at the World Series. With the exception of Eddie Cantor, who had five daughters with his Jewish wife and stayed married to her for life, they not only defied the cultural expectations of the dominant caste but also flouted its moral conventions, most conspicuously by frequently marrying and divorcing, usually with pretty chorus girls and actresses, none of them Jewish. It's as if they were making up for the time lost in their impoverished early years, enjoying the unhindered gratification denied their parents and grandparents who had been forced to live such shriveled, unexciting lives. Their elders strove for survival and respectability; they sought fame, fortune, and fun. They helped make America more vulgar, morally looser, but also more open-minded, more "multicultural," to use a much later expression. They fostered the crossbred, mixed-up, hybrid culture that became deeply, uniquely American even as it captured the world.

* * *

We needn't document every one of Jolson's steps as he achieved his own celebrityhood—just the highlights. After his stint touring with Joe Palmer in "A Little of Everything," he made it into the world of vaudeville circuits, the companies that toured the country performing in an established network of theaters. He went to San Francisco and Oakland, Detroit, all over, even to Butte, Montana, where the local newspaper said he "was greeted with an unusual amount of applause and laughter." In Oakland, he met an eighteen-year-old "Minstrel Maid" named Henrietta Keller, who had "very pronounced Scandinavian features," according to Herbert G. Goldman, and a former sea captain father who hated Jews, which forced them to postpone their marriage. Meanwhile, Al signed up with a vaudeville circuit for $150 a week, traveling to El Paso, Chicago, Minneapolis, Duluth, and Lincoln, Nebraska. "A pair of very useful and versatile lips . . . [that] emit all manner of queer sounds and frame all kinds of ridiculous expressions are possessed by Al Jolson . . . who received a veritable ovation by an audience that refused to release him until he had exhausted his repertoire," read one typical review in 1907. Reflecting the growth of his fame, the *El Paso Times* in 1907 called him "the greatest monologist in the business."

That was Al's life for the next few years, a one-night stand here, a couple of days, maybe even a week or two there, traveling long distances by train. It must have been exhausting and also gratifying that his dream was being realized. The stock phrases that stuck to him for decades began to appear in local newspapers—the world's greatest entertainer, the funniest man on earth. But the lifestyle took its toll. Jolson was prone to spasms of anger. He could be violent. Sometimes the boy from Seredzius who used his fists in fights with schoolboys used his fists even after he'd achieved success in America. Once he was standing in line after breakfast in the Sinton Hotel in Cincinnati, impatient to pay his bill, and he asked the man in front of him to hurry up, please. "I don't hurry up for kikes," the man growled, whereupon Jolson laid him out with a punch.

A year after meeting Henrietta, Al married her in a civil ceremony in Oakland. There is no indication that he informed any of his family in advance, surely knowing that they would feel betrayed by his choice of a gentile, wanting to spare himself, and perhaps them too, the grief. Sometime later, Harry, in San

Francisco for some shows of his own, chastised him for his aban-
donment of the tribe. (A couple of years later, Harry married a
non-Jew himself, and, unlike Al and Henrietta, they stayed married for life.) The newlyweds moved into a hotel but there was no
honeymoon. A few days after the wedding, according to the *Star
Tribune,* Al "convulsed" Oakland at the Bell Theatre, which, the
paper continued, "has presented many comedians, but never one
that was the equal of Al Jolson." After his success in Oakland,
the Wigwam Theatre in San Francisco offered him $250 for a
two-week engagement, but Jolson insisted on twice that amount,
and he got it. Then, with Henrietta now accompanying him, he
spent the first half of 1908 in Los Angeles, Denver, Chicago, and,
in his first appearances in the South, Nashville and Little Rock.
"His stories are new and refreshing, his songs original, and his
personality a great asset," the *Knoxville Sentinel* said.

We're not talking about high culture here. We're talking
about a certain middle-brow, crowd-pleasing brilliance. When he
was on a bill at a theater in Oakland or Little Rock or Butte, Jolson was one act among many, preceded by, to take the Little Rock
example, Slives, the clown baseball player; Pollard, the juggler;
Will Cross and his "stunning beauties" in a "musical montage";
followed by Dumont, the Chinese impersonator, meaning a white
guy in a parody of an Asian man. Finally, there was Al Jolson,
the rising star of "negro storytellers." Jolson's always-on-the-move
style of life, his fondness for late-night card games, the races, and
boxing matches, combined with his chronic anxious excitabil-
ity, which arose out of what Jean-Paul Sartre called "authentic
angst" in the sense that it exists apart from objective conditions,
all this caused difficulties for his marriage, which took only a few
short years to go bad. He and Harry, who fell farther and farther
behind in the fame and money sweepstakes, had periodic fallings-
out, followed by fallings in, and then more fallings-out, like a

married couple who couldn't live without each other or with each other either.

The one consistent, unchanging thing in Al's life to which he devoted himself with relentless attention was his pursuit of stardom, "the big time," which the small regional theaters where he played definitely were not. But it was coming. Harry told the story: He, Al, and Henrietta had dinner together during which Henrietta pleaded with Al to save some money, which he was never able to do. "Why should I save money?" Al said. "I'm the greatest entertainer in the world. Some day I'll be a millionaire. You watch and see." Years later, Henrietta said, "I always thought [Al] was a little crazy. We couldn't understand that he was telling the truth. He was the only one who knew of his greatness."

In Little Rock (or possibly Seattle, the accounts differ on this detail), Jolson got picked up by Lew Dockstader's Minstrels, perhaps the most famous of the traveling vaudeville troupes. Dockstader, born in Hartford, Connecticut, in 1856, was an overweight, hard-drinking comedian and singer famed for his Theodore Roosevelt impersonations, which he did in blackface. To be part of Dockstader's company was to go about as far as it was possible to go in vaudeville, and Jolson stayed with it for a couple of years, traveling with Henrietta from one venue to the next, getting paid $125 a week. Al was in New York when the Dockstader troupe took four weeks off, and a booking agent named Arthur Klein got Jolson a four-week engagement at Hammerstein's Victoria Theatre.

It would be his first solo performance at a major New York venue, and he was gripped with anxiety. The Victoria was known as a tough place to perform because important people in the theatrical trade came there to view new acts. When he got onstage on a Sunday night in 1909 he found the audience talking among themselves, not paying much attention to what was taking place. Jolson whistled through his fingers to get everybody's attention. "If you want to talk to each other you could have stayed home and saved yourself a nice piece of change," he said. He had a couple of jokes to tell, he continued, and a couple of songs to sing, and then everybody could go home, which he wanted to do too, since his wife, "a real cute trick," was waiting for him in his hotel, and "you wouldn't want me to keep the little lady waiting any longer than necessary, would you?" After he performed, the applause was wild. Jolson wanted to celebrate with Henrietta, but she didn't want to go out so late, so he called Klein and didn't come back until dawn.

In 1910, Jolson's stature increased when the songwriter Harry Von Tilzer wrote "Hip Hip Hypnotize Me" expressly for him. Tilzer was born Aaron Gumbinsky in 1872 in Detroit, the son of Jewish immigrants from Poland. At fourteen he left home to join a circus in Chicago as a singer and tumbler, adopting his mother's maiden name, Tilzer, adding a "Von" to give it an aristocratic touch (talk about self-invention!). He went to New York, became a pianist in a saloon, and wrote songs. He was unsuccessful at the last of those until he was discovered by Maurice Shapiro and Louis Bernstein, the founders of one of the most storied of music publishers on Tin Pan Alley, Shapiro, Bernstein & Co., who hired Von Tilzer and paid him handsomely to write songs for them. Tilzer's first big song, "My Old New Hampshire Home," sold a million copies. In 1900, he had another hit with "Bird in a Gilded Cage," lyrics by Arthur A. Lamb, a sentimental ballad about a pretty girl who marries for money ("And her beauty was sold for an old man's gold / She's a bird in a gilded cage.")

Two years later Von Tilzer left to form the Harry Von Tilzer Music Publishing Company, which produced hundreds of successful songs, perhaps the most famous of them being "I Want a

Girl Just Like the Girl Who Married Dear Old Dad." And then, as we've seen, Von Tilzer introduced Al and Harry to an agent at the Morris Agency. Eight years later, in 1910, Tilzer wrote "Hip Hip Hypnotize Me," lyrics by William Dillon, for Jolson, who turned it into a risqué hit.

> *A hypnotist once in a vaudeville show*
> *Was admired by a maid in the very first row.*
> *She said, "If you hypnotize me, then I won't know . . .*
> *I don't care what you do.*
> *I'll take my chances with you, if I'm*
> *Hip hip hypnotized."*

It was the last song Jolson sang on the program with the Dockstader Minstrels, and *Variety* reported that he "pulled down something close to a riot of appreciation . . . a fire of insistent applause." What happened next suggests his knack for establishing a kind of complicity with the audience. He did that sometimes with Jewish-inflected humor—"If those three dollar seats are filled, we're out of trouble already," he would say, pointing to the front rows. "Wait a minute," he says to another character when he first appears in *Bombo,* one of his long-running Broadway shows. "Let me say hello to the audience. After they paid $3.30 you ought to say something to them." On the occasion of "Hip Hip Hypnotize Me," he told the orchestra with mock severity not to play it again because it was "a dirty song," according to a disapproving account of the incident in *The American Magazine*. When the audience responded with laughter, Jolson said, "Ah hah! That's what you want!" And he sang it again. "Now your wife might have been in that audience," the magazine warned. Jolson is "coming to your town, wherever it is, and if he hasn't been there yet—Jolson and all his kind."

The magazine's warning about looming moral perdition went largely ignored, or at least sufficiently ignored for Jolson to continue moving up the ladder of celebrity. He stayed in New York where he made $500 a week doing two shows a day at two or three of the twenty-six vaudeville houses in the city, working and living furiously, as was his wont, staying out while Henrietta stayed home. He turned down an invitation to audition for the Ziegfeld Follies on the grounds that he didn't "do auditions," and, anyway, "there will be bigger opportunities."

* * *

One day in the spring of 1910, the theater owner and impresario J.J. Shubert was strolling in New York when the American Horse Exchange on Broadway and Fiftieth Street came into view. Shubert, like Al Jolson, with whom he was soon to enter into a close, sometimes tense, extremely profitable relationship, was one of the more prominent of the Jewish immigrants for whom show business was a ladder to stratospheric success. New York's Broadway was cutthroat, greedy, and unforgiving, but it was also in its way progressive, a kind of urban frontier democracy, a place of a "roughneck sort of egalitarianism," in Irving Howe's phrase, at a time when Jews were mostly excluded from the more genteel realms of American life. The most famous Jewish person in America at the time was Louis Brandeis, who was named to the Supreme Court in 1916 after a confirmation battle that was bruising in part because his Jewishness was not welcome to the WASP establishment. Brandeis belonged to the older generation of Jews who were already making it in America, despite the obstacles. His German-speaking ancestors had come from Prague, waxed prosperous in Louisville, Kentucky, before the Civil War, and were able to give their children a cultivated, assimilated home. Louis's grades at Harvard Law School were the highest in the history of the school up to that point.

But Broadway was for a different class, the poor and scrappy, many of them Jews like Asa Yoelson and Jacob Schubart—Shubert before its orthographic reform—who didn't go to Harvard Law or even City College, where many poor and middle-class Jews were getting the educations they were denied at more prestigious institutions. They could be called Lower East Side Jews, even if some of them didn't literally live there, who grew up in tenements or their equivalents, with the common kitchen down the hall and the toilet in the backyard. What they had in common, aside from their Jewishness, was what Howe called "a coarse hunger for success and few scruples in their climb to reach it." Broadway was a place of American possibility. It was untrammeled, unregulated, absent WASP aristocrats, where what counted was talent, ambition, and grit, not pedigree or family advantage. It was also a place where Jews gained power, and while Jews competed against other Jews and even sometimes stabbed them in the back, they didn't discriminate against them. Popular entertainment was a kind of fractious club, competitive, manipulative, mercenary, but it was also a domain where tribal membership carried an advantage.

Jacob Schubart arrived in New York in 1881 in steerage from Poland, with his wife, three boys, and three girls. He was a religiously Orthodox, erratic, abusive father. The family settled in Syracuse, New York, in a house sandwiched between another house and the railroad tracks, so they were never far from the sound of locomotives and the smell of coal smoke. One of the sisters died of malnutrition during the family's first winter in America.

They lived in Syracuse's Seventh Ward, where "the Israelites," as the local newspaper called them, formed a ghetto. The boys' father pulled Levi, the oldest of the brothers (later known as

Lee), out of school when he was ten years old, so he could peddle housewares to local farmers. He did the same to the middle boy, Sammy, when he was eight. The youngest of the brothers, Jacob (later J.J., who was walking up Broadway that spring day in 1910) stayed in school to a reasonable age, which was fourteen. After a while Levi began running numbers for a cigar factory owner who had a gambling operation on the side. Jacob sold newspapers on the Syracuse-to-Rochester train. Sammy, thin, small, delicate, clever, audacious, and ambitious, went to work at the Grand Opera House in Syracuse, where he distributed programs to patrons, earning a salary of $1.50 per week.

By the early twentieth century, the brothers were among the richest and most powerful theatrical entrepreneurs in America, founders of the Shubert Organization, which remains the biggest owner of live-performance theaters in New York. Led by Sam, they acquired theaters in several cities in upstate New York and in Manhattan. They were also impresarios, financing and booking variety shows—singers, dancers, chorus girls, jugglers, magicians, animal trainers, comedians, and the like—into their theaters, shows that featured some of the biggest names, both American and European, in the world of entertainment.

And that's why on that walk in 1910, the American Horse Exchange was of interest to J.J. It was a bit too far uptown compared to other Broadway theaters, but it was lofty and spacious and, J.J. thought, could be converted into a spacious, elegant, state-of-the-art theater that could serve as a home base for the revues and extravaganzas that the Shuberts produced in New York, which they then packaged for tours to Shubert theaters throughout the country. When J.J. learned that the Horse Exchange landlord was the financier William K. Vanderbilt, he went straight to Wall Street to see him, and, according to J.J.'s version of events, they scribbled a deal on the back of an envelope right away: a forty-year rental for $40,000 a year.

Two years later, on March 20, 1911, the majestic, lavishly decorated, 1,750-seat Winter Garden Theatre, as it was and still is called, opened. Its inaugural event was a four-hour variety show marathon with hundreds of performers and dozens of acts, one following another onstage, some of them imported from Europe. It was the most anticipated theatrical event of the season. The newspapers disclosed the lavish program days in advance; they sent reporters to rehearsals. It was news when opening night was postponed for a couple of days because the Shuberts didn't feel it was ready. The theater was sold out weeks in advance. The crowds of people looking at the people going into the theater were so large that extra detachments of police were called out. The lines of carriages and automobiles stretched for two blocks. There was a mock Chinese opera; a Russian dance; a ballet called *The Pretty Milliners;* Consuelo Tamayo, a Spanish singer and dancer known as La Tortajada, starred in one featured act; another was a two-act musical comedy called *La Belle Paree,* or *A Jumble of Hilarity,* with dozens of performers telling the story of a wealthy widow and her encounters with characters as she journeys to Paris.

Just a few weeks after Jolson had turned down an audition for the Ziegfeld Follies, waiting for "a bigger opportunity," the Shuberts offered him a role as one of those characters. Jolson played what was called "a colored aristocrat" named Erastus Sparkler, who met "a colored queen," Eczema Johnson, played by Stella Mayhew, on a Paris street. The two of them sang a half dozen songs, including a duet with the cringeworthy title, "Paris Is a Paradise for Coons," the music composed by the young Jerome Kern. The song title sounds terrible; it would clearly fail abysmally by the standards of today, but its content was actually better than

the title suggests, a rhymed enumeration of the types of racial violence common in America that were happily absent in Paris. By
the time Jolson's number came on, it was after midnight and the
audience was sleepy, some of the critics already gone, which made
Jolson feel that he'd bombed.

The reviews that first night were mixed. "Jolson's 10-minute
turn passed in good shape, but no more," *Variety* said. *The New
York Times* called the show "a very flashy toy full of life and go
and color and with no end of jingle to it." The Jolson-Mayhew
part of it was among its "very best features," the *Times* continued,
but the whole glittery extravaganza "lagged where by all the rules
it should have moved more briskly," a flaw the paper blamed on
"a tired, overworked company on the nervous edge." Though Jolson emerged from opening night in pretty good shape, critically
speaking, he and some of the other players were dismayed by the
reviews and thought they might be dropped from the bill. Some
of them were, but J.J., a keen observer of audience reactions, not
only did not fire Jolson, he moved him to an earlier slot on the
bill, and Jolson turned it to good advantage. "Lots of brave folks
out there," he said to the audience on the second night of *La Belle
Paree*. Then, alluding to the reviews the show had gotten: "Either
that or you can't read. Come to think of it, after the reviews we
got there's a lot of brave folks up here on the stage."

With the show more compact, and Jolson coming onstage
earlier, *La Belle Paree* turned into an event. Jolson was not the
featured or most famous performer—others got more press and
more enthusiastic notices—and yet, over the next weeks and
months, he became the undisputed linchpin of the Shubert productions and the Winter Garden, staying until 1926, when he left
to do the movie *The Jazz Singer*. After his years of struggling, his
experiments in Yiddish dialect skits, his touring the country in
vaudeville, all those "restless nights in one-night cheap hotels,"

as T. S. Eliot might have put it, was in the past. Within a couple more years, Al Jolson was the most famous popular performer in the country and reputedly the highest paid. It was a remarkable rise for the motherless Yiddish-speaking boy from Lithuania to go in a little over fifteen years from busking in front of the Raleigh Hotel in Washington to becoming rich and famous on New York's Great White Way.

"Basically, J.J. would present two kinds of musicals at the Winter Garden: those with and those without Al Jolson," Foster Hirsch, the historian of the Shubert Organization, wrote. The shows featuring Jolson were essentially vehicles for him; nobody else really mattered, except as necessary props. Over the years, his salary grew to $5,000 a week, an extravagant sum in those days when the average working person made around $500 a year. Nobody in American show business was paid more; nobody had more star power.

At first, there was a new show every year or so at the Winter Garden, but because any show that had Jolson in it could basically run forever, the intervals stretched out to roughly every three years. After *La Belle Paree* in 1911 came *Vera Violetta,* starring a French singer and comedian named Gaby Deslys, who was a sensation at the time. In 1913 came *The Hollywood Express,* after which Jolson signed a five-year contract with the Shuberts, paying him $1,500 a week, a signing bonus of $10,000, and 10 percent of the profits of the shows he appeared in. He was at the beginning of the long stretch of time during which Babe Ruth and Charlie Chaplin dominated baseball and silent films and Jolson musical comedy. All these enterprises flourished as never before.

The year after *Hollywood Express* brought *Dancing Around,* the first show in which Jolson got top billing. Next was *The Whirl of Society,* which marked the first time Jolson took on a blackface character that he played again in other shows. This character was

"Gus," a Black underdog who is, as Gilbert Seldes described him, "the scalawag servant with his surface dullness and hidden cleverness." He's a classic underdog, disadvantaged but smarter than the supposedly superior characters around him, about whom, as Goldman put it, he "shares private jokes with the audience." In *Bombo,* for example, Gus was a sort of jester to Christopher Columbus; it is he, not the buffoon-like Columbus, who is responsible for the "discovery" of America. In *Big Boy* he was a picked-on stable boy on a Kentucky horse farm who triumphs over a group of nefarious rivals by winning the Kentucky Derby (which the bad guys were trying to fix).

The mere fact that a megastar like Jolson would take on the persona of a Black man and play him over and over in one production after another was surely rooted in the pathological fixation of white America on blackness, which made minstrelsy the most popular form of entertainment in the country from roughly the mid-nineteenth century to the early decades of the twentieth. But Jolson's impersonation of Gus actually subverted the stereotypical elements of the usual minstrel character. Gus was very different from a Zip Coon or a Jim Crow, and even from Amos 'n' Andy of later years. He was, to be sure, an outsider. But he was a shrewd outsider who felt no inferiority compared to the insiders, and, indeed, understood their game, and he manipulated it for his own benefit and for the benefit of what was good and just as well. The character wasn't intended to be a disguised piece of political or racial commentary, but the underlying message of Jolson's impersonation was one of equality in which Jews and Blacks, both outsiders, punctured the pretentious self-satisfaction of the insiders' world. The fact that Jolson played Gus in several stage comedies, as well as in the movie version of *Big Boy,* suggests that audiences were receptive to that implicit message, as well as to the fact that

Jolson had the sort of star power that allowed him to do pretty much whatever he wanted.

"Jolson now had all the trappings of a major star—a valet, a chauffeur, a manager, a wife he kept in California, and money," Goldman writes. In 1918, he signed a new contract with the Shuberts guaranteeing him $2,500 a week and 15 to 25 percent, not of profits as before, but of gross receipts. Jolson developed his signature techniques, running back and forth on a runway built into the center aisle that put him in the lap of the audience, getting down on one knee and extending his white-gloved hands in front of him, belting out his song's final refrain. Audiences truly went wild, delaying scenes with prolonged applause, hats thrown into the air, demanding that Jolson sing for them and never mind what else was supposed to take place on the stage.

* * *

What was it that made him so successful? Watching footage of him today—and there are plenty of videos on YouTube—he's certainly good, but is he *that* good? Of course, the fact that he mostly performed in blackface already makes him seem like a historical curiosity, an artifact of a discredited era rather than a cultural monument. Others from his era, like George Gershwin, Irving Berlin, even such disparate figures in the world of entertainment as Harry Houdini and the columnist Walter Winchell, seem somehow to have left a more permanent legacy. Some of the songs that were among Jolson's biggest hits—"Swanee," "My Mammy," "Toot Toot Tootsie," and "Rockabye Your Baby with a Dixie Melody"—seem corny, and, in the case of "Mammy," schmaltzy by today's standards. Many of them are very clever and tuneful, but not more clever or tuneful than the songs other people were singing, and Jolson's style of singing them seems outdated now, like fins on cars, brassy, flashy, a touch bombastic (though not always), even vulgar in their sentimental gladness, their pasted-on poignancy, especially compared to the amplified coolness and sleekness of the popular music fashions that have followed him. Jolson was loud. "He sang in California; you heard him in Altoona," George Burns once quipped. Have people listened to Jolson since the sixties? Some of his contemporaries—Caruso, Louis Armstrong, blues singers like Bessie Smith and Ethel Waters—are listened to more than he is. As of 2022, the International Al Jolson Society, which publishes a quarterly journal of photographs, historical sketches, and reminiscences, has fewer than five hundred members worldwide.

And yet, from the early 1910s to the late 1940s, there was nobody more beloved, more in demand, more celebrated, bigger than Al Jolson. His voice had a broad range, an instantly recognizable timbre, a vibrato, that set him apart, and there was a natural passion to his style. Like Sinatra later, though without a microphone, Jolson seemed to incarnate a song, to stroke it almost sensuously, breathe immediacy into it. And there was a tremendous energy to everything he did, or, perhaps by today's more laid-back standards, overdid. He would trot onto the stage from the wings and start singing right away, arms, legs, and slender body all in motion. "Watching Jolson come on the stage was like watching a duck hitting water," Samson Raphaelson, who wrote the short story and the play that was turned into the movie *The Jazz Singer,* said. The image is a bit mysterious, but the suggestion is of an impact, a sudden disruption of a smooth surface. Raphaelson spoke of Jolson's "amazing velocity," his "fluidity." There was always something playful in the quick rhythms of his songs, the short phrases alternating with elongated words—"I'd give the *wooooorld* to be," and then the quick trip down the scale, "among the folks in

D-I-X-I-E," the letters spelled out quickly. The critic Seldes used the word "demonic" to describe Jolson (and his contemporary Fanny Brice); Raphaelson described him as "possessed," delineating the difference between Jolson and the other singers and comics who were also becoming famous in America.

"They seemed very much alike, but they weren't," Raphaelson said years later. "There was nobody like Jolson. . . . You could take Jessel, Cantor, Berle, Lou Holtz—there's a generic resemblance—but [Jolson] loomed way above them." Raphaelson called Jolson "the most electric theatrical personality I'd ever encountered," adding that the electricity didn't come across in the movies. You had to be in the theater to feel the charge that accompanied Jolson's appearance on a stage, in person, he said. "To have heard Al Jolson sing 'Swanee' is to have had one of the few great experiences which the minor arts are capable of giving," Seldes wrote. "To have heard it without feeling something obscure and powerful and rich with a separate life of its own coming into being is—I should say it is not to be alive." And beyond that: "On the great nights when everything is right, Jolson is driven by a power beyond himself. . . . In those moments I cannot help thinking of him as a genius."

* * *

On March 21, 1926, Jolson, now thirty-five years old, performed in a celebration of the fifteenth anniversary of the Winter Garden. He was onstage for an hour—"he sang and talked, talked and sang," according to *The New York Times*. The theater was filled to capacity. People who couldn't get tickets milled about in the theater's spacious lobby "receiving tidings of the doings within from volunteer dispatch runners." Jolson "was the center of a distinguished audience's frenzied cheers."

Jolson's stardom was such that in 1926, when Warner Bros. decided to make a movie version of *The Jazz Singer,* they assumed that Jolson was too big to take the lead role. "Jack Warner never dreamed they could get Jolson," Raphaelson remembered years later. "Jolson was unobtainable." What the Warners didn't know was that Jolson already had a long history with Raphaelson and *The Jazz Singer,* a deeply personal attachment arising out of the fact that he regarded the Raphaelson short story and the play based on it as his own story, which, in a remarkable coincidence, it was.

5

The Good Story

The title was "Day of Atonement," subtitle: "A Dramatic Story of Filial Devotion," by Samson Raphaelson. The story was published in the January 1922 issue of *Everybody's Magazine,* a handsomely illustrated, general interest periodical devoted mostly to contemporary fiction. "If it's a good story, it's in *Everybody's,*" was its slogan.

Raphaelson's was a good story, following in the magazine just after "The Mystery of Ravensdale Court" by J. S. Fletcher ("It grips. You won't want to put it down.") and *The Circle* (a "brilliant and witty play" by W. Somerset Maugham). But what might now be called its ethnic flavor made "Day of Atonement" unusual for *Everybody's,* which aimed at a kind of generic, educated, American Main Street readership. And yet here was a story sprinkled with Hebrew and Yiddish terms—*chazonoth,* the cantorial liturgy; shiksa, a gentile woman; Yiddishkeit, Jewishness—none of them explained or translated into English, as if the writer and his editors felt the readership would understand them, would need no explanatory guideposts as it made the journey. That knowledge, that familiarity with the other, was a sign of changing times. The year 1922 was at the end of the four-decade-long period of massive immigration to the United States that had begun in the 1880s and brought new populations to the country, with new anxieties and new "good stories."

"Day of Atonement" was one of the first short stories published by Raphaelson, then twenty-three years old, a bright and
eager "skinny kid with glasses," as he liked to put it. He was
destined for considerable success as a New York playwright and
Hollywood screenwriter. Born in New York in 1894, the eldest of
eight children, his breeding ground was the same as that of the
others of the Jewish cohort that was making it in the world of
American popular entertainment. He spent his early childhood
on the Lower East Side where, as he said, "all I knew were Jewish
kids. . . . It was all Jewish, everywhere." When he was eleven, he
moved to Chicago—his parents had relocated there a few years
earlier, leaving him in the care of his grandparents in New York—
eventually studying at the University of Illinois. Later, when he
was established in Hollywood, he would write witty, repartee-rich
romantic comedies like *The Shop Around the Corner,* directed by
Ernst Lubitsch, as well as *Suspicion,* directed in 1941 by Alfred
Hitchcock. He also wrote nine plays that made it to Broadway,
and dozens of short stories.

None of that later work had much if anything in the way
of Yiddishkeit in it, reflecting Raphaelson's general observance of
the rule among Jews, which was to keep their Jewishness at bay,
private, out of the public sphere. In Raphaelson's long career—he
died in 1983 at the age of ninety-one—only "Day of Atonement"
and the play, *The Jazz Singer,* which he later wrote as a theatrical
version of the story, seem directly connected with his own life and
to any concern about Jews. "Day of Atonement" was connected
to the life that Al Jolson also kept private, though the story was
truly and by intention modeled on Jolson's own. In writing "Day
of Atonement," Raphaelson created a kind of feedback loop that
connected America's greatest entertainer to his Jewish roots and
to the Jewish struggle with assimilation. It brought that struggle

into the open, universalized it as a theme in a culture that, under the influence of millions of immigrants, was becoming wider, deeper, more capacious.

"I thought it would have universal appeal," Raphaelson said years later, speaking of the theme of "Day of Atonement." The occasion was his transformation of the story into *The Jazz Singer,* which had a successful run in 1926 and 1927, both on Broadway and on tour across the country. Raphaelson continued:

> Because to me it wasn't a play about a cantor and about synagogues. To me it was a play about the orthodox religious faithful, the older generation, and the young, radical, broken-away-from-faith generation . . . whether it was a Jew, a German—whoever it was—the Irish people, with their worship of the priest and so on. I thought it was universal . . . and that people would respond. . . . It was parent and child, and it was America.

Indeed, it was America, or, as applied to Raphaelson's own group, it was the Jews becoming American and America becoming Jewish, but not without struggle and anguish. The main character in "Day of Atonement," and in its future theatrical and cinematic versions, is Jakie Rabinowitz, whose father, Yosele, like Jolson's father, Moshe, is an Orthodox cantor who, as Raphaelson's story put it, "had Europe in his bones," the Europe of stubborn religious identity and practice that had survived centuries of Jew hatred, pogroms, and ghettos.

"For ten generations, in Russia and now in America, the name 'Rabinowitz' had stood for devout, impassioned *chazonoth,* and Jakie's father was animated by the one desire that his son should become even a greater cantor than himself," the narrator of "Day of Atonement" says. The cantor, it should be noted, was a figure of nothing less than magnificence in the Jewish world in those days. A great cantor was a commanding figure, the one who gave musical voice to the pleadings and prayers of the congregation, who gave the rituals of the synagogue their beauty and aesthetic meaning, who made going to shul the transporting experience it was meant to be. For a cantor to wish for his son to follow in his footsteps was to want not just community respect for him, or the perpetuation of tradition, but a kind of glory compared to which secular riches and fame are trivial, insignificant. That glory was the real-life Moshe Yoelson's wish for both of his sons, Hirsch and Asa. But the fictional Jakie, like the real-life Jolson, belongs to the "broken-away-from-faith generation" that, living in the bracingly free air of America, sees the tradition not as glorious and revered, but as cramped and defeatist and yearns for success in the broad and deep arena that is non-Jewish America.

"What our Jakie needs is a God," Cantor Rabinowitz tells his wife. "What I need," Jakie says, "is a song number with a kick in it."

Jakie gives himself the anglicized stage name Jack Robin and he achieves success in vaudeville, though his success is modulated by a tug on his spirit exercised by the old ways. Cantor Rabinowitz, his off-kilter syntax reflecting his foreign birth, tells him, "Music is God's voice, and you make your papa and mama happy, Jakie, if you grow up to be a great Chazan like your grandfather in Vilna, *olav hasholom*." It's not clear how many of *Everybody's* readers knew that *olav hasholom* is Hebrew for "peace be upon him," but Jakie knows it, and he never entirely escapes the feeling that "his lyric voice" had all along been destined "to cry the sermons of Israel in a Russian synagogue."

Despite the tug, Jack pursues his ambition, and after some struggles his career begins to take flight. He falls in love with a shiksa chorus girl. Things are good. If the joys of being alive smote him, what could more sweetly ease the ache of happiness than the plaintive blues of Irving Berlin's "Alexander's Ragtime Band"—

Come on and hear, come on and hear
Alexander's Ragtime Band.
Come on and hear, come on and hear
It's the best band in the land.

—in which Raphaelson's narrator hears what Yosele Rabinowitz is unable to hear, namely, that "this grave-eyed boy with the ways of the street was sincerely carrying on the tradition of plaintive, religious melody of his forefathers." What Yosele derisively calls "ragstime," sung only by "bums," actually incarnates the tragic Jewish tradition "with the gay trappings of Broadway and the rich vulgarity of the East Side." Raphaelson, the American English major, draws on a famous metaphor of the poet Matthew Arnold to find commonality between Yosele's *chazonoth* and Jack's "ragstime." When Jack sings his American tunes, he is "translating the age-old music of the cantors—that vast loneliness of a race wandering 'between two worlds, one dead, the other powerless to be born'—into primitive and passionate Americanese."

Raphaelson may well have been stretching a point here. It's hard to believe, for example, when Jolson sang his "Mammy" songs that he was feeling anything specifically Jewish in them, much less that he was translating the age-old music of the cantors into an American idiom. But the notion that American musical theater, as incarnated by Jews like Jolson, was in its way like the Hebrew liturgy, Americanized but imbued with the same poignant spirit, was a fixed idea for Raphaelson, and it was there from the beginning of his long encounter with Jolson. When he was seventeen, a student at the University of Illinois and eager to make an impression on a young woman, he took her to see Jolson at a theater in Champagne, where he was touring in one of his musical comedies—*Robinson Crusoe, Jr.*

Robinson Crusoe, Jr., which some critics described as Jolson's apotheosis in musical theater, opened in 1916. Like other of his musical comedies, the story was a scaffolding for Jolson's songs, the story in the case of *Crusoe, Jr.* about a bored millionaire who dreams of exotic travels—to an island with an enchanted forest, on a pirate ship crewed by chorus girls—to which he is escorted by "Gus," his "good Friday." Jolson, playing Gus in blackface, was at the center, mixing up jokes with sardonic commentary and being the smartest character on the stage, then belting out his musical numbers, supported by about two hundred dancers and other singers. Among the songs was "Where Did Robinson Crusoe Go with Friday on Saturday Night?"

> *On this island lived wild men and cannibal crimmin*
> [criminals?]
> *And you know where there are wild men, there must be wild*
> *women.*

and "Yaaka Hula Hickey Dula," perhaps the most famous supposedly Hawaiian song in Broadway history.

> *Beside the sea at Waikiki you'll play for me*
> *Yaaka Hula Hickey Dula, Yaaka Hickey Hula Du.*

"I shall never forget the first five minutes of Jolson," Raphaelson said, remembering years later his attendance at that 1917 performance. "That figure in blackface kneeling at the end of a runway that projected him into the heart of the audience, flinging out his white-gloved hands, was embracing that audience with a prayer—an evangelical moan—a tortured, imperious call that hurtled through the house." Raphaelson, his spirit brushed by something mystical and religious, turned to his date and declared, "My God, this isn't a jazz singer. This is a cantor!"

* * *

Not everyone would have seen anything quite so religiously uplifting in Jolson's voice and gestures. There's nothing in the lyrics to these songs that seem to suggest an evangelical moan. And yet, for a boy from the Lower East Side for whom "it was all Jewish, everywhere," the sentiment is credible. Listen to a 1916 recording of Jolson singing "Yaaka Hula" and it's not outlandish to detect something cantorial in the Jolsonian lilt, the way his voice slides clarinet-to-trombone-like at the end of phrases, lingering on rhyming lyrics—"a Hula maiden plaaaay. . . . She stole my heart awaaaay." Listening to that song, it's possible to imagine Asa Yoelson chanting the Hebrew liturgy in Seredzius less than twenty years before, his father standing over him as he sang the prayers he rarely sang anymore but never forgot. If you want to hear Yiddishkeit in "Yaaka Hula Hickey Dula," Yiddishkeit will be there. Jolson himself seems to have made no allusion to that possibility. He never said that only a Jew whose background was cantorial, who knew the deep melancholy of *Hineni* or Kol Nidre, who heard the voices of the past whispering to him down the corridors of the generations, could have sung "Rockabye Your Baby with a Dixie Melody" the way Jolson did, with, as it was often said of him, "a tear in his voice."

There was also of course Dixie and especially the Black influence, which pervaded almost everything Jolson did, from the songs themselves to his use of blackface, which, among white people, became nearly a monopoly of the Jewish entertainers. The affinity was also in what were called "coon songs," a term that is now correctly seen as a racial insult. George Gershwin, who wrote "Swanee," "blended Yiddish folk tunes and black melodies into a blue union," as Irving Howe put it. "Put Yiddish and black together and they spell Al Jolson," one of Gershwin's biographers, Isaac Goldberg, wrote. The Jews were not the only people in America whose music was weighted with historical suffering. And yet, it is hard to imagine a white Episcopalian Anglo-American taking on the tonality of a Jolson. Listen to recordings of Cantor Josef Rosenblatt, the leading cantorial celebrity in the golden age of the cantors, the 1920s and 1930s. The style of Jolson and Rosenblatt couldn't have been more different. Rosenblatt, who did what Jolson's father wished his son had done, did not frolic onstage; Jolson did not wear a long black beard and skullcap. The one stood stolid and nearly motionless as he chanted in Hebrew and Yiddish; the other rocked and quick-stepped, dropped to one knee and threw back his head as he sang in southern-accented English. But there is something in the voices of the two men, born in the Russian Empire four years apart, suggesting that they branched off from the same aesthetic and cultural root. The Yiddish word applied to Rosenblatt is *krekhz,* defined as "the sobbing crack in his voice that evoked a conversation with God." There was *krekhz* in Jolson's voice as well. When Raphaelson exclaimed on hearing Jolson, "This is a cantor!," he wasn't inventing something out of thin air.

The night that he heard Jolson in *Crusoe, Jr.,* Raphaelson went backstage. Jolson invited him to his dressing room and told him "about how religious and strict his father was and how the old man only wanted his sons to sing in the synagogue . . . and I decided to put it in a story." Raphaelson probably didn't know that a couple of years before, Jolson himself was enacting some real-life scenes that could have been in "Day of Atonement." On a Friday night in 1915, President Woodrow Wilson was due to attend a performance by Jolson in *Dancing Around,* on tour in Washington, D.C. Jolson sent front row tickets to Moshe and Hessi, but he could see from the stage that while the president of the United States and his wife were in the audience, the Yoelsons, father and stepmother, weren't.

"You didn't come to the show last night, Papa," Jolson told Moshe when he went to see him in the apartment above the store soon afterward.

"Asa, it was Friday night."

"So?"

"I am at the synagogue. You forget, I see, the faith of our people."

"Papa, I'm sorry. I knew that, but I thought you'd make an exception. I was singing for the president."

"I was singing for God," Moshe said.

Did this episode actually happen? Only the people in the room would know for sure, though it appears in the first biography of Jolson, written by Pearl Sieben, who became a confidante of Jolson after he met her in the early 1940s. No such episode is in "Day of Atonement." But whether apocryphal or not, the story seems accurately to reflect Jolson's relationship with his father and the conflict between father and son that is at the heart of that story. The father never stops hoping that the son will return to the fold. "Maybe when he gets older he'll see how beautiful is Yiddishkeit," the old man tells his wife, Rivka, Jakie's adoring mother, instead of "hanging around music places and singing these ragtime songs what all the bums they sing." And Jack never stops longing for his father's respect, or entirely sheds the hold of the tradition that he angrily tells his father is "dead." On a visit to his parents, he goes with his father to shul, where he finds himself touched by "the blessedly familiar and peaceful." It's not hard even today to experience the hold of the ancient rites. No matter how educated,

secular, and assimilated an American Jew may be, once he or she
has experienced the ravishing, tragedy-tinged minor-key beauty
of Kol Nidre or *Eli Eli,* the effect will never entirely disappear.

Jack Robin was susceptible to that effect, but when it came
down to the practical conflict in his life between the old-fashioned
wishes of his father and his own American dreams, it seems inevitable that he will grit his teeth and choose the latter. And, of
course, the whole point of "Day of Atonement" is that it does
come down to such a choice. A powerful producer offers Jack the
chance he's been striving for, to move from vaudeville to the big
time. "I'll put you on Broadway in electric lights," the producer
tells him. Meanwhile, Cantor Rabinowitz collapses, and Jack's
mother pleads with her son to come to the synagogue on Yom
Kippur to chant the Kol Nidre prayer in his father's absence. But
Jack's Broadway opening is on that very night, the one and only
time in the year when Kol Nidre is sung, and to miss the opening
would be to give up on the future he's worked so hard to achieve.

Then, on the day of the show, a friend of the family, Yudelson,
comes to Jack's hotel to tell him that Cantor Rabinowitz has died.
Jack rushes to the apartment on Hester Street where Rivka tells
him that it was his father's dying wish that he take his place in
the synagogue that night, so the chain linking ten generations of
Rabinowitz cantors who chanted Kol Nidre on Yom Kippur won't
be broken. And now Jack has to confront his impossible dilemma:
whether to "sing ragtime songs while his father lay dead, and
thereby to force his mother to suffer an unbearable double grief,"
or to wreck his chances for secular success by not showing up for
his Broadway show.

This is a contrivance, of course. No Broadway producer would
ever have opened a show on the eve of Yom Kippur, not in a city
that was 25 percent Jewish. But the contrivance does represent
the enduring conflict in the Jewish American soul between tradi-

tion and modernity, Jewishness and assimilation. How would an American reader of 1922 have wanted Jack to resolve this conflict? The 1920s was the heyday of the melting-pot ideology, the powerful conviction that the only way to deal with the millions of new arrivals in the country was to require them to shuck their particularity, their old-world habits and customs, and become "one hundred percent American." Now that "diversity" has come to be valued as an end in itself, at least by the Democratic party and most liberal-minded people, it's hard to remember that in the late decades of the nineteenth century and the early decades of the twentieth, diversity was seen mostly as a danger to the nation, its character, and its democratic values. The nation's challenge, as the social reformer Lillian Wald put it, was "to fuse these people who come to us from the Old World civilization into . . . a real brotherhood among men." In 1915, Henry Ford, wanting his immigrant workers to become 100 percent American as quickly as possible, set up the Ford English School that foreign workers were required to attend if they wanted to work on a Ford assembly line. The first sentence they learned to repeat in their very first lesson was "I am a good American." To instill the benign concept of the melting pot, the school invented a ceremony whereby foreign-born workers wearing all sorts of outlandish garb would file into a great pot placed on the stage for the purpose—labeled "Melting Pot" for those who might otherwise miss the point—and then march out wearing identical suits and carrying American flags. Ford, as is well known, was a ferocious antisemite, one of whose prejudices arose from the Jewish insistence on retaining a separate identity. He was unlikely to have sympathized with Jakie Rabinowitz's dilemma.

It's hard to know for sure of course what readers would want Jack to do—sing Kol Nidre in a little synagogue on New York's Lower East Side or do "ragstime" in a grand Broadway theater and achieve the American dream—but it's quite certain that most people, Jewish or gentile, if actually faced with a similarly impossible choice in their real worlds of paying the rent and feeding their children, would have gone for the career and sacrificed the tradition. But not in Raphaelson's story. In "Day of Atonement," Jack yields to his mother, to his father's dying wish, and to the commands of the religious Orthodoxy. He dons the cantorial apparel and chants Kol Nidre in his father's shul, filled to the rafters, like it has never been sung before, and he continues to lead the Yom Kippur prayers the next day, "swathed in the great folds of a black striped *tallis* [prayer shawl] an elaborate and stiff black-plush skull cap on his head, his thin, handsome face deadly white, his dark eyes afire."

The suggestion is that Jack has made the correct moral choice, a spiritual one over a materialistic one, and he makes that choice having to assume that in doing so he has ruined his Broadway dreams. Perhaps he's even consigned himself to lifelong service as the cantor of a dingy shul on New York's Lower East Side patronized by a disappearing generation. But the moral bravery of his choice saves him. Unbeknownst to him, his producer, at first furious at Jack's failure to show up, reads in the papers of something remarkable taking place at the Hester Street Synagogue. (In fact, it's unlikely that Jack's appearance in his father's shul would have been reported in the press, but never mind.) Incognito, he goes there and hears Jack in his liturgical splendor, after which he runs to a phone at the corner drugstore. There, he summons his partner to the shul where he's going to hear "the greatest ragtime singer in America." During his moment of fury that morning, the producer had chosen a replacement for Jack, whom he intended to fire. Now he tells his partner to take down the replacement's name from the marquee and put Jack Robin's back up there instead.

6

Different and the Same

Among the entertainers who emerged to prominence during the Roaring Twenties, George Jessel was surely one of the brightest lights, even as he was also one of the most complicated and conflicted. "It would be foolish to pretend he is not a mixed-up fellow," his friend, the playwright William Saroyan, wrote in a preface to one of the several memoirs published over the years by Jessel. He was "a great storyteller," Saroyan continued, "not a great writer but, occasionally, the energy and eagerness and loneliness of the man come through with a power that is both rare and touching."

"Jessel held court," George Burns said, remarking on Jessel's natural command of an audience. When the comedians were gathered at the Hillcrest Country Club in Los Angeles, "they all *listen* to Georgie," Eddie Cantor said. "He was the great jester of our time."

"He was toastmaster at his own *bris,*" Bob Hope quipped at a Friars Club testimonial for Jessel in 1948. The reference was to Jessel's status as the most in-demand after-dinner speaker in America, well paid to offer testimonials, sometimes to people he didn't know. In spite of that, as Saroyan said, he always seemed "as sincere as the next man."

Jessel was famous for his comic routines, his improvisational wit, his many movie roles—bridging silent films and the

talkies—and his Rabelaisian appetites. He was a womanizer (he
married and divorced three times), a drinker, a jokester, a big
spender, a bon vivant. When he was interviewed on television by
Mike Wallace in 1957, several of Wallace's questions had to do
with Jessel's failed marriages and his pursuit of much younger
women—Jessel's third wife was sixteen years old when he married
her; he was forty-two. Jessel said that he was "on more front pages
and more gossip columns than any of my contemporaries," and,
while it's impossible to verify that statement, his blatant violations
of the rules of middle-class propriety kept him in the public eye
as much as his talent. "If it was not for their divorce in 1921, their
remarriage in 1922, divorce in 1923, and remarriage in 1924," a gossip columnist in the New York *Daily News* said, speaking of Jessel
and the silent film actress Florence Courtney, "the separation of
Mr. and Mrs. George Jessel might not make such a ripple in the
life of Hollywood." George Burns told the story of seeing Jessel in
The Jazz Singer on Broadway one night, probably in 1925 or 1926,
and being moved literally to tears when Jessel sang Kol Nidre at
the end of the play.

"I ran back to tell Jessel how great he was," Burns said, but
the theater attendant told him he couldn't go to the dressing room
because Jessel had his clothes off.

"I've seen a naked Jew before," Burns said.

"He's got a dame in there with him."

"I thought nothing could follow Kol Nidre, but I guess that
could," Burns said.

Jessel was born in New York in 1898. His father, a sometime
playwright of modest success, died when George was ten, leading Georgie, as he was called all his life, to get a job as a song
plugger at the Imperial Theatre on 116th Street, where his mother
was the ticket seller (a song plugger sang from the orchestra pit
as the audience waited for the silent feature to go on). Jessel was

the youngest member of a group called the Imperial Trio, one of whose other singers was the future gossip columnist Walter Winchell, whom Jessel described as "a handsome little guy with a fairly good voice and the heart throb of 116th Street." Both Winchell and Jessel eventually auditioned for *Kid Kabaret,* a traveling minstrel show created and produced by Gus Edwards (born Gustav Schmelowsky in German Silesia in 1878), a songwriter and impresario now largely forgotten but a major figure in vaudeville at the time. As the name suggests, *Kid Kabaret* engaged young performers for its shows, some in their late teens and early twenties, but others, like the twelve-year-old Jessel, legally underage, which meant it fought a kind of guerrilla war with what Jessel later called "that damned Gerry Society." Another boy in the *Kid Kabaret* troupe was Eddie Cantor, a few years older than Jessel, who, like Jessel, had grown up poor and fatherless (and, as we've seen in Cantor's case, motherless as well). They did skits, songs, imitations of famous people (especially of Jolson, who was already very famous), Yiddish monologues, and other acts. *Kid Kabaret* incubated more than a few major careers, not just that of Jessel, Cantor, and Winchell, but Will Rogers, Groucho Marx, Phil Silvers, and many others not quite as famous. There was a kind of natural progression, from *Kid Kabaret* to the Ziegfeld Follies, where both Cantor and Fanny Brice became famous, or to one of the vaudeville circuits.

In 1916, Jessel and another former *Kid Kabaret* performer named Lou Edwards created an act called "Two Patches from a Crazy Quilt," in which, among other things, Jessel did an imitation of Charlie Chaplin. They "jumped from the Beacon Theater in Boston—a ten cent vaudeville theater—to the Victoria Palace in London with eight weeks' bookings at $250 a week," Jessel remembered. Then it was back to New York where, after some struggle and a lot of persistence, he got parts in second-rank vaudeville theaters. He did that for a couple of years traveling the country. When he was in New York, he went to the Sunday night concerts that Al Jolson regularly gave at the Winter Garden, during which, as Jessel liked to put it, "Prince Al tore his heart out in song about his relations in Dixie." During 1917 and 1918, the time of American participation in World War I, the American theater was put largely on hold. But soon after the war, Jessel was hired to perform in *Gaieties,* a Shubert spectacle opening at the 44th Street Theatre in New York.

It was Jessel's breakthrough to Broadway, and he made the most of it, singing songs, some of his own composition, like "Oh How I Laugh When I Think How I Cried About You," and getting praise from critics for his ad-libs. Jessel was always among the more explicitly Jewish of the major comics, something of a throwback to the days when Jewish dialect comedy was a minor craze. Or, put it this way: He rode the old tradition of the "Hebrew comic" to national fame. Among his inventions, much imitated, was "Hello Mother," in which Jessel, using an old black telephone with separate mouth and earpieces as a prop, made filial calls:

"Hello mother, how did you like the bird I sent you."

Pause.

"Oh no! You cooked it?"

Pause.

"But it was a South American parrot. It spoke five languages!"

Final pause.

"It should have said something?"

Or there was the story of the gangster from Chicago, "a real tough guy who, every Friday night on Shabbos eve, would go to his mother's house for soup and chicken. On this particular occasion, as he gets out of his armored car, somebody shoots him. He has just enough strength to climb up and knock on his mother's door. She says 'Hello Morris,' who's lying on the ground near death. 'Mamma, they got me,' he gasps. She says, 'First you'll eat, then you'll tell me all about it.'"

But of all his acts, songs, routines, and after-dinner speeches, Jessel was proudest of the dramatic role he played in the stage version of *The Jazz Singer.* It was 1925, and Jessel's star had continued to rise. After his stint with *Gaieties,* he wrote a musical revue called *Jessel's Troubles,* about an East Side kid who persuades his mother to loan him her meager savings so he can produce a musical revue, which is then afflicted by all sorts of "troubles," including dunning creditors, an actors' strike, and the demands of a chorus of "twelve pretty trouble-makers," as a critic put it. Jessel traveled with the show for two years, to Los Angeles, San Francisco, Sacramento, Oakland, Memphis, Montreal, Kansas City, Philadelphia, and elsewhere, getting pretty good reviews for what one reviewer called "a pleasing bit of entertainment," and another "a nonsensical hash of claptrap." Al Lewis and Max Gordon, the show's producers, were immigrants from Polish shtetls, both of whom had done "Dutch"—meaning German—comedy skits on vaudeville before creating their own booking and production agency, becoming, in Jessel's words, "the most important of the vaudeville producers of the time." With Jessel's career blossoming, Lewis and Gordon approached him with the idea that he play a serious role in legitimate theater. Specifically, they'd bought the rights to do a stage version of "Day of Atonement," and they wanted him to play the character of Jakie Rabinowitz/Jack Robin.

According to Raphaelson, Lewis and Gordon, as Jessel's agents, wanted "to give Jessel a chance to find himself not merely as a comedian but as a great dramatic actor." Since publishing his story, Raphaelson had gone to New York to try to make it as a writer. One of his friends was a jazz musician named Peewee Byers, who knew Jolson. Byers told Raphaelson that Jolson had read "Day of Atonement" and wanted to talk to him about it.

And so, one night, Raphaelson, who described those early years in New York as "very lonely," went to the Café Royale, on the corner of Second Avenue and Twelfth Street in Manhattan—the heart of the Yiddish Theater district—where Byers brought him to Jolson's table.

"He was there with Mary Lewis, a young and beautiful opera singer in a mink coat," Raphaelson remembered later. "He was charming to me. He said, 'Listen boy, you got something there. You got something there, and I'll play it. Now I'll tell ya just what to do, and you got yourself a show.'"

Jolson went on to describe the songs he'd want Raphaelson to write into what he imagined to be a musical comedy, an opportunity that Raphaelson might have been expected quickly to embrace. Instead, he told Jolson that if he wrote the play Jolson's way, it would be just another vehicle for Jolson, like *Crusoe, Jr.* or *Bombo,* but if he wrote it his way, Raphaelson's way, it wouldn't be for Jolson at all. At that point, Raphaelson says, Jolson might have "told me to get the hell out of there. Instead, he put his hand on my shoulder and said, 'I like you. Now, you go ahead and do it the way you want. It won't be for me. But if you need any money, you need any help—let me know.'"

Now, three years later, Raphaelson went to work with Lewis, Gordon, and Jessel to adapt "Day of Atonement" for the theater. It wasn't a harmonious collaboration. Raphaelson complained that Jessel wrote "very slick and smooth little vaudeville jokes" into the script, and Raphaelson hired a lawyer to demand that the jokes be removed. Jessel, who, according to newspaper accounts of the time, came up with the new title "The Jazz Singer," treated Raphaelson patronizingly, like an amateur who didn't understand the first thing about theater. "Like most young authors, Sampson Raphaelson didn't want his brainchild touched," he wrote. Raphaelson described himself "as this agonizing, aspiring kid"

whose "genius" was being fouled by a "jungle of vaudeville men."
He stayed up all night one night taking out some of the material
that Jessel had written in, which infuriated Jessel. "I know this
guy," he said of Jakie/Jack. "It's me. I would be a wisecracking
guy."

The play opened in Stamford, Connecticut, in the middle
of September 1925, in a version that still included "the slick and
smooth little vaudeville jokes" that Raphaelson hated. The audience response was warm, which prompted Jessel, the future
national toastmaster, to give a little speech expressing appreciation "for your wonderful reception of me and my little play,"
making no mention of Raphaelson. "The great lesson we must
learn from this play is, 'Honor thy father and thy mother,'" Jessel
continued, a statement about the play's meaning that Raphaelson
found "pious." It also missed the point by a wide margin.

"It killed me hearing him say 'my little play'—because that
was the night when all the jokes were in, the bad jokes," Raphaelson said. He describes his relations with Jessel at the moment as
"violently hostile."

But then, disgruntled as he was, Raphaelson had a moment
of redemption. In an incident that he mentions but that is absent
from Jessel's account of that night, suddenly from the third row
of the audience someone stood up and shouted "Author, author!"
It was Jolson. "Do you think I'd miss this opening?" he'd told
Raphaelson shortly before the curtain went up. But the appar-
ently shy Raphaelson was in the shadows at the back of the theater
and made no effort to make himself visible. "'Well, the author
doesn't seem to be around,' Jessel said finally," as Raphaelson
remembered it, "'but I want to express my gratitude to him,' or
whatever it was."

Jessel played the lead role in Raphaelson's play for nearly three
years, in New York and in Los Angeles, San Francisco, Chicago,

and other cities, garnering the sort of commentary normally reserved for undisputed classics. "One of the most powerful dramas that have come upon the American stage of late years," a *Wisconsin State Journal* reviewer wrote. A critic for a Kansas City, Missouri, paper, *The Lathrop Optimist,* called it a "great dramatic triumph." What does it say about the America of the 1920s that a play about Jewish generational conflict would play so well in middle America? In answering that question, some of the commentators stressed, like Raphaelson, the universal dimension of the theme. "The orthodoxy whose pull and tug through the generations is the theme of the play, but the arguments were just as dramatic if the illustration were Roman Catholic, Evangelistic, Mormon, Mohammedan, or Buddhist," wisely intoned the *Chicago Tribune* critic when *The Jazz Singer* came to the Harris Theater in the fall of 1926.

Often the reviews reverentially cited one of the climactic lines in the play. As in Raphaelson's original story, Jack forsakes Broadway in order to chant the Yom Kippur prayers at his father's modest shul. The director of the Broadway show and Jack's shiksa girlfriend follow him there in order to dissuade him from his foolish decision. They arrive just as Jack, accompanied by a chorus, sings Kol Nidre, and its solemn beauty is not lost on them. "A great blackface comedian is singing to his God," Jack's girlfriend murmurs to the Broadway director, an observation that puts the shallow ephemera of secular fame and fortune into the trivial place where they belong, or so *The Jazz Singer* seems to be saying. "It is a near and yet far cry from the tinny rhythms of Alabammy Mamma to the chants of *Kol Nidre,*" the reviewer in New York *Daily News* observed. The play is "shoddily directed," the review allows, but the play itself, "mixed with the lamentations and pathos of the Jewish race, proved tense and stirring."

In other words, the deep respect accorded to Raphaelson's play about Jews seems to have reflected a broader American yearning to recapture a sense of the sacred in the secularizing, materialistic society of the Roaring Twenties. There is an irony here. In real life, people like Jack Robin didn't choose the sacred over the profane. Certainly Jolson, whose life situation inspired Raphaelson's story, didn't choose a life of devotion to Torah. He chose a life of fast money, the racetrack, lots of non-Jewish women, the Stork Club over B'nai B'rith, even if at times he felt "the pull and tug" of Orthodoxy, as embodied by the mother he lost when he was a child and by the father who disapproved of the life he led. Jolson liked *The Jazz Singer* even though Raphaelson's play depicted the character he inspired making a traditionalist choice that, in fact, Jolson didn't make himself and never would have made, and that Jews in America in general weren't making. In his memoirs, Jessel talks about performing one time "for a thousand priests," and, indeed, a *New York Times* reporter in February 1926, a few months into the play's run on Broadway, wrote that "a thousand ministers of all denominations . . . from Hartford, New Haven, Bridgeport, Newark, Jersey City, Trenton, and Camden came to a special performance," after which "the play's star [Jessel] received thirty-seven invitations to occupy pulpits"—presumably to speak in churches. *The Jazz Singer* "became a subject for sermons in every city we played," Jessel said.

Certainly the Jewish press liked it, in part because of the promise that it would increase tolerance for Judaism. "The theater may impress on countless thousands the deepest emotions and highest inspirations of religion," a commentary in *The Modern View,* the English-language paper of Missouri's German Jewish community, said. "It's probably the only play ever produced that shows the traditions of the Hebrews in a serious vein," *The Wis-*

consin Jewish Chronicle pronounced. "Every prominent rabbi in
Chicago has delivered a sermon on this wonderful play and urged
his congregation to see it."

* * *

People, whether Jewish or not, loved *The Jazz Singer* for its
reaffirmation of tradition, but that was not what the American
theater's depiction of Jews did much of to that point. Raphaelson's play marks a departure, and, in some ways, a turning back,
from the way in which the Jewish encounter with America had
been generally portrayed onstage and in the movies. It's likely
in this sense that because *The Jazz Singer*—especially the movie
version that was to come after the Broadway play—occupies a
special place in American cultural history, that other aspects of
that cultural history have been forgotten. The theatrical version of
The Jazz Singer—different, as we'll see, in one important respect
from the movie version—unambiguously affirmed and validated
the tradition. The play itself and the commentary on it approved
the choice Jack Robin makes as he heeds his mother's plea and,
he thinks, gives up his Broadway career. "The mother pleads and
something melts in the actor's heart and soul," the commentary
in *The Modern View* said. Jack Robin "abandons the stage forever;
the jazz singer becomes a cantor."

But if that's seen as the right thing to do, it is not what Jewish characters on the American stage had been doing in the years
before *The Jazz Singer*. The scholar Harley Erdman has compiled
a list of the plays with significant Jewish characters that were performed in America from 1860 to 1920. There were 167 of them,
among them numerous versions of Shakespeare's *Merchant of Venice,* with the character of Shylock portrayed as everything from

hatefully avaricious to sympathetic. There were numerous plays imported from England, including several theatrical renditions of Charles Dickens's *Oliver Twist,* with its hateful Jewish character, Fagin, portrayed as a hateful Jewish character. In the first half of the nineteenth century, when there were roughly fifteen thousand Jews in an overall American population of seventeen million, there was literally not a single piece of theater produced with a Jewish character. It was only starting in the 1860s, after the immigration of some German Jews, that, as Erdman put it, "the Jew came to be noticed" in the popular culture. Stage Jews were not all alike; as early as the 1860s there were sympathetic portrayals of Jews, mostly in revivals of English plays, like *The Mendicant's Son, or, the Jew of Southwark,* by the prolific Victorian playwright Edward Stirling, about a poor but heroic Jew wrongly accused of a crime.

By the late nineteenth and the early twentieth centuries, Hebrew comics, as Erdman writes, had become "a regular feature in vaudeville and could often be found doing character comedy in Broadway musicals." While steeped in stereotype, this comic Jew at least was no longer a detestable Fagin- or Shylock-like character, but someone to be laughed at or even pitied. Any number of the comics playing these roles, whether the clever, fast-talking Jew or the world-weary, pathetic Jew, as one scholar categorized them, became famous and wealthy. Among them, for example, was Julian Rose, who developed the character Levinsky. There was "Levinsky Buying a Car," "Levinsky at the Beach," and most famously "Levinsky at the Wedding."

Well, I guess Abe's lucky, now he's married. I'd like to do it, too, but every time I fall in love with a girl I find she's got no money, so what can I do? One thing I didn't like about Abe's wedding was right away it said at the top, "your presents is requested." They can't wait to let you know you must help pay the expenses.

But that was the low culture, and it came at a time of the more general influx of other European nationalities, with the ethnicity-inspired humor and lampoonery that resulted. Skits involving Irish, German, Italian, and Chinese stereotypes were often in the same shows on the same stage as the Jewish ones. But in the legitimate theater, there was a change. Starting at least as early as 1881, the play *Sam'l of Posen* achieved great national success. It was the invention of the Hungarian-born actor M. B. Curtis, who commissioned the Irish American playwright George H. Jessop to write it. Curtis played Sam'l, the central character, who was born in Posen, Poland, and worked as a "drummer," or traveling sales-man in America. Sam'l is cocky, brave, resourceful, and likable, as well as clean-shaven and erect in posture, nothing Shylock- or Fagin-like or greedy or unscrupulous or lamentable or unkempt about him. "He carries his exaggeration of the commercial trav-eler's audacity to the limit of burlesque," a *New York Times* critic said of Curtis, "but the fun of the thing is irresistible, and the piece is likely to draw great crowds." Erdman notes that even the character's name, Sam'l Plastrick, marks a departure. It is still "noticeably Jewish," but it "departs from the codified practice of having stage Jews signified as 'Solomon,' 'Levi,' or 'Moses.'"

Curtis, whose real name was Moritz Bertrand Strelinger, was, thanks to *Sam'l of Posen,* one of the most famous actors in America, his fame augmented both by a knack for publicity—when Congress dithered about appropriating funds to light the brand-new Statue of Liberty, Curtis covered the cost out of his own funds—and a sensational criminal case. In 1891, Strelinger was charged with the murder of a police officer in San Francisco.

He was acquitted after three trials and a life's savings spent on lawyers' fees, but his acting career was never fully restored, and he died in 1920 a broken man. But he was fully, if tragically, implicated in American life, and so was his Sam'l, perhaps the first fully realized American Jew to be depicted in an American play. That the play was written by the Irish American Jessop, also an immigrant, perhaps shows a sort of common trans-ethnic identification, the newcomers against the old-timers.

Other plays with Jewish themes followed, among the most successful of them *The Auctioneer*, played by David Warfield (born David Wohlfeld in San Francisco in 1866), possibly the most renowned stage actor of his time. Warfield started in an ordinary burlesque company doing a "Jewish specialty act," as a *New York Times* writer described it, "in a greasy black frock coat with a black derby pulled over his ears." There remains a residue of stereotype in his character in the play, an auction house proprietor named Simon Levi, who, despite his "codified" name, to use Erdman's term, continues the trend away from the Jew as comic buffoon toward the Jew as a fully developed, complex figure. In the story, Simon and his wife move to a non-Jewish neighborhood in upper Manhattan. There, Simon's brother, anxious to conceal his own Jewishness from his neighbors, perpetrates a fraud on Simon, who loses his home and becomes a lowly street peddler. Another Jewish character might have fallen into liturgical, Joblike lamentations at his misfortune, but Simon remains genial and warm. "The audience repeatedly sees, beneath the mask of canny salesman, the loving family man sympathetically engaged with the plights of those around him," Erdman writes, even as he stays "always faithful to his roots."

The burlesque Jew remained a fixture of the traveling variety shows in the early years of the century, but in the late 1910s and early 1920s, some playwrights further depicted complex Jewish characters sympathetically, struggling as they try to adapt to an often hostile new land. Like Simon Levi, these Jews have the standard Jewish names and engage in the standard early twentieth-century Jewish professions—they are variations on Lower East Side merchants, not justices on the Supreme Court—but they embody goodness, not ridiculousness. *Welcome Stranger* by Aaron Hoffman is about Isadore Solomon, "a generous, sympathetic, and far-seeing Hebrew," in the words of Alexander Woollcott, the critic at *The New York Times,* who tries to set up a shop in a town in the Northeast where "anti-Semitic prejudice runs so strong that it is all he can do to get inside its gates." Solomon rises above this prejudice by virtue of his character; he is "an embodiment of mellowness and humanity and charm." The play, Woollcott wrote, was a "haphazard jumble of very good and very bad" that "provided an almost continuously amusing piece of theatrical entertainment." It had a long run in Chicago before it arrived in New York. A silent movie version came out in 1924.

To be sure, characters like Sam'l of Posen, Simon Levi, and Isadore Solomon have an unmistakable foreignness to them. They try to survive with dignity, cleverness, and humor in an alien land, but survival for them involves no conflict with their Jewishness, which a hostile world would prevent them from relinquishing even if they wanted to, though they don't. As Jews attached to a tradition and an identity, they're more in the generation of Rabinowitz the father in *The Jazz Singer* than in that of his son. There's no shiksa temptation in plays like *The Auctioneer* or *Welcome Stranger,* no generational conflict, no anguish over what would be lost through assimilation because assimilation for these characters is purely transactional, a necessity for them to make their livings, not threatening to their very identity.

But the plays do demand acceptance in the theater and silent films of the 1920s of Jews as fully human, even admirable figures who endure and sometimes fight prejudice and ignorance, almost to the point where a bad Jew, a Shylock or Fagin, seemed to have become forbidden. This was due in part to the simple fact that Jews were too powerful in both the world of legitimate theater and the movies for antisemitic stereotypes to have much chance. There was now also an organized Jewish resistance to antisemitism, specifically the Anti-Stage Ridicule Committee and the Anti-Defamation League of B'nai B'rith, both founded in 1913, the former making itself known by organizing protests in Chicago against the worst sorts of depictions of Jews in vaudeville and burlesque. The Jews were well enough established and confident enough by then to fight back. Paradoxically perhaps, the end of the mass wave of immigration in the mid-1920s meant that there were fewer foreigners with strange accents, clothing, and customs around "for performers to parody or audiences to recognize," as one scholar has written. The fashion for raw ethnic humor came to seem an artifact of an earlier, less enlightened time.

One consequence of this when it came to the Jews and the Irish was a whole genre of plays about intermarriage. For the Jews especially, a small persecuted minority, this has always been the most dreaded threat posed by assimilation, that Jewish boys and girls will participate in secular society by marrying non-Jews, forsaking the tradition altogether by having and raising non-Jewish children, replacing menorahs with Christmas trees, Kol Nidre with "Silent Night." The threat applies especially to boys, because Jewishness by rabbinic law passes through the mother, so when a Jewish boy marries a gentile girl, his children will not be recognized as Jews by other Jews. Or, as it's said, "A Jew is somebody whose grandchildren are Jewish." To want to sustain the tradition, the sense of ancestral belonging, moreover, is not a backward, antiquated ambition. It is defensible, understandable, and the question of intermarriage worthy of deep and serious exploration.

But probably because intermarriage at the time was too rare to be perceived as a dire communal threat, that is not what the intermarriage plays and movies did. They presented the issue in comic form, but they also elevated the image of Jews, especially Jewish men; they took a universalist, deep-down-we're-all-the-same attitude that made light of the question of tribal survival even as it took the portrayal of Jews farther than ever from the invidious caricatures that had predominated only a generation before.

The prototypical production along these lines was *Abie's Irish Rose* by Anne Nichols, a Georgia-born Baptist. It started as a play about a Jewish boy, Abraham Levi, and an Irish girl, Rosemary Murphy, who fall in love and get married, to the consternation of their families. The play was sensibly denounced as treacle by the more highbrow critics—it's "about as low as good clean fun can get," Robert Benchley wrote—but it was an immense popular success, enjoying the longest run of any American theatrical production ever at its time, some 2,327 performances starting in 1922 and lasting until 1927. It was revived in movie versions in 1928 and 1948. It set off several copycat productions, including the movie *Kosher Kitty Kelly* and a series, "The Cohens and Kellys," involving similar Irish Jewish intermarriages, that was produced between 1926 and 1933 and included *The Cohens and Kellys in Paris,* in Atlantic City, in Scotland, in Africa, in Hollywood, ending with *The Cohens and Kellys in Trouble.* Another movie in that genre was *Private Izzy Murphy,* starring George Jessel.

The success of *Abie's Irish Rose* and these other plays and movies depended on audiences taking delight in the younger, Americanized generation defying the old-fashioned prejudices of their parents, their sticky adherence to tribal identity. Abie and Rosemary meet during World War I, "over there," specifically in a French hospital where he is a wounded American soldier and she a nurse. They get married by a Protestant minister, but when they come home, to conciliate Abie's widowed father they arrange to be married again, by a rabbi. At the ceremony, however, Rosemary's father turns up with a priest. A conflict seems about to break out, except the rabbi and the priest recognize each other from their service as chaplains "over there," and so they do two marriages, one Jewish, one Catholic. The rabbi and priest overcome the families' anguish by talking about the soldiers they buried of the other's faith. "They all had the same God above them," intones the priest. "Catholics, Hebrews, and Protestants alike all forgot their prejudice and came to realize that all faiths and creeds have about the same destination after all."

The message of this is pretty obvious: that the stubborn insistence on a tradition or on a historical, tribal, or religious identity is mere "prejudice." At a time when the Ku Klux Klan was enjoying a renewal of its power, and when, in reality, there was generally not much love lost between Irish and Jews—witness Father Charles Coughlin's rabid, antisemitic broadcasts in the 1930s—this was perhaps a noble sentiment. But it was also maudlin and shallow, reaching its sentimental height when Abie and Rosemary give birth to twins, thereby relieving them of the terrible decision of whether to raise their children as Catholics or Jews. They simply make one a Jew, the other a Catholic. The era of the Hanukkah bush is born.

In historical reality, it should be noted, the Baptist Anne Nichols married a Catholic and converted. At a time when doctrinal religious differences were taken more seriously than they are now, her *Abie's Irish Rose* might have been an extrapolation of her wish for a kind of love-conquers-all triumph over narrow tribal affiliation. It's a Romeo and Juliet sentiment transcribed to early twentieth-century America, and, like in Romeo and Juliet, the audience's sympathy is for the young lovers separated by a senseless clinging to particularity, the obvious difference being that in *Romeo and Juliet,* the young lovers meet with tragedy while all the American plays have happy endings. Shallow as this is, it marks a departure for the theatrical presentation of Jews. Unlike the feminized Jewish caricatures that came before, Abraham Levi is masculine; he's brave, handsome, and dashing, a soldier who risked his life for his country, not a bent-over Shylock counting his shekels or trembling in fear before antisemitic bullies. The new generation of Jews in *Abie's Irish Rose* are admirably assimilated and represent an advance over their elders, whose heavy Yiddish accents mark their old-fashioned love-does-not-conquer-all customs.

Private Izzy Murphy, the Warner Bros. silent movie of 1926 that starred George Jessel (who took some time off from *The Jazz Singer* to make his movie debut), took a similarly casual attitude toward the question of ancient attachments. The main character, Isadore Goldberg, adopts the name Isadore Patrick Murphy in order to fit in with the Irish neighborhood where he owns a store, and that's the name he uses when he falls for an Irish girl, Eileen Cohannigan. Like Abraham Levi, Izzy Goldberg becomes a soldier, volunteering to fight in Europe during the Great War, and, also like Abraham, he is valorously wounded. Deciding to come clean with Eileen, he writes to her from the hospital and confesses his secret: He is a Jew. She loves him anyway, she replies, and when Izzy comes home from the war, they get married. The sentiment that makes this movie "a dignified fourth cousin of 'Abie's Irish Rose,'" as a *Times* writer put it, comes when a fellow soldier squashes Eileen's father's objections to the marriage, saying "'If Izzy was good enough to fight for his country, he's good enough for any girl.'" *Private Izzy Murphy* did well enough at the box office for Warner Bros. to make a sequel, *Sailor Izzy Murphy,* described in an advertisement as "the most outrageously uproarious comedy ever screened." The plot: "A passionate perfumery peddler [Izzy, played again by George Jessel] who is kicked out by his prospective father-in-law, pursues him and his daughter in a yacht which is manned by maniacs."

Reducing the question of Jewish identity to farce perhaps had its beneficial side, since farce has a leveling effect; it makes us all victims of a joke. In any case, the movies of the 1920s were produced mostly by Jews more interested in using heartwarming sentimentality to make profitable entertainments than they were in deep explorations of Jewish American ambivalence or, more generally, the dilemmas of assimilation.

Samson Raphaelson had another idea, deeper, more tinged with tragedy, about the brutal bargain imposed by the melting-pot idea, the lacerating price that the demand to be the same as everybody else was paid by people, Jews in this instance, faced with the agonizing choice between one meaningful life, drenched in an ancient and beautiful heritage, and another. With *The Jazz Singer,* the culture took a deeper look at the problems of identity and assimilation, not so easily resolved by recourse to Hanukkah bush accommodation, and in taking that deeper, harder look, it awoke something in the collective consciousness. The struggle over identity and the competing and irreconcilable demands of tradition and Americanness became Americanness itself, no longer an amusing, heartwarming affirmation of our essential sameness but an examination of what it means to be different and the same simultaneously.

7

From Lithuania to "Alabammy"

All along Jolson was convinced that he had a kind of star power that went beyond ordinary star power. "I don't think you are treating me fairly in regard to my salary," he wrote to J.J. Shubert in May 1912, soon after he began performing in the Winter Garden. "You know as well as I do that my value has increased considerably. . . . If I'm not worth at least $750 a week for the remainder of the season and all of next season I'm not worth anything." Jolson tells J.J. that he can get $1,250 a week if he were to go back to vaudeville, leaving the threat that he might do so implicit. "I am realy [sic] sincere in my demands this time."

That entreaty was near the beginning of a partnership that, sometimes affectionate, sometimes fraught and uneasy, was to last for the next thirteen years and would make both parties rich and powerful. The musical comedies that came one after the other from 1912 to 1926 had two things in common: One, they were very successful, with long runs on Broadway and on tour from Boston to San Francisco. And two, their success depended almost entirely on Jolson's presence in them, Jolson putting on the costume of a Black character whose roots were in the American South.

Unlikely as it may seem, the most successful cultural properties of the 1910s and 1920s emerged from this almost weird combination. It was the Jews, the singers and the songwriters, Jolson,

Irving Berlin, and George Gershwin most prominent among them, who transformed the plantation South into a place for which Black people and white people were presumed to have a sentimental yearning. The most common explanation for this has to do with the disruptions caused by mass immigration, urbanization, industrialization, and the onset of a new, modern America, with its strikes, its economic downturns, its slums, its criminal subculture, and its on-the-edge economic precariousness, not to mention the first of the great world wars in which tens of thousands of American soldiers gave their lives. All of this gave rise to a yearning for the simpler, peaceful, more soulful rural place associated with mammy and a mother's love. Stephen Foster, who was born in Pittsburgh and lived most of his life in the North, was the most perfect expression of this nostalgia, with songs like "Swanee River" and "The Old Folks Back Home." Jolson, Berlin, Gershwin, and others, like Foster, who preceded them by half a century, had no experience of the South, but they built on Foster's cleverly sentimental edifice while they redirected their own nostalgia for the simpler life of their own ancestors, even as they knew that their ancestors had happily escaped to America from centuries of oppression. Neither the shtetl nor the tenement ghettos the Jews lived in after escaping the Pale of Settlement were any more a paradise than the southern plantations, but there is something about the childhood longing for a lost and innocent time that is subjectively poignant and moving even if it is objectively ridiculous.

Just think of it: A Jewish population newly arrived from the Russian Empire creates Tin Pan Alley and musical theater in America by imagining an American time and place of which it had no experience whatsoever. Scholars have come up with a plausible psychoanalytic interpretation of this, according to which the

Jewish entertainers, needing to conceal their Jewishness in order
to be accepted as Americans, sublimated the minor-key poignancy
of the Hebrew liturgy and fused it with the minor-key poignancy
of Black music. The Jews could change their names from Isko-
witz to Cantor, Borach to Brice, Yoelson to Jolson, marry non-
Jews, escape from the trammels of tradition, but, as the scholar
Irving Saposnik has written, "they could never deny their shadow
selves." Jolson never performed the Yiddish favorite, "Meine Yiddishe Mama," onstage, but one of his most famous songs, the one
that ends the movie *The Jazz Singer,* is "My Mammy," sung in
blackface.

> *I'd walk a million miles*
> *For one of your smiles*
> *My Mammy*

"'My Mammy' transposes the Yiddish-inspired longing
for home into a Southern setting," Saposnik writes, "and con-
verts the Yiddishe Mama into a black Mammy, and the nurtur-
ing, sweet-tempered, long-suffering, Black mammy, epitomized
by the happy, comforting, domestically skilled Aunt Jemima
of the pancake mix, was, as other scholars have pointed out, at
the very center of longing for the disappeared past. "Meine Yiddishe Mama" begins with a remembrance of "Our humble East
Side tenement / Where my childhood days were spent." It wasn't
much like paradise, but the sweetest thing in it was the eponymous mama, the figure of love and protection absent from the
faraway world of today. How nearly identical that is to the world
of "My Mammy," which is about the emotional price of seeking
adventure and fortune away from home. "Everything is lovely /
When you start to roam; / The birds are singin', the day that
you stray, / But later, when you are further away, / Things won't

seem so lovely / When you're all alone." The fact that Jolson sang "My Mammy," not "Meine Yiddishe Mama," perfectly symbolizes the larger choices that he made in his life. But there seems little doubt that the sentiment of both songs had a special poignancy for the man whose mother, not from a fictitious "Alabammy" but from a very real Lithuania, died when he was nine years old. On a trip to Washington in 1913, after visiting his father, Jolson went down the rickety stairs of the apartment above the store, walked to the synagogue where his father sang, then to the Jefferson School where he once held his mother's hand terrified of his new life in America, then to the cemetery where his mother's grave was, the first time he'd been there since she was buried nearly twenty years before, and he dropped to his knees and wept.

"My Mammy," which Jolson always ended on one knee, his hands stretched out toward the audience in a kind of supplication, didn't just transfix American audiences; it also helped to elevate Jolson to a plane unoccupied by any other entertainer of his time. Reflecting the extraordinary stature he had attained, for the opening of *Bombo* in 1921 the Shuberts built a new theater on Fifty-ninth Street in Manhattan, and they named it Jolson's 59th Street Theater. Jolson took thirty-seven curtain calls on *Bombo*'s opening night there. He was thirty-five years old.

* * *

There was always a greediness to Jolson that bespoke an inability to take true satisfaction from his success, as if what he really wanted always remained just out of reach. He constantly referred to himself as the "world's greatest entertainer." He told everybody what a star he was, including his father and stepmother on his dutiful visits to them in Washington. In 1912, after he'd gotten glowing notices in the show *Vera Violetta,* Jolson paid for a New Year's greeting in *Variety* saying in part: "Everybody likes me. Those who don't are jealous," which comes across more as a desire to be universally loved than a conviction that he really was.

He was nervous, fretful, prone to hypochondria, worried that his voice would desert him. "Many a night I saw him in the wings before his first entrance, wringing his hands nervously, wiping the cold sweat from his face, even throwing up," his friend and accompanist Harry Akst remembered. Performing was a kind of addiction for him; he was insatiable, greedy for the spotlight and the applause. "He was never able to stop proving his greatness," Akst said, "whether the audience numbered a thousand, a hundred, or just one—himself." Raphaelson was fond of him but unsparing in his description of Jolson's narcissism, his hunger for attention. "There was no conversation," he said. "Nobody knew how to talk to him. He'd tell me how rich he was, the trouble he had with Harry Cohn [evidently a generic stand-in, not a real person], or something like that, always something—but . . . he was constantly living in a little cosmos of his own."

Accounts of him say that before shows, prostitutes would sometimes be brought to his dressing room so he could relieve his tension. During shows, buckets were kept backstage so that he could throw up into them between numbers. Stagehands knew to keep the water running in his dressing room while he was in there during other performers' acts, the water creating a blocking noise so he wouldn't hear the applause going to other people.

He worked extremely hard, especially when shows went on tour. Jolson, like the rest of the cast, moved from city to city by train, sometimes in a series of one- or two-night stands that he found exhausting. He was driven to do it by his quest for fame, money, and applause. Especially in the early years of his Shubert period, he aroused nothing short of consternation on the part of the Shuberts and just about everybody else in the organization by behaving as if he were the only person who really mattered. At one point, J.J. wrote him a scorching two-page, single-spaced letter, followed the next day by a five-page expanded version, warning Jolson that his unpredictability and capriciousness were throwing the whole organization "into a state of turmoil."

"Every performance varies from the preceding one, and you cannot expect to be successful under conditions of that kind," Shubert says, going on to warn that the whole enterprise will be ruined

> if you continue to change your business, change your position, change your lines, and change your songs when you desire. You upset the musical director by telling him one thing and then turning around and telling him another; you upset the stage manager, because he does not know what you are going to do; and you upset the actors, because they don't know how long you are going to remain on that stage or what you are going to say. . . .
>
> Remember you are a young man, and what I am telling you is to your own interest. It is all right for you that they like you in New York, but remember that I have seen reputations come and go like the shifting of the winds. You are on top, and I want you to remain there. You are a big asset to us, and your remaining as the pivot all depends upon yourself.

Shubert is ready to attribute Jolson's unsettling behavior to what he calls his "temperamental" nature and to his habit of "listening too much to the quack doctors you meet in all those towns." "The idea of your getting nervous and not being able to sleep nights and walking the floor, and the other things that you

told me, shows you are conscientious . . . but all that is unneces-
sary if you would give a little more time and attention to what you
are going to do yourself and to editing the things you are going to
say onstage before saying them."

"I know your condition better than you do yourself," Shubert
writes on another occasion, when Jolson was complaining that his
voice was deteriorating because of his demanding schedule. "You
always want something to worry about. These worries get on your
nerves and it certainly does not do you any good."

The constant refrain in these exchanges—all of which took
place when Jolson was on the road—consists of Jolson complaining that he's tired and needs time off, and Shubert, alternately
scolding and affectionate, stern and conciliatory, attempts to
cajole him into staying the course. "As we will have played over
forty weeks, and believe me I am tired out," Jolson writes in 1917
from Cincinnati, where he was on tour with *Crusoe, Jr.,* possibly
the same tour that brought him to Illinois and his meeting with
Raphaelson. "I know there are many thousands more to be made
by playing further, but it is beyond me to keep on." Shubert's reply
to Jolson's plea for time off: "You know that is impossible, as we
have contracted for all the western time . . . and it would put us in
a terrible hole as we have no other show to take its place." He adds:
"Remember, Al, my whole interest is for you. I do not wish to do
anything that will hurt you, physically or financially, so please
reconsider this and try and play the time."

A few weeks later, Jolson tells Shubert he wants a few days
off so that he can attend the World Series, which was in Chicago
that year. Shubert grudgingly cancels some shows, but he warns
Jolson that he'll get a bad reputation if "you open and close shows
just as you see fit." He continues, "You are the most popular man
in America. Why not keep that title? Hold onto it." Still later,
Jolson asks for time off for the Jewish holidays. "After all is said

and done, you are still a son of Abraham," Shubert writes, in a rare reference to their shared Jewishness. "Am trying to arrange to cancel Oct 6 and 7 but it will cost us five hundred dollars to do so." Along the way, J.J. chastises Jolson for his prima donna attitude. "When you cannot have your way it doesn't make it all wrong," he writes to Jolson, now in Dayton, Ohio. "We all think we are right, otherwise you would have a great deal more if you did not play the races. The horse that you think will win doesn't always win. It applies to business judgment the same as to racing, and in all other forms of life."

Jolson's pleas for time off might have seemed like contractual breaches to Shubert, and, as he frequently reminded his big star, they were bad for business. It's a virtual certainty that any other member of the cast who complained the way Jolson did would have been quickly told to seek work elsewhere. From the point of view of Jolson, on whom the main burden of the performance fell, the schedule was indeed grueling. His biographer, Herbert G. Goldman, has tabulated the performance schedules for all of Jolson's shows. Over a fourteen-month period, from roughly September 1916 to November 1917, *Crusoe, Jr.* played in 113 different cities and towns in the United States and Canada, and Jolson continued to protest about the hardship that that entailed. There is this stream of consciousness fulmination to J.J. from Flint, Michigan, written with a lot of missing punctuation (a consequence of his having left school when he was twelve) and a keen sense of urgency:

> Now JJ, there is no use beating around the bush. I have played thirty-one one nighters in succession and I don't think I can stand up much longer the food is terrible, the hotels worse, I have had one good meal this month . . . I love hard work but I must have regular food and sleep . . . and the past month has been a horrible nightmare. . . .

You say I'll get the reputation of canceling towns Good
God! Have I not the right to close after being out eighty
weeks playing every terrible town in the country, no heat
in the theaters no hot water to wash up with and no actors
to play with. If I don't get a good meal pretty soon you can
use me for a Xylaphone.

During all of this, Jolson made, and spent, staggering
amounts of money. In 1918, he signed a new five-year contract
with the Shuberts paying him $2,500 a week ($40,000 today) and
15 to 25 percent of *gross* theatrical receipts, this at a time when a
new Ford automobile cost $875. *Big Boy,* for example, grossed an
average of $5,000 per performance, which meant that Jolson got
between $750 and $1,220 for each time he went onstage, which
was eight or nine times per week. A note buried in the correspondence file in the Shubert Archive in New York shows what Jolson
made for a nine-month period of performing in *Bombo:* $74,000
in salary and $104,547.42 in his share of the profit (this was when
the contract called for him to share net, not gross, receipts); Jolson
could probably have made a lot more if he'd accepted other offers.
In July 1926, he got an offer of $600,000 to perform in a theatrical
circuit for forty weeks. He turned it down.

Jolson's self-centeredness and emotional insatiability ruptured
his private life, especially his marriages and other sentimental
relationships, which were with one chorus girl after another, Jolson often displaying his neurotic tendency to devalue what he had
once he had it, and then to want it back once he'd lost it. Everybody knew that Henrietta, Jolson's first wife, was rarely invited to
accompany him, not only when he went on tour but even when he
was at home. Henrietta, more or less banished to her hometown,
Oakland, as Jolson lived the high life in New York, sued him for
divorce in 1918. She persuasively recounted instances of physical

abuse by Jolson, saying that he had once punched her in the face, giving her a black eye.

Jolson clearly preferred the company of men as he went about his recreational pursuits, especially horse racing and prizefights. But once his divorce from Henrietta came through, he was tireless in his efforts to win her back, not, it can be assumed, because he genuinely loved her but because her decision to leave him was an intolerable blow to his ego. Jolson lived at a time when reports of spousal abuse short of actual murder put nary a dent in celebrity reputations, and though her accusation received its share of press coverage during the divorce hearings, it had no discernible effect on his career. All along, whether married or not, Jolson was sexually voracious. "He had virtually no 'love affairs'—just one-night stands with chorus girls or, more frequently, prostitutes," Herbert Goldman writes.

Ray O'Brien, who was the pianist for at least two of Jolson's musicals, said that when the shows were on tour, "[Jolson's train] compartment was never empty at night. There was always a girl with him." Three years after his divorce, Jolson married again, this time to a twenty-two-year-old chorus girl whose stage name was Ethel Delmar, whom he'd met in 1919 when she was in a Broadway show called, ironically, *Scandals.* Jolson treated his new wife more or less the way he'd treated his ex, mostly ignoring her as he went about his hectic life but also, according to O'Brien, giving her the occasional slap across the face. They were divorced in 1926 after four years of marriage.

* * *

In 1913, Sime Silverman, the editor of *Variety,* asked Jolson to write something for the paper on the heavyweight championship boxing match between the Black champion Jack Johnson

and James J. Jeffries, the "great white hope." A lot of the hatred of
Johnson came because he was a Black man triumphing over white
men, getting well paid in the process. Some resented that he was
married to a white woman and was reputed to have had white girlfriends. Some of the antipathy was simply because Johnson was
the most famous Black man in America, perhaps in the world.
Johnson knocked Jeffries down three times in the final round and
won by a TKO.

In his account of the match, which appeared in *Variety* five
days later, Jolson emphatically repudiated the widely repeated
canard that Jeffries, otherwise undefeated, had lost because he'd
had to come out of retirement to fight Johnson and that if the
match had taken place a few years before, he would have won.
"It's all right to say that if Jeff were in his prime what he would
have done to Johnson, but believe me, it would have been just the
same," Jolson wrote. "You know that old gag about only two blows
hit. Well, that goes. Johnson hit Jeff, and Jeff hit the floor. . . .
The majority at ringside must say that Johnson is the greatest
fighter who ever lived. Jeffries did not hit him one good punch."

Jolson doling out what might have been an unwelcome truth
about the fight of the century is a good reminder of the fraught
topic of race in Jolson's time, and to his renown as a blackface
entertainer, sometimes as a "mammy singer" or a "coon shouter,"
which is what singers doing what was recognized as Black music
were called. Jolson wasn't a deep thinker on the issue, but, as his
account of Johnson's defeat of Jeffries indicates, he was instinc-
tively in favor of the idea, formative as it was in the early years
of the twentieth century, of racial fairness. Jim Crow, the Klan,
lynchings, the systematic suppression of Black people—all of this
was at its height at the time. But Jolson, like many other entertainers, notably many other Jewish ones, belonged to a nascent
bohemian-bourgeois culture that was burgeoning, especially in

northern cities like New York. These were the early years of the
Harlem Renaissance when some Black entertainers were crossing
over for the first time to white audiences—not as objects of pruri-
ent curiosity in a circus sideshow but as the musical and comedic
geniuses they were, worthy of due respect and admiration.

For Jews who believed as Jolson did, there was a natural identification with the Black struggle, for the obvious reason that Jews
knew exclusion and bigotry from the inside, which led many of
them to sympathize with the Black struggle for equal rights. Jewish organizations like the Anti-Defamation League of B'nai B'rith,
formed in 1913, four years after the creation of the NAACP, gave
vocal support to the Black struggle for equal rights. More generally, the world of popular entertainment was a sort of natural
arena for racial mixing and acceptance. It wasn't at that point
a matter of articulated principle or of organized protest, but a
kind of natural recognition that talent will out and that to stifle it
on racial grounds was retrograde, backward, counterproductive,
no fun.

It's almost uncanny in this sense how similar the backgrounds,
the points of origin and the trajectories of the Jewish and Black
entertainers were in the late nineteenth and early twentieth centuries, with the obvious difference that the Jews were recent arrivals
to America and the Blacks had been there since the seventeenth
century. For the most part, Jews and Blacks in the "theatrical
trade" made their way from poor backgrounds, started as child
street performers, had very little in the way of formal education,
went into vaudeville on their way up, and found themselves in
popular entertainment because so many other avenues to success
were sealed shut to them, more tightly closed for the Blacks than
for the Jews who, despite the power of antisemitism, had the benefit of being white.

Ma Rainey, to take one example, was born Gertrude Pridgett

in Columbus, Georgia, in 1886, the same year that Jolson was
born in Lithuania. Her initial musical education took place in
the First African Baptist Church, which is similar in its way to
Jolson's childhood training in the Hebrew liturgy at the insistence
of his father. By the time Gertrude was twelve she was performing in minstrel shows. Later, she and her husband, "Pa" Rainey,
joined the Rabbit's Foot Company, a Black vaudeville troupe that
performed all over the South, where they were billed together
as "Black Face Song & Dance Comedians, Jubilee Singers, and
Cake Walkers."

Similarly, Bessie Smith, born in 1894 in Chattanooga, Ten-
nessee, sang on street corners with her six brothers and sisters, just
as Harry and Al sang in front of the Raleigh Hotel. Smith danced
in front of the White Elephant Saloon in Chattanooga while one
of her brothers played the guitar, this before she became one of
the great blues singers of the century. Louis Armstrong, born in
New Orleans in 1901, was raised partly by a Yiddish-speaking,
Lithuanian Jewish family named Karnofsky. He got started as a
musician playing a tin horn to attract customers to his adoptive
parents' junk wagon.

The first Black talent to become a star on Broadway was Bert
Williams (born in Nassau, the Bahamas, in 1874), who performed
with the Ziegfeld Follies in blackface alongside Fanny Brice,
who also did her skits and songs in blackface. When Ma Rainey
and Bessie Smith toured with tent shows in the South they also
"blacked up," as the saying went. Shelton Brooks, born in 1886,
the composer of ragtime hits including "Some of These Days"
(made famous by Sophie Tucker), learned music on the organ in
a Canadian church where his father was a preacher. He went into
vaudeville as a kind of Bert Williams imitator before finding his
métier as a songwriter. Ethel Waters, known for hit songs like

"Stormy Weather" and "Heat Wave," a huge star at the Cotton Club in Harlem, was raised in the early years of the twentieth century by her grandmother. She started singing when she was nine years old, eventually joining a traveling Black vaudeville troupe.

There was a fashion among some whites in the days of the Harlem Renaissance to "stream up to Harlem's integrated jazz clubs in the 1920s to experience 'hot,' 'primitive' music," as one scholar put this, and this even led some of them "to actually identify with the struggles of real African Americans." Certainly white audiences were important for business in hot spots like the Cotton Club.

Of course, during the long era of Jim Crow, most white Americans didn't stream up to Harlem or identify with the struggles of Black people in any way. But Jolson did, and that was recognized by Black performers and others who, of course, knew who he was. According to Goldman, Jolson was the only white man ever admitted to Leroy's, the Black cabaret on 135th Street and Fifth Avenue in Harlem, during the five years of its existence, 1910–15. In fact, it's not certain that other whites were banned from Leroy's, which was described by nightlife guides at the time simply as "one of the most popular places in the city and home of the cabaret." In any case, Jolson, an indefatigable night owl, was a regular at the Harlem nightclubs.

In 1921, while Jolson was headlining in *Bombo,* a rival Broadway show was *Shuffle Along,* written by the composer Eubie Blake and the lyricist Noble Sissle. It was the first hit Broadway show written by a Black composer and lyricist with an all-Black cast, the first show that showed a Black romantic relationship, the first one where Black members of the audience sat in orchestra seats rather than in the balcony, often the only location where Blacks were allowed. The show ran for 504 performances in New York and then went on a tour that lasted three years. *Shuffle Along* was one of those cracks that were appearing in the white edifice; it originated several hit songs, including "Love Will Find a Way" and "I'm Just Wild About Harry" and it gave a big boost to the careers of Black entertainers like Josephine Baker, Paul Robeson, and Florence Mills.

A year or so before *Shuffle Along* opened, Sissle and Blake were on tour in Hartford, Connecticut, with their own two-man show, and they were turned away by the owner of a restaurant who reportedly told them, "We don't serve colored people." Jolson, who was performing in Hartford at the time, saw an account of the incident in the *Hartford Courant*. Jolson contacted Sissle and Blake at their hotel and invited them to dinner that night. "He was so sore about that story he wanted to make it up to us," Sissle later said.

From then on Jolson and Blake were frequent men about town together, going to the fights especially. They had much in common, including being members of a discriminated-against minority who had triumphed over adversity. Blake, born in Baltimore in 1887, was the only surviving child of two former slaves. His mother, like Jolson's father, was deeply religious. When Eubie was fifteen, without his parents' knowledge, he was playing piano at a local bordello. In his early twenties, he went into vaudeville, eventually meeting up with Sissle, with whom he formed a musical act known as the Dixie Duo, the act they were most likely performing in Hartford when they were denied service at that restaurant. And so, here were two men, Blake and Jolson, born one year apart, musicians of extraordinary talent, with deeply religious backgrounds, who had come up from the streets, living twentieth-century American lives that their nineteenth-century parents couldn't have imagined. When Jolson died, Sissle represented the Negro Actors' Guild, of which he was president, at his funeral. Many Black performers and friends were there.

Jolson reacted viscerally and impulsively to discrimination against Jews and Blacks both. In 1911, still a relative newcomer to the Shubert Organization, he sent an impassioned telegram to J.J. Shubert imploring him not to fire a fellow actor, Harry Wardell. The details are sketchy, but Wardell, who later became one of Jolson's cohorts, appears to have committed an act of aggression against another person, and the Shuberts, always conscious of their public image (J.J. once reprimanded Jolson for going onstage in a provincial town without a collar) were ready to let him go. "There's a lot of prejudice owing to his race that of being a Hebrew and that prejudice seems to predominate," Jolson wrote to Shubert. "I assure you he is innocent and I beg of you to consider his dismissal as he only got back at a drunken bum who called him a dirty Jew. Do this favor for me and I will do anything you ask of me."

A few years later, Jolson very publicly quit a Westchester country club, the Biltmore, when he was told not to bring a friend, a cabaret entertainer named Harry Richman, as a guest. "Jolson was given the Jew reason for Richman being deemed 'undesirable,'" *Variety* reported, which is somewhat mysterious given that Jolson himself was Jewish, though perhaps he was exempt from the "Jew reason" because of his celebrity and the fact that he was an early club member. In any case, *Variety* said, he "carried the matter before the club board of directors where he hotly presented his resignation."

Jolson was no civil rights campaigner, but over the years he did what he could to promote Black entertainers; he befriended them; he liked them. The newspapers, including the Black papers, reported on various gestures he made that showed his essentially progressive attitude on racial matters. Florence Mills, one of the

stars of *Shuffle Along,* was well-known for championing racial
equality. When she died at the end of 1927 at the age of thirty-
one, Jolson sang a solo at her funeral, accompanied by a chorus
of six hundred and an orchestra of two hundred musicians at
the Mother African Methodist Episcopal Zion Church on 137th
Street. A few weeks later, he led a cohort of "Broadway stars" to
her memorial service at the Alhambra Ballroom in Harlem. Perhaps he felt a special kinship with Mills who, like Jolson, started
as a child performer singing duets with her sister in Washington,
D.C., then traveled in vaudeville shows before she achieved success in New York.

At the Clef Club on 155th Street at Eighth Avenue, a gathering
place for Black musicians, something called the Al Jolson Silver
Loving Cup was awarded to the winner of a Charleston dance
contest. Jolson was supposed to have attended a fundraiser for
the club and to bring members of the cast of his ongoing show at
the Winter Garden, but he fell ill and went to Florida, as he often
did, for some rest; the silver loving cup was in lieu of his personal
appearance. One year, the cup was presented by Garland Anderson, a former bellhop at a Los Angeles hotel. Anderson, who was
Black, had written a play called *Appearances* and sent it to Jolson,
who, having read it, covered the cost of Anderson's trip to New
York when he went there in search of a producer. In 1925, the play
was performed on Broadway, where it was acclaimed by much of
the Black press. It "shows the intellectual, cultured, and spiritual
side of the Negro as no other play in the history of the American
stage has done," a *New York Amsterdam News* critic wrote. After
three weeks, the play closed for lack of funds, whereupon some
noted figures from the New York entertainment world went on a
fundraising campaign so the performances could resume. David
Belasco, the theater director, was the first to make a donation,

$1,000 (equivalent to about $15,000 today), Jolson the second with a gift of the same amount (Florence Mills was among the many Black entertainers who also contributed).

* * *

If Jolson was so progressive on race, how could he have performed in a guise that was intrinsically demeaning to Black people? The main answer to that question is that Jolson, a man of the early twentieth century, didn't see things the way we see them in the first quarter of the twenty-first, and neither did society as a whole. Even Black society at the time seems to have accepted blackface as a kind of given without much in the way of protest, though, as we'll see in a minute, that may have been more a matter of practicality than absence of feeling. Perhaps Jolson and the others who adopted blackface, including the Black performers who also "blacked up," should have known better. But, surprising as this may seem, Jolson seems to have received no message, not even from Black reviewers and commentators, that what he was doing, his very stock in trade, was a racial offense.

Now, a century later, things are different. Any number of writers, especially in academia, most of them white, many of them Jewish, have engaged in a deep exploration of this topic, seeing blackface as a way for white performers to demarcate themselves from Blacks, to assure white audiences of their superiority, and, more generally, to fit into the image of an America fundamentally and inescapably deformed by racial bigotry. And since many of the leading blackface performers were Jews, this academic subculture attaches a special blame to them for perpetuating the enduring racial misdeeds of American history. Nic Sammond, a professor of cinema studies at the University of Toronto, has written that wearing blackface "forged an allegiance with the white Protestant majority." Similarly, Michael Rogin, a political scientist at the University of California, has called blackface "an act of ventriloquism, a speaking for, through, and instead of mostly absent and silent blacks." It was an "appropriative identification," which is a kind of ownership of people, an especial insult given that these same people were once actually owned. For Rogin, when Jolson, his face covered in burnt cork, sang "My Mammy" in the closing scene of *The Jazz Singer,* he was "condensing into a single figure the structures of white supremacist racial integration that built the United States: black labor in the realm of production, interracial nurture and sex . . . in the realm of reproduction, and blackface minstrelsy in the realm of culture."

In this view, for Jews to put on blackface was to enable them to conceal their Jewishness and to assert their whiteness. Blackface, with its long history, was the most uniquely American of all cultural expressions, so that for the Jews to adopt it was part of their effort to be accepted as Americans, because what could be more American than asserting whiteness over blackness? "Paradoxically, by donning blackface, the Hebrew becomes Caucasian," one scholar, Matthew Frye Jacobson, has written. "The burnt cork at once masks Jewishness and accentuates whiteness; in playing black, the Jew becomes white."

Jolson in this sense may have thought of himself as an ally of the Black community, but his blackface persona was nonetheless an embodiment of his white privilege. "I have had the dream where I hold Al Jolson wearing a dark coat of blackface under the water of an old bathtub," the essayist Hanif Abdurraqib writes in his book *A Little Devil in America* (2021). "I scrub at his face with my hands until the scrubbing becomes clawing, trying to remove the layer of caked-on dark skin, to address the man underneath."

It's not hard to understand Abdurraqib's sentiment. The most common image of Jolson is of him with his face covered in burnt cork, exaggerated white lips, and a woolly skullcap, and given his remarkable fame, many people today find it impossible to forgive him, even if in private life he was, as this has been put, "a friend of the Negro." Given the brutal history of American racism, it's natural to see in blackface, with its roots in nineteenth-century minstrelsy, an expression of contemptuous denigration of "the Negro," a cultural reflection of the physical oppression of Black people. To see Jolson's face covered in burnt cork is to see an actor in apparent willing complicity with that oppression, exploiting it for his own benefit.

But consider another image: Early on in the movie version of *Big Boy*, Jolson's blackface character, Gus, stands in front of a white-pillared Kentucky plantation house. Sitting around him are a group of Black men who have been freed from slavery recently, since the time is shortly after the end of the Civil War. The men, led by "Gus," in overalls, a white shirt, a straw hat in his hand, sing a deeply resonant and stirring version of the spiritual "Go Down Moses."

> *Go down Moses,*
> *Way down in Egypt land.*
> *Tell old Pharaoh*
> *To let my people go.*

There is something conspicuously odd in this scene, the white man impersonating a Black man and leading other Black men (actual Black performers, not whites in blackface) in an uplifting spiritual, as if they need Gus to show them how to be authentically Black. "Thus blacks were taught their place in life, a bit of their history, and a sample of their music by a company of white writers and a singer under cork," as the cultural historian Thomas Cripps has written. But the spiritual is a song about the yearning for freedom being sung, supposedly, in the aftermath of the abolition of slavery, and in this sense, Jolson's leading the chorus seems both to illustrate the persisting racial hierarchy of American life and to protest against it at the same time. In fact, the principal moment of racial caricature in the movie comes when the arrogant, imperious, bigoted "Old South" villain of the story arrives on the scene. Bully John Bagley, a stupidly imperious former plantation slave master who, ignoring that abolition has occurred, begins to order Gus and another Black character (played by a Black actor) to do menial tasks for him, like polishing his shoes. Gus tells the other Black character to pay no attention. "You're any man's equal now," he says, the whole scene probably written into the script so Jolson could utter that line. When Bagley tries to abduct the daughter of the plantation owners, Gus leaps on a horse and gallops to her rescue. If the standard iconic racial offense stemmed from the Black man's sexual desire for a white woman, here things are inverted. In *Big Boy,* the Black man saves the white girl from a villainous white man and is profusely thanked for his service in a kind of idealized southern society in which white plantation owners and Black former slaves mingle on a cordial, if not entirely equal, basis.

The film, made in 1930, was the cinematic version of the musical comedy of the same name that was a Jolson vehicle in the mid-1920s, playing for two lengthy engagements at the Winter Garden and in more than thirty cities across the country. In the stage production, Jolson performed with a Black orchestra onstage, rather than in the pit, the orchestra made up of singers drawn from the Clef Club where the annual Al Jolson Silver Loving Cup was awarded. *The New York Times* noted in a worshipful portrait of Jolson in *Big Boy* in 1925 that "the only distinguished numbers are the negro spirituals sung against banjo accompaniment by Al and the Jubilee singers," this at a time, as the scholar Charles Musser notes, when spirituals, being revived and presented as a project of the Harlem Renaissance, were struggling to achieve popular recognition, something that Jolson, well-connected with the world of Black entertainers, probably knew. When Jolson temporarily canceled the show because of illness, the ten Black performers in the musical, calling themselves Al Jolson's Jubilee Singers, brandishing guitars and banjos and broad-brimmed hats, went on tour performing what one newspaper writer called "an entertaining melange of syncopated melodies, favorite tunes of the South, as well as the latest jazz harmonies."

Big Boy, both the staged and cinematic versions, reflect the lower-class reality of the Black American condition. Gus is a stable boy; he accepts an inferior social position vis-à-vis the owners of the horse farm who are, needless to say, white and patrician, though they are trusting and appreciative of him. But he is clever, resourceful, and capable. He foils a plan conceived by some grifters to fix the Kentucky Derby by having the plantation's racehorse, the eponymous Big Boy, ridden by a white jockey who will intentionally lose the race. Gus, who has tended to Big Boy since he was a colt, displaces the bad guy's jockey and rides the horse to victory.

This doesn't justify Jolson's impersonation of a Black man, and yet, given the pervasiveness of both racism and antisemitism at the time, his portrayal of Gus in *Big Boy* suggests more a gesture of sympathetic than "appropriative" identification. For decades, American Jews have sung the spiritual "Go Down Moses" at their Passover seders. It's a gesture of solidarity or at least commonality being expressed by a people whose most cherished tradition, the Passover seder, is a celebration of their liberation from the condition of unfreedom—four hundred years of bondage in Egypt—

just as the Negro spiritual itself was an expression of identification by enslaved Blacks with the enslaved Hebrews of the Bible, and the hope that their own Moses might someday lead them to freedom. "A Jew using blackface to play a black man who sang spirituals with black singers about the plight of the ancient Jews: this was a powerful assertion of shared experience and unity," Musser writes. Jolson's acts in general, he continues, "were exercises in cultural fluidity and mutual longings for freedom." For much of his career, starting in the late 1930s and extending through the 1950s, Paul Robeson, the celebrated performer and champion of Black equality, sang an eighteenth-century Hassidic chant as a regular part of his concert repertory, using the same Hebrew words, *yis'gedal v'yiskadash sh'may raboh* (glorified and sanctified be God's great name), that the cantor Josef Rosenblatt sings in a cameo appearance he makes in *The Jazz Singer*. Robeson, who called the chant "a tremendous sermon-song declaration-protest," was making a reciprocal gesture of sympathetic identification.

As in *Big Boy*, so in the several other productions where Jolson played Gus, he is smart, resourceful, and funny, not the butt of jokes but a wry commentator on the foibles and pretensions of other characters. He's a bit like the later Groucho Marx, the wisecracking subversive of the established order, making a mockery of convention. The musical *Bombo*, for example, tells in burlesque style the story of Christopher Columbus at the court of Ferdinand and Isabella of Spain. Gus, who is Bombo, is Columbus's servant. He convinces the Spanish monarchs to support Columbus's proposal to sail west to India, quipping all the way. When Ferdinand asks why the world moves, Gus replies, "Because it's cheaper than paying rent." When the king, angered because Gus has sat on his throne, announces that he'll have him beheaded at sunrise, Gus tells him he doesn't get up that early. A beautiful Moorish princess, Baobadella, falls in love with Gus; she disguises herself as a boy so she can go on Columbus's voyage and be near him. On the voyage, Gus foils an attempted mutiny. When the ship makes landfall, Gus, in a not so sly smidgen of Yiddishkeit, greets the local king with "*Sholem Aleichem.*" The king returns the Hebrew greeting, whereupon the scene ends with Gus telling Columbus, "You aren't the first one here. The Hebrews are ahead of you," a line no doubt intended as a wink of complicity with Jews in the audience. Gus is there for fun. He's the underestimated underdog who turns out to be smarter than everybody around him. He's a Black man who sees through cant and conventional wisdom and outwits his pretentious, racist rivals, very much like a Jew does, or wishes to do, with what many Jews saw as the social disdain and exclusivity of WASP society.

To be sure, all blackface was rooted in minstrelsy, in which white actors played Black characters in lighthearted burlesque entertainments, thereby incarnating the American racial hierarchy in which even a poor, ignorant white was superior to any Black. The fact that many Black entertainers of the late nineteenth and early twentieth centuries also appeared in blackface doesn't make it less objectionable, though it is true that for the first quarter of the twentieth century almost all of them, from the vaudevillian Bert Williams to blues pioneers like Ethel Waters and Ma Rainey, played in traveling "tent shows" wearing blackface before both Black and white audiences. This was because Black entertainers had little choice; their survival as performers depended on giving the white audiences what they wanted. "African-Americans gained the mainstream stage only because white audiences demanded they be there," Lynn Abbott and Doug Seroff write in their illustrated history of Black popular entertainment. Their fortunes "remained subject to the coon-song loving disposition of the dominant race and the inherited conventions of minstrelsy."

But minstrelsy was complicated. It was invented in the 1830s in the rough quarters of New York by a young man named Thomas Dartmouth Rice, who was a kind of precursor to the sort of street performer Al Jolson was seven decades later. Rice created the character Jim Crow, a name now synonymous with racial caricature, but was originally a tough, clever, two-fisted rascal, not an improvident simpleton.

> *As I caution all white dandies, not to come in my way,*
> *For if dey insult me, dey'll in de gutter lay.*

Or so ran one of Rice's verses, as he rode Jim Crow to national success. Minstrelsy had many varieties, just as the depiction of Jews had its varieties, many of them stereotypical, insulting, and harmful. When mass immigration brought ethnic diversity to America, not minstrelsy itself but its spirit of satire and travesty was applied to all the groups that now made up the raucous, tense, wary American panorama. Ethnic and racial caricature and lampoonery were its chief pop cultural attributes. Entertainers like Jolson, Sophie Tucker, Eddie Cantor—indeed, practically all of the white vaudevillians—did blackface, but they also did what might be called Jewface, Yiddish dialect humor with its Jewish stereotypes—*Amos 'n' Andy* with an East European accent—and they did it with a kind of equal opportunity abandon.

In "blacking up," Jolson, Tucker, Cantor, Brice, and others took what was available from the American cultural shelf; blackface was ubiquitous, a stock image, one of the main prototypes of American history, identified by the culture historian John Strausbaugh as the Yankee, the frontiersman, and the blackface minstrel. In enlightened, post-civil-rights-movement America, blackface has come to be like the swastika and the N-word, banned from public spaces. But at the time that Jolson adopted it, it was taken for granted; it was a sort of stock image, a cliché, alongside what

Strausbaugh calls "various other brands of broadly played ethnic stereotypes and impersonations, for equally low laughs—the brawling Irish, wheedling Jews, oily Italians, thick-headed Germans, inscrutable Chinamen, gullible country rubes and so on." What makes this tricky is that Blacks were suffering from a pervasive discrimination unlike that suffered by other groups, at least the white ones. But while this is clear in retrospect, it wasn't clear to people from humble backgrounds half a generation removed from Old World pogroms striving to claw their way out of the poor, crime-ridden, filthy neighborhoods where they'd spent their own far from privileged childhoods.

What Jolson was actually guilty of—if guilty is the right word—is his adoption of the paradoxical post–Civil War collective nostalgia for the very South that so many had sacrificed so much blood to defeat. Jolson, Berlin, Von Tilzer, Caesar, Gershwin, and the other songwriters adopted this nostalgia, then improvised on it because, like blackface, it was an available cultural paradigm, like the Old West. There was an audience for it. They weren't striving to perpetuate whiteness. They were simply striving to get out of their own ghettos and to make it in America.

Which brings us to the notable absence of much in the way of overt objection to blackface in the commentary of Black writers and journalists. There were complaints about blackface in the 1910s and 1920s in the main Black newspapers like *The Pittsburgh Courier, The Chicago Defender,* and the *New York Amsterdam News,* but the complaints weren't so much that blackface was an insult; they were that whites had stolen blackness and were being more successful at it than Blacks were. In 1924, a chorus girl named Bessie Allison won a contest for the best essay on the topic "How the Negro Has Helped the Theatrical World." Allison noted that "aspiring competitors are being made every day to sing, dance, talk, act and execute Jazz more like the Negro; but there are so few who truly succeed in their attempts to imitate that one might venture to conclude that the Negro is yet unrivaled." IMPOSTERS STEAL RACE MATERIAL, was the headline on a 1930 column in *The Pittsburgh Courier*. "There was a day when white stage performers could put over their lines to an audience and get a laugh and draw a living salary with their own white skin," the paper's commentator said. "But that day seems gone." Whites "want the Negro form of entertainment—they want the original comic or the soul-stirring inborn expression such as the Negro alone can give."

As for Jolson, the columnist continued, "I know at least ten actors who . . . can beat Al Jolson singing a 'mammy song' the best day he ever lived." Another criticism was that white blackface performers tended to get "the Negro dialect" wrong, exaggerating it, "much like a New Yorker or a Yankee going to Florida or the Carolinas for the first time and there trying to talk southern," as a writer in the *New York Amsterdam News* put it in 1926. The article gives the example of one Jay C. Flippen, an "easy-going blackface comic," who, after being informed that his imitation of blackness was off the mark, studied the diction of Jolson and Eddie Cantor. "He observed that they spoke good American with the slightest intonation of Negro dialect—or just enough to stay within the character." That Jolson was a "blackface comedian" served some Black commentators as an element of exhortation to other Blacks to do better. "When you realize that Al Jolson is the highest sala-ried comedian on the American Stage (imitating a colored man), doesn't that prove that the colored man has the goods if he would only deliver them!" said a commentator in *The Chicago Defender*.

That the African American press didn't call attention to blackface as a racist offense doesn't mean that Black people didn't find it insulting; it may be that they felt themselves too vulner-able and powerless in American society to call attention to insults that were so common that white people scarcely noticed them. The impulse at the time was to live with it, somewhat the way Jews, until more recent times, hesitated to protest antisemitism out of the fear that complaining would only make matters worse. But this may portray the Black community as more passive in the face of cultural offense than it actually was. As Thomas Cripps has pointed out, among the early major projects of the NAACP, founded in 1913, was to organize boycotts of D. W. Griffith's *Birth of a Nation,* released in 1915 and correctly seen by Blacks "as a Gothic horror tale haunted by black brutes." It was too late to stop Griffith's movie, but, from that point on, the Black press "raged whenever white moviemakers flirted with racism." The newspapers, joining forces with the NAACP, "demanded censorship of racial slanders."

But when it came to Jolson, the Black press's treatment was one of respect and even affection: his identity as a "blackface performer" simply taken for granted, not worthy of much note, or perhaps, just understood as an inescapable trope, a resignation that a man like Jolson, whose good will was assumed, couldn't be expected to be light years ahead of his time. *The Pittsburgh Courier* tagline for Jolson was "the world's foremost entertainer," a phrase used without any apparent bitterness or resentment. "Undoubtedly one of the greatest of all entertainers," a contributor to the *New York Amsterdam News* called him. If they felt there was something intrinsically wrong in his use of blackface, for whatever reason, they didn't mention it.

8

Warner Bros. Takes a Chance

The big movie studios were making so much money and the technical difficulty of synchronizing pictures and sound was so daunting that the major figures of the movie business were happy to keep things as they silently were, the profits rolling in. So it's probably not surprising that it was the smaller, more precariously positioned Warner Bros. studio, with the eager collaboration of Al Jolson, that produced the first "talkie," *The Jazz Singer*.

There was a bit of serendipity in the way the event unfolded. "The fact is we were barely breathing," Jack Warner, the fourth of the four brothers, wrote in his memoir, summing up, albeit with some hyperbole, the state of the studio in the months and years before *The Jazz Singer* was produced. "It was a freak roll of the dice . . . which took us from a net income of $30,000 for the first eight months of 1927 to a staggering profit of $17,000,000 for a similar period only two years later."

The Warner brothers—Harry, Albert, Sam, and Jack in order of birth, four boys out of a total of nine children—grew up mostly in Youngstown, Ohio, where their father, Benjamin Wonskolaser, had established a modestly successful grocery and butcher business. Benjamin and his wife, Pearl Leah Eichelbaum, emigrated in 1883 from Krasnosielc, a small, mostly Jewish town, that is, a shtetl, that was the private possession of a rich Polish nobleman and, like Jolson's Seredzius, part of the Russian Empire. Benjamin was a devoutly Orthodox man who eked out what must have been a modest living as a shoemaker, with part of his earnings paid as taxes to the Polish overlord. The oldest of the boys, Harry, born Hirsch Mojzesz Wonskolaser, was the only one of the future Warner Bros. to be born in Poland, which, as Neal Gabler writes in his collective biography of the Jews who "invented Hollywood," was perhaps the reason he remained closest to his father, including in the depth of his Jewish attachment, in contrast to the American-born brothers whose degree of attachment seems to have attenuated in the order of their birth.

The four sons, three born in America, formed a kind of family corporation, like other sets of brothers—the Rothschilds come to mind, the Shuberts of New York, the Sassoons of Asia—whose family cohesion and geographical dispersion were the foundations of great business empires. The Wonskolasers went first to Baltimore, then spent a couple of years in Canada before winding up in Youngstown at the dawn of the twentieth century. It was there that Sam met a woman who ran a boardinghouse whose son had gone on the road with an Edison kinetoscope, the primitive movie projector of the time, and, having failed to make a go of it, wanted to get rid of it. Sam was working as a railroad foreman, with no connection to entertainment or the movies, but he very presciently saw the potential in the device, and he persuaded the family members to pool their resources to buy that very kinetoscope. Soon the brothers were traveling to towns throughout Ohio and Pennsylvania charging admission to see the sole movie they owned, *The Great Train Robbery,* a ten-minute silent classic. By 1910, the four boys were producing movies of their own. By 1916, they were making real money. In 1918, Sam and Jack were in California to run the Warner Bros. new studio there while Harry and Albert took care of the film distribution and exhibition business from New York.

Sam and Jack were relative small fry in Hollywood—"rather a dim speck with a rundown studio at Eighteenth and Main and an unimpressive roster of performers," Gabler writes, which may be the reason for the Warners' special, iconoclastic character. "Our new studio looked like the city dump," Jack Warner wrote in his autobiography. "It was so unimpressive that we waited for a long time before we publicly proclaimed it as the home of Warner Brothers Pictures." He describes a number of failed ventures, all silent films undertaken in the early to mid-1920s, including one called *Babe Comes Home* in which Babe Ruth played himself, badly. According to Jack, they "bombed" with several other attempts, including *Ashamed of Parents, Parted Curtains,* and *Your Best Friend,* though they did have some successes, most notably a total, eventually, of nineteen movies starring a German shepherd named Rin Tin Tin, without which, as Jack put it, though, again, with some dramatic license, "we would have closed up the lot and gone back to the meat market in Youngstown."

There's a picaresque quality to the Warners, in their combination of caution, calculation, and audacity—Harry and Albert more cautious, Sam and Jack more brash, freewheeling, sybaritic. In the mid-1920s, when the studio was still struggling, Jack was traveling in Michigan on business when he ran out of money. He called Sam long distance and asked him to wire $500. Sam, saying the phone connection was poor, pretended not to hear, whereupon the operator came on the line. "I can hear your brother in Michigan perfectly well," she said. "You can?" Sam replied. "Well, maybe you can send him five hundred dollars."

Despite their financial worries, the Warners were successful enough to move to another lot, thirteen acres on Sunset Boulevard, and soon after that, they decided to produce *The Jazz Singer,* with synchronized sound. This was the happy bit of serendipity that made movie history.

The road to the movie version of Samson Raphaelson's story and play was far from straight or predictable. In 1925, Sam and Jack decided to start a radio station, copying what at least two other studios had already done as a way of promoting their movies. To get the project going, the brothers hired a prominent sound engineer named Nathan Levinson to build a transmitter on the Warner lot. Levinson was the West Coast representative of Western Electric, the company that manufactured telephones and other electric equipment for Bell Telephone. Like the Warners themselves, Levinson was the son of Polish Jewish immigrant parents. He'd grown up on the Lower East Side, worked as a telegraph operator in New York when just fourteen years old, then joined the army signal corps during World War I, rising to the rank of major. Later he became semi-famous in Hollywood, nominated for a dozen or so Academy Awards and winning one, for *Yankee Doodle Dandy,* in 1942.

While he was working on the Warners' transmitter on their Sunset Boulevard lot, Levinson had occasion to visit the Bell Labs in New York, where he saw what he called "a talking picture," and he urged Sam to go see it. Sam acted on Levinson's enthusiastic suggestion. At Bell Labs he saw a series of short films in which the sound—an object falling on a table, voices, music—came from loudspeakers placed behind the screen that were perfectly synchronized with the corresponding images on the screen. This had amazed the tech-savvy Levinson, and it amazed Sam as well.

Until then, the silent film era had not actually been silent at all. There was plenty of sound accompanying the pictures that were shown in the thousands of movie theaters that dotted the American landscape of big cities and small towns alike, but it was extraneous from the action on the screen, provided by a piano player onstage, or "song pluggers" in the orchestra pit, or by a small ensemble, or, in the case of the big, opulent movie theaters, whole orchestras with famous conductors.

"From the beginning, the cinema abhorred silence," Scott Eyman writes in his history of sound in the movies. "The cinema needed some sort of sound, if only to cover up the distracting noises of the projector and the shuffling of the audience." According to Eyman, movie theaters "were the foremost employers of musicians in the country." As we've seen from the example of George Jessel and Walter Winchell, furnishing music to go with a silent film was a major source of employment for poor, upwardly mobile young performers.

That was what made the movies different from vaudeville or legitimate theater. In the movies, the performers spoke only in mime; they weren't heard, which meant it didn't matter whether they had squeaky voices or heavy accents or couldn't speak English. Actors learned to pause the action at certain points when dialogue boxes, known as titles or title cards or intertitles, flashed on the screen telling spectators what was being said. Everybody in the world knew what Charlie Chaplin, Douglas Fairbanks, Mary Pickford, and the other big silent-era stars looked like, but only their friends and associates knew what they sounded like, and nobody could be sure that if they converted to sound they would be any good, if their voices or accents might not match audience expectations.

Even if the major studios were content to leave things as they were, there were plenty of others who understood that there were fortunes to be made in combining pictures and sound, and inventors had been trying to do that for a long time. In 1913, Thomas Edison, having invented the phonograph some thirty years before, unveiled what he called the Kinetophone. It was a Rube Goldberg sort of contraption, a projector in a booth at the back of the theater connected by an overhead belt and pulleys to a phonograph placed behind the screen at the other end. It didn't work very well. The synchronization was off, and the volume of the sound was inadequate because Edison's phonograph was a mechanical, not an electrical, device. The acoustic horns familiar from photographs of the early phonographs were used to record sound and to play it back, but there was no amplification, no speakers, and in a theater with large audiences, the sound had to be loud.

But the technology kept advancing. Vacuum tube amplification was improved; the condenser microphone and the electrical loudspeaker were invented, and by 1924, Western Electric had constructed what came to be the device used in the first talkies. It was a turntable and a movie camera both attached to a motor that turned at a constant speed, so that sound was recorded by a stylus on a wax disc at the same time as the images were captured by the camera. When the movie was shown the process was reversed. Both the projector and the turntable were in the projection booth at the back of the theater, and the turntable was connected by electrical wires to speakers at the other end of the room behind the screen. Western Electric made some test films, but none of the major studios were interested in the epochal and risky switch to sound movies.

Sam Warner, however, understood the revolutionary potential of the device he saw that day at the Bell Labs in New York. Still, in a famous part of the Warner lore, Harry, the president of the company, rejected the idea of talking pictures, feeling it an expensive gimmick that would not attract an audience. He refused even to go to Bell Labs and see the Western Electric demonstration. But the clever Sam, as the story goes, set up a benign trap for his older brother, inviting him to what he said would be a meeting with bankers at Goldman Sachs, who had become the Warners' chief source of financing, perhaps because the Jew-

ish bankers were more willing to take a flier on an upstart Jewish movie company than the WASPy banks were. In 1925, in an
important step for Warner, Goldman had financed Harry's purchase of the ornate 1,500-seat Piccadilly Theatre on Broadway and
Fifty-second Street in Manhattan, and renamed it the Warner.

The meeting, which Harry attended, turned out to be a showing of a short film of a jazz band, and Harry was enthralled. The
demonstration at first made him think more of filmed musical
events than talking pictures, but he soon realized that everything
from vaudeville to grand opera could now be shown to audiences
with no need for actual musicians to be present. "If it can talk, it
can sing," Harry said to his Goldman Sachs banker. Things then
moved quickly. With Goldman's backing, Warner entered into
an agreement with Western Electric by which it got an exclusive
license for the sound process, both to use in making movies and
to sell to theaters, which would have to have it if they were to
show movies with sound. According to Jack Warner, they exam-
ined four hundred different possible names for the device, eventually settling on Vitaphone.

Warner Bros. set up a soundproof studio in Brooklyn to produce short films of the sort that were shown in theaters before
the main feature. Problems immediately presented themselves,
mostly in the form of what Jack Warner called "aggravating
noises" that got picked up by the recording device. The camera
itself made a whirring sound; the nearby elevated subway train
made a rumbling sound; the arc lights used for filming made "a
sizzling sound, like bacon frying." The camera was put into an
insulated booth to eliminate the whirring sound; incandescent
lightbulbs replaced the arc lights; to get away from the subway
noise, Sam moved the whole operation to the Metropolitan Opera
House in Manhattan.

LEFT: Al Jolson, American singer, comedian, and actor, circa 1915.
(Photo by Keystone-France / Gamma-Keystone via Getty Images)

RIGHT: Rabbi Moses Rubin Yoelson and Chyesa (Ida) Yoelson, Jolson's father and his father's second wife, in a photograph taken in Washington, D.C.
(Library of Congress, Prints & Photographs Division / Harris & Ewing)

LEFT: Jolson was born in 1886 in an Eastern European shtetl, something like the one shown on this postcard, which dates from circa 1916 to 1917.
(Lebrecht Music & Art / Alamy Stock Photo)

ABOVE: Jolson's parents' house, at 713 4½ Street, S.W., Washington, D.C.
(*Library of Congress, Prints & Photographs Division / Harris & Ewing*)

BELOW: Jolson and his father, photographed in Yonkers, New York, at the home of Jolson's sister Etta, during a family reunion in 1931.

BELOW: Jolson (*right*) and his older brother, Harry, in "The Hebrew and the Cadet," a comedy skit they performed early in their vaudeville careers.

LEFT: Sheet music for "Swanee," one of Jolson's biggest hits, written by George Gershwin and Irving Caesar and published by T. B. Harms and Francis, Day & Hunter, Inc., New York, in 1919.

BELOW: Jolson in blackface, getting ready for the musical comedy *Big Boy* with members of the Jubilee Singers, who performed in the show on Broadway in 1925 and later in the movie version.
(Bettmann / Getty Images)

LEFT: American comedienne and actress Fanny Brice (1891–1951) in the early 1920s. She and Jolson were singled out by the critic Gilbert Seldes for possessing something "demonic" in their ability to give audiences "a genuine emotional effect."
(Library of Congress, Prints & Photographs Division / Bain News Service)

BELOW: Samson Raphaelson, whose short story and play were the basis for the movie *The Jazz Singer*, circa 1960.
(Courtesy of the University of Illinois Archives)

BELOW: Songwriters Eubie Blake (*left, at the piano*) and Noble Sissle, 1930s. Jolson very publicly invited them to dinner after a restaurant refused to serve them.
(Pictorial Press Ltd. / Alamy Stock Photo)

RIGHT: George Jessel in the stage production of *The Jazz Singer*, 1925. *(White Studio / Billy Rose Theatre Division / The New York Public Library)*

BELOW: Jacob J. Shubert, circa 1900. The youngest of the three Shubert brothers, theater owners and impresarios, he was the one closest to Jolson, their biggest star. *(Billy Rose Theatre Division / The New York Public Library)*

BELOW: Jolson with his Mercedes-Benz Roadster on the Warner Bros. lot, where he filmed *The Jazz Singer* and other Warner films, 1930. *(Pictorial Parade / Hulton Archive / Getty Images)*

ABOVE: Outside the Warners' Theatre, October 6, 1927. *(RBM Vintage Images / Alamy Stock Photo)*

BELOW, LEFT: Jolson and Ruby Keeler, probably on their honeymoon in London in 1928, when *The Jazz Singer* was playing there. *(Walter Bellamy / London Express / Getty Images)*

BELOW, RIGHT: Jolson and his close friend Walter Winchell, gossip columnist extraordinaire, at the Stork Club, New York, circa 1944. *(Courtesy CSU Archives / Everett Collection)*

ABOVE: A scene from the film *The Jazz Singer* (1927) with Jolson as Jakie Rabinowitz, Eugenie Besserer as Sara Rabinowitz, and Warner Oland as Cantor Rabinowitz. *(Bettmann / Getty Images)*

BELOW: Jolson singing "Kol Nidre" in *The Jazz Singer*. *(Everett Collection)*

ABOVE, LEFT: Jolson entertaining U.S. troops at Pusan Stadium during his visit to the Korean front, September 17, 1950. He made the trip at his own expense. *(Everett Collection Historical / Alamy Stock Photo)*; ABOVE, RIGHT: "Al Jolson, wearing G.I. uniform and Air Force patch, returned from the Korean War front . . . today. He was the first entertainer to go to Korea. Jolson was greeted at the airport by his wife." September 28, 1950, *Los Angeles Herald Examiner. (Herald Examiner / Los Angeles Public Library)*

BELOW: "From all walks of life, the humble and the mighty came today to pay final respects to Al Jolson, the great show-man, whose songs thrilled three generations. Traffic outside the Temple Israel [on Hollywood Boulevard], where funeral services [were held,] was jammed, and the streets were thronged by thousands. Photo shows part of crowd outside the temple." October 26, 1950, *Los Angeles Herald Examiner.* Jolson had died three days earlier. *(Herald Examiner / Los Angeles Public Library)*

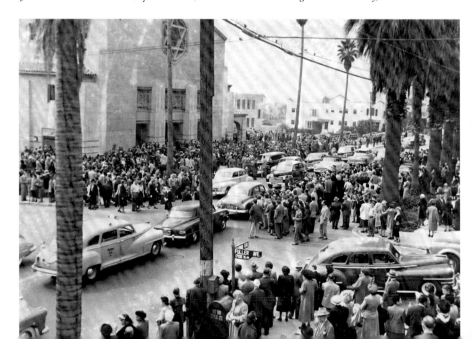

There, eight shorts were produced, including one of the New York Philharmonic playing the overture to *Tannhäuser,* the violinist Mischa Elman playing Dvořák's "Humoresque," and the Metropolitan Opera soprano Marion Talley singing an aria from *Rigoletto.* Meanwhile, at the studio in Los Angeles, Jack oversaw production of a full-length feature, *Don Juan,* starring John Barrymore, which the Warners had originally planned as a silent movie. While the filming took place on the Warner lot in California, a grand symphonic score specially composed for the movie was recorded by the full New York Philharmonic in the Vitaphone studio at the Metropolitan Opera House in New York.

The world premiere of all of this, preceded by an enormous publicity campaign in which the Warners promised "a new era in motion picture presentation," took place at the Warner Theatre in New York, and the response exceeded even Sam Warner's expectations. "A marvelous device . . . stirred a distinguished audience," *New York Times* critic Mordaunt Hall gushed, extolling the quality of the sound and the "uncanny" timing of "sound to the movement of lips and the actions of musicians. . . . The future of this new contrivance is boundless, for inhabitants of small remote places will have the opportunity of listening to and seeing grand opera as it is given in New York." But the era of talkies hadn't quite started. *Don Juan* had its impressive score but no audible spoken dialogue. It still used the familiar silent-film-era intertitles, like dialogue balloons in cartoons, to indicate spoken words. John Barrymore could be seen but he couldn't yet be heard. Nonetheless, it was clear that the spectacular success of the Warner premier had put the movie business on the precipice of a new era. Jack Warner later noted that several executives from rival movie studios attended the *Don Juan* premier, and, he wrote, they "would soon be thinking of cutting their throats because they had ignored sound films as a crackpot idea." Now, Jack continued, "the pros knew that Armageddon was at hand."

* * *

Jolson quickly got into the act. After the *Don Juan* premier, the Warners made more shorts, including one called *A Plantation Act,* in which Jolson sang three songs. He appears, in blackface, from behind what looks like a farm shack somewhere in the South, wearing striped overalls and a shirt whose loose sleeves flap around his elbows. He sings "Red Red Robin Comes Ba Ba Bobbin' Along," after which he looks into the camera and says, "Wait a minute, wait a minute, give me a chance, folks. You ain't heard nothin' yet." Then he sings "April Showers" and "Rockabye Your Baby with a Dixie Melody," his hands over his heart, then clenched, then outstretched toward the audience.

A million kisses I'll deliver,
If you'll only play that Swanee River.
Rock-a-bye, your rock-a-bye baby,
With a Dixie melody!

The important thing about *A Plantation Act* is that Jolson came across well on film, or, at least, well enough, and this may have come as a surprise to him. In 1923, three years before making that short, Jolson agreed to act in a movie that would be made by D. W. Griffith, now on the historical dustbin because of his notorious *Birth of a Nation,* with its ugly racist images of Blacks and its favorable portrayal of the Ku Klux Klan. But at the time, Griffith, an important cinematic innovator, was a powerful and influential movie director. Jolson agreed to participate in a silent

movie to be called either *Mammy's Boy* or *Black Magic*. It told the
story of a white lawyer who disguises himself as a Black man in
order to clear a Black client of a murder charge.

It seems strange that Jolson, America's most famous singer
and comedian, would want to play a role in a silent film in which
he could neither talk nor sing. He asked for a screen test, and
he took one at the Griffith studios in Mamaroneck, New York.
Jolson hated what he saw, though it's not clear exactly what it
was, whether the screen test showed him in blackface—the white
lawyer posing as a Black man—or not. Whatever the case, he
nonetheless told Griffith that he'd do the movie, and Griffith went
about preparing to shoot it, including building a set that Griffith
said cost $70,000.

Then, on the day screening was to begin, Jolson spent most
of the day at the Aqueduct Racetrack. The next day, without any
notice to Griffith but with the newsreel cameras whirring, he,
together with J.J. Shubert, boarded the ocean liner *Majestic* and
sailed to Europe. End of movie.

The incident was avidly covered by the press—Jolson's "walk-
out" was "the sole talk of Broadway circles this week," *Variety*
announced—and it led Griffith to sue Jolson for $571,696. The
matter dragged on for a couple of years until, in 1926, a jury in
federal court in New York awarded Griffith a mere $2,627.28, evi-
dently accepting the argument of Jolson's lawyer that Jolson had
never actually signed a contract to make the film. At the time, Jolson, explaining his decision to back out of his verbal agreement,
declared that he'd been "rotten" in his screen test, and he vowed
never to attempt another movie.

But just around the time the lawsuit was being decided, there
was Jolson, excited by the prospect of talking movies, making his
film debut in *A Plantation Act*. And he was good in it. His layered,

resonant voice reproduced well, and his "you ain't seen nothin' yet" recapitulated his famous rapport with the audience, his ability to break the barrier between spectator and performer in favor of an atmosphere of cordial complicity.

Shortly after Warner introduced Vitaphone to the world, the French poet Paul Valéry invented the concept of what he called "the conquest of ubiquity." Thanks to the new technology, Valéry wrote in a 1928 essay, works of art "will not merely exist in themselves, but will exist wherever someone with a certain apparatus happens to be." Just like gas or electricity, there could now be "the home delivery of Sensory Reality," and this would be the case for music especially, which "will be made instantly audible on any point on earth, regardless of where it is performed."

Up to the time of the Vitaphone, probably only Charlie Chaplin was ubiquitous in Valéry's sense of the term. With *A Plantation Act* the word applied to Jolson too, with the important difference that he could be heard musically as well as seen by audiences in all of America's estimated twenty-five thousand movie theaters. It marked a new vista of fame for a performer who had already come a long way from his modest beginnings. Jolson's fame, moreover, was about to grow even further with the movie version of *The Jazz Singer,* which was significant for two reasons: It was the Armageddon that Jack Warner predicted for the movie business, and it marked a new stage for Jews, Jewishness, and America in a culture that was undergoing an Armageddon of its own.

9

"A highly unlikely prospect for immortality"

In the mid-1920s, a promising, handsome young actor in New York named Frederich Meier Weisenfreund, born in 1892 in Lviv, now in western Ukraine, made a game-changing career move. He abandoned the Yiddish theater in which he'd successfully performed and took a part in an English-language production on Broadway.

He wasn't alone. The Jewish press even had an expression for what was becoming a common occurrence in Yiddish theater circles—*avek tsu di goyim*, gone off to the gentiles. The suggestion was obvious and the implied judgment harsh: that to leave the Yiddish theater for the fame and fortune of Broadway was a kind of betrayal, and, in this sense, the trend mimicked the plot of *The Jazz Singer*, which is about a young man who sees better, certainly far more lucrative and glamorous prospects singing on Broadway than in a synagogue. The Yiddish theater, with its dozen or so venues, mostly along Second Avenue in Manhattan but in Brooklyn and the Bronx as well, served some of the same functions as the Jewish places of worship: It was one of the things that gave Jewish immigration its sense of community, and it both preserved and developed Yiddishkeit.

But now assimilation, that inevitable and ultimately necessary consequence of immigration, was driving the second generation of eastern European Jews both out of the ghetto and away from Yiddish, hence, in the theatrical trade, the move from Second Avenue to the Great White Way. Weisenfreund, whose stage name had been Muni Weisenfreund, changed his name again, this time to Paul Muni, and was soon a Hollywood matinee idol, known for his roles as an Italian immigrant gangster Tony Camonte in *Scarface* (written by another Yiddish-speaking child of immigrants, Ben Hecht).

But when Al Jolson took on the role of Jakie Rabinowitz/Jack Robin in *The Jazz Singer,* he was moving in a different manner, staying closer to his roots. Everybody knew that Jolson was Jewish, foreign-born, the son of a cantor. It was in all of the profiles of him devoured by his adoring public. Here and there in his stage appearances he'd make a gesture of complicity with the Jews in the audience by letting fly a little Yiddishism, as in *Bombo,* when he greets a Native American chieftain with "Sholem aleichem." He does that again in the play *Wonder Bar* when he greets the Chinese hatcheck girl. In the movie version of *Wonder Bar,* released in 1934, there's an extravagant Busby Berkeley–choreographed minstrel show in which Jolson, in blackface, goes to heaven (while singing "Goin' to Heaven on a Mule"), whose inhabitants, including Saint Peter and Saint Gabriel, are all also in blackface. In one fleeting scene, Jolson reads a mocked-up Yiddish newspaper called *Gan Eden Star* (Paradise Star) showing a banner headline, "Two Runaway Angels Ran into the Comet," in Yiddish.

It's impossible to know how many members of the audience would have gotten this little joke about a Yiddish newspaper in an all-Black heaven, but the mere fact that it was in there shows an affectionate attachment to an identity. In the 1931 theatrical version of *Wonder Bar,* Jolson sang "Khasndl Oyf Shabbos" (A Cantor on the Sabbath) in Yiddish, and that scene was filmed for the movie version, though it didn't make it through the final cut.

When Jolson first met the generation-younger Eddie Cantor and George Jessel, who had come to see him in Los Angeles in an act of worshipful obeisance, he took them to a kosher restaurant.

Jolson never concealed his Jewishness, but in public he mostly kept it in the background. Figures like Cantor, Jessel, Fanny Brice, and Sophie Tucker frequently performed in Yiddish or in "Jew-face," using made-up Yiddish accents as ethnic shtick, in what was perhaps the last incarnation of the stereotypical stage Jew, tinged with a kind of mocking sentimentality over the disappearing world of their elders. When Brice used her Yiddish accent to sing "Second Hand Rose," she "testified to the romanticization of the ghetto that most New York Jews no longer lived in," as the theater historian Ted Merwin has put it. The song is about a girl from the Jewish quarter of Second Avenue who can't afford anything new—her shoes, her hose, even her beaus are used. But Brice lived on Park Avenue, wore the most expensive fashion, and didn't speak Yiddish. The Jews who moved away from the Lower East Side retained a kind of mocking affection for the place. It was the humble cradle of their new American lives; it rang of a certain authenticity and folksy charm; and it played well in the Ziegfeld Follies. Funny Yiddishisms and Yiddish sentimentality could be monetized, in the same way that the warm and fuzzy image of the Old South was. But nobody wanted to go back to the Lower East Side any more than they wanted to return to their Russian Empire shtetls or to the banks of the Swanee River.

Jolson spoke Yiddish and knew the Hebrew liturgy and, as we've seen, he made identifying gestures, but his personal rupture with the ways of his ancestors couldn't have been more complete in his lifestyle, his marriages, and in his impersonation of a Black man evoking the South. Since his youthful stints with brother Harry in "The Hebrew and the Cadet" and his touring with Joe Palmer in "A Little of Everything," he did no Jewish impersonations, no Yiddish or Yiddish-accented songs (with the single known exception of "A Cantor on the Sabbath" in *Wonder Bar*), nothing explicitly Jewish beyond the briefest allusion here and there. But now, in early 1927, Warner Bros. offered him the role of Jakie Rabinowitz/Jack Robin in a movie version of *The Jazz Singer,* which it had chosen as its next Vitaphone feature. As we've seen, Jolson had been interested in Samson Raphaelson's "Day of Atonement" when it first appeared in *Everybody's Magazine* in 1922, and he'd even proposed that Raphaelson write a musical version of the story just for Jolson. Now there was going to be such a version, and that meant many things for him, including the start of a very successful career as a movie star, during which he returned to the character Gus, which he'd played in the Shubert-produced musical comedies. For the moment, though, *The Jazz Singer* gave him a chance to go not away to the gentiles, like Paul Muni, but back to the Jews.

* * *

George Jessel reminded people all his life that he was supposed to have played the lead role in the movie *The Jazz Singer,* as he had in Raphaelson's stage version, and all his life he claimed that Jolson, in cahoots with the Warners, had engaged in subterfuge to deny him the part. As he told the story, after his success in the play and in *Private Izzy Murphy,* there was an unambiguous understanding with the Warners that he would take on *The Jazz Singer.* The Warners even agreed to postpone production for a year so Jessel could finish his tour in the theatrical version, which was doing extremely well as it moved around the country, ending with a two-week run in April 1927 at the Century Theatre in New York, with seats for an audience of 2,300 people. All the trade publications announced that Jessel would do the film. A price was agreed on, $5,000, according to Jessel in his memoirs (though this seems to be a typo; other accounts say $50,000). But when Jessel found out the film would be a talkie, he asked for a bonus, which he says Harry summarily rejected. But Harry and Sam felt the deal could be salvaged, and Jessel traveled across the country to Hollywood to start work on the film. There, he went to see his friend Jolson, who was in a show in Los Angeles. Jolson invited Jessel to stay the night in his suite at the Biltmore Hotel. The next morning, he told him he was going to play golf. The morning after that, Jessel writes in his memoirs, "I picked up *The Los Angeles Times* and read that Jolie had signed a contract the previous day—the day he was supposed to be playing golf—to star in *The Jazz Singer*. It threw me for a loop, and I couldn't even get Jack or Darryl on the telephone"—Darryl being Darryl Zanuck, the star Warner producer.

Jack Warner's version of the story differs on key points. He says that he agreed to pay Jessel a bonus of $10,000 (over and above his base fee, which he gives as $30,000, though he seems to have confused that amount with the fee Jessel got for two more Izzy Murphy movies he made later). But Jack took offense when Jessel demanded a binding letter regarding the additional payment, rather than accept Warner's word. But written contracts were standard in Hollywood at the time and there was nothing unusual about Jessel wanting one. It's possible, of course, that Jack refused because, as Herbert G. Goldman maintains, he already knew that Jolson was interested in the part. Still, Jack claims that he was desperate to find a substitute for the suddenly unavailable Jessel. He gave a screen test to a young actor already on the set, but he turned out to have "a voice like a tired spoke." He asked Eddie Cantor to play the Jakie/Jack role, but Cantor refused on the grounds that the part ought to go to Jessel. Then, Jack claims, not entirely convincingly, the idea of Jolson suddenly came to his mind. He tracked him down in Denver where he was on tour with *Big Boy,* and had an associate see him in his hotel to offer him the part. Jolson quickly agreed, for $75,000.

Whatever the truth about the switch from Jessel to Jolson, the Warners must have been very pleased by it. As one film historian put it, "Jessel was a vaudeville comedian and master of ceremonies with one successful play and one modestly successful film to his credit," whereas "Jolson was a superstar." The deal was that Jolson, "the world's greatest entertainer," would sing six songs in the movie and record them for separate sale. It was the smartest deal the Warners ever made.

Jolson was enthusiastic about taking on the role. Perhaps it was his ego, since Jolson liked the world revolving around him, and *The Jazz Singer* was *his* story, inspired by *him,* based on *his* actual life. Given that, it's not hard to imagine that lurking behind Jolson's eagerness to take on the Jakie/Jack role was a desire to return to his roots, to do things over, to have a chance to reconcile himself to his father and, perhaps more important, to resurrect his mother. *The Jazz Singer* was going to be a movie that celebrated the haunting beauty of cantorial music. It would bring Jolson back to his childhood in Seredzius, to the house with the hemlock needles on the floor, and to the rooms above the store in Washington where he had been a cantorial apprentice, before his mother died. For Jolson, *The Jazz Singer* would be personal, even as it would extend images of religious Jewish life into the heart of gentile America, like that ramp projecting into the first few rows of the audience that he performed on.

It would in that sense be a kind of religious coming out for Jolson, and not only for Jolson but for the Warner brothers as well, and that raises the question of why these Hollywood Jews, striving for assimilation and acceptance in America, chose a property like *The Jazz Singer* to be their first full-fledged talking movie.

It's a paradox in its way. The Jews who "invented Hollywood" didn't generally make movies about Jews, or, at least, they didn't make many of them compared to the movies they made about other kinds of people. Among those they did make were the Warners' own *Private Izzie Murphy* and *Sailor Izzy Murphy*, starring George Jessel. Carl Laemmle, born in 1867 in the Jewish quarter of a small town in Württemberg, Germany, and cofounder of Universal Pictures, produced the Cohens and Kellys series, one of whose screenwriters was Alfred A. Cohn, whom the Warners hired to adapt Raphaelson's *The Jazz Singer* for their movie version. Two years before, Cohn wrote the script for *His People*, a powerful drama of generational conflict among Lower East Side Jews that had a good deal of thematic overlap with *The Jazz Singer*, including the Lower East Side scenes that start each movie, the rigid father repudiating a wayward son, the doting mother, the heartwarming reconciliation at the end.

But movies with Jewish themes were a very minor element of Hollywood's vast production. In 1927, hundreds of films were released, all of them, with the notable exception of *The Jazz Singer*, silent, and only a very small number of them telling stories of Jews or depicting Jewish life, and those tended to be light comedies— *Sailor Izzy Murphy* or *Clancy's Kosher Wedding*, the latter declared by *Moving Picture World*, a weekly devoted to the film business, to be a "familiar racial character comedy" with "nothing new" in it. Directors like Alfred Hitchcock, Fritz Lang, F. W. Murnau, Josef von Sternberg, and Cecil B. DeMille were in their silent film heyday in the mid- to late 1920s, but none of them made Jewish movies. Fritz Lang's classic *Metropolis*, about class conflict in a city of the future, was released in 1927, the same year as *The Jazz Singer*. Hitchcock made half a dozen thrillers that year. There were westerns like *Buffalo Bill, Jr.*, and any number of movies about love affairs across class lines. The great silent comedians

Mack Sennett and Buster Keaton had new movies in 1927, Keaton in *College,* about a nerdy student who tries to become an athlete. *The Mystery of the Louvre* featured a phantom stalking Paris; *Wings* was a war drama about two men in love with the same woman; there was a DeMille extravaganza, *King of Kings,* telling the life of Jesus. A movie called *Dr. Wu* starring Lon Cheney, "the master of makeup," told the grim story of a Chinese mandarin who murders the daughter he loves rather than allow her to marry an Englishman, one of a minor fashion of movies in the silent film era that can legitimately be called racist, the endless series depicting the villainous Fu Manchu chief among them. In 1927–28, Warner Bros. made twenty-seven movies, including *The Bush Leaguer, The Desired Woman, Slightly Used* (with May McAvoy, who played Jolson's girlfriend in *The Jazz Singer*), *One-Round Hogan, A Reno Divorce, The Fortune Hunter,* and others, as well as four Rin Tin Tin productions (*Jaws of Steel, Hills of Kentucky, Tracked by the Police,* and *A Dog of the Regiment*). But aside from the silly *Sailor Izzy Murphy, The Jazz Singer* was the only one of its Hebraic kind that the Warners produced that year.

Unlike vaudeville, where a large proportion of the performers were Jewish, the big stars of Hollywood were almost all not, though the studio owners, producers, and even financiers may have been Jews. The male stars included Rudolph Valentino, John and Lionel Barrymore, Douglas Fairbanks, and Lon Chaney; there were the great comedians—the Chaplins, both Charlie and his half brother Syd, Mack Sennett, W. C. Fields, Harold Lloyd, Buster Keaton. The most glamorous and highly paid women included Mary Pickford, Clara Bow, Lillian Gish, Greta Garbo, and Louise Brooks, none of whom appear to be Jewish or to have played Jewish characters.

One historian of the silent film era, Kevin Brownlow, argues that the movies of that time didn't just paint a trivialized, innocu-

ous, wholly entertaining picture of America. Hollywood was a liberal, socially progressive place that made movies exposing crime,
poverty, child labor, unwanted pregnancy, and political corrup-
tion, or presenting in a favorable light causes like the women's
struggle for suffrage, such that conservatives complained about
how the movies were casting a perniciously progressive influence
over the country. But given the persistence of the old antisemitic
prejudices of the era, Brownlow says, "is it any wonder that the
Hollywood producers avoided the subject of their own people?"
Many of the Hollywood Jews, he adds, "believed that any treatment might spread anti-Semitism."

The Jazz Singer was the exception. It was also a high-stakes
gamble for the Warner studio, one on which their risky invest-
ment in Vitaphone, including installing the equipment in the
theaters they owned, would depend. They had the encouraging
example of some of the other Jewish-themed movies of recent
years, especially the variations on *Abie's Irish Rose,* but those movies were light, crowd-pleasing romantic comedies about non-Jews
as much as Jews, not the unsparing look at generational conflict
of *The Jazz Singer,* and they were both intellectually and technically undemanding. *The Jazz Singer,* moreover, with its scenes of
caftan-clad rabbis and cantors, and real Torah scrolls and praying
in Hebrew, and its emotional climax, the chanting of Kol Nidre in
an actual Orthodox synagogue, was going to go much deeper into
Jewish religious life and observance than any other of the Jewish-
themed movies that preceded it, and that religious life would be
shown realistically. Jews might provide a kind of audience base,
as they no doubt did for the staged version of *The Jazz Singer,* but
the movie would have to cross over to the gentile majority to be
a commercial success. Given the stakes, the Warners could have
chosen a safer, more garden-variety property, perhaps a romantic
comedy starring John Barrymore, who had played Don Juan in

the studio's first full-length Vitaphone feature. *The Jazz Singer* was "a very unusual choice," Neal Gabler writes, "one that, at first or even second or third blush, seemed a highly unlikely prospect for immortality." So again, why did they make it?

The Warners themselves seem never to have fully explained their decision. Harry, the brother most attached to his Jewish origins, told Jessel that *The Jazz Singer* might, if nothing else, "be a good picture to make for the sake of racial tolerance." According to Jack, Harry "desperately wanted the screen rights [to the Raphaelson property] for Vitaphone," and soon after the success of the first Vitaphone demonstration he swept them up for $50,000—Raphaelson getting the happy news while vacationing in Europe. In the Warners' mind, the surprising success of the theatrical version of the story no doubt played a part. Certainly if Jessel's *Jazz Singer* had failed, Harry would never have gone ahead with a movie version. The play, as performed before full audiences all over the country, was powerful evidence that a drama centering on Jewish generational conflict could sell and that it could sell beyond Jewish audiences.

In this sense, the Warners' decision to make *The Jazz Singer* showed a certain conviction that America was open-minded enough to welcome a story like that of Jack Robin and his father. This alone is remarkable. The America of the 1920s was still the America of the Ku Klux Klan, the antisemitic fulminations of Henry Ford's *Dearborn Independent*, with its Protocols-of-the-Elders-of-Zion lie that a secret Jewish cabal was taking control of the minds of America, in part by making movies and feeding them to an unsuspecting public. The America of the upstart Jews who created Hollywood and Tin Pan Alley was the America that didn't admit Jews to fancy country clubs and erected quotas to keep their numbers in the elite universities to a minimum. The Warners knew the anxiety of being Jewish in America in 1927, but they had succeeded there, and they had a certain confidence that *The Jazz Singer* would make its way. And, as it turned out, they were right. Or perhaps they were just lucky that the movie came along at a time when America was becoming the best place in the world for Jews; yes, it was still a place afflicted by the ancient prejudices, but the Jews as a whole were making it in a way that had eluded them for centuries in the Old Country.

The Raphaelson story and play were not about antisemitism in America, or prejudice against the Jews, or Jewish suffering at the hands of others, even though everybody knew that all of that existed. That topic would have to wait twenty more years, until 1947, to be made into a mass-circulation movie, *Gentlemen's Agreement,* in which Gregory Peck plays a newspaper reporter pretending to be Jewish in order to experience firsthand the anti-Jewish bigotries of the time. For the Warners, there was a personal element in the choice of *The Jazz Singer* as their first talkie, but it had nothing to do with a complaint about the wider society.

As Gabler writes, the Warners themselves were intimately knowledgeable about the kind of conflict put on display in the movie, the conflict between generations, between Jewishness and assimilation, the worry of the older generation that the very welcome the Jews had received in America would destroy Judaism and its beauties. The four Warner brothers experienced the conflict among themselves, between the more conservative, religiously attached older boys, Harry and Albert, and the fast-living, entirely assimilated younger ones, Sam and Jack. Harry may have seen the movie as a way to advance religious tolerance, but, as Gabler has put it, for Jack and Sam, who supervised the production of the film at the Warner studio in Los Angeles, "*The Jazz Singer* was . . . a highly personal dramatization of the conflicts in their own lives and within their own family."

Perhaps for both Jolson and the four Warner brothers, choosing *The Jazz Singer* as the foundation on which to construct their Vitaphone venture was a kind of affirmation of Jewishness as compatible with Americanness. It was a homecoming, maybe even an act of expiation for the sin of assimilation that all of them had committed, if to different degrees. One of the bit players in the film, a Jewish actor from Poland named Joseph Green, told Kevin Brownlow that for the scenes in the synagogue, Sam and Jack "put their father in charge," meaning Benjamin, who came to Los Angeles for the purpose. Yossele Rosenblatt, the famous Orthodox cantor who played himself in *The Jazz Singer,* singing in a concert of liturgical music, was there as well. "For that day," Brownlow says, "they all refused to use English and all spoke Yiddish on the set. Even the director [Alan Crosland] spoke Yiddish"—though Green is likely to have remembered this detail incorrectly, since Crosland wasn't Jewish and almost surely didn't speak Yiddish. But all of them that did were going back, symbolically speaking, to the Lower East Side and the world of their fathers and mothers.

* * *

"All is ready for Warner Brother's [*sic*] effort to turn out the first feature motion picture that talks and sings," *Moving Picture World* announced in a news column on June 11, 1927. The paper reported that May McAvoy, one of the better-known silent film actresses of the time, had been signed for the role of Mary Dale, Jack Robin's shiksa girlfriend. "Cantor Rosenblatt is on his way to Hollywood," the paper said, having signed a contract to play himself giving a concert of Jewish liturgical music, a scene that also shows Jack Robin sitting in the audience thinking longingly of his father singing the same songs in his synagogue in New York. The role of the elder Cantor Rabinowitz went to Warner Oland, the Swedish actor later famous as the Chinese detective Charlie Chan. "The work of building two sound-proof stages is near completion," *Motion Picture World* announced, having earlier published a detailed account of the construction of the stages on the Warner lot that could accommodate Vitaphone technology.

In late June, Alan Crosland went to New York to film the street scenes on the Lower East Side that open the movie. Some weeks later, the whole crew boarded the cross-country train for the long ride to New York, where they filmed scenes outside the Winter Garden, causing a near stampede as hundreds, then thousands, of pedestrians, hearing of Jolson's presence, massed at the theater striving for a view. In August, Jolson recorded his songs on the soundstage, now evidently ready for use. A month later, *Moving Picture World* carried two pictures of Jolson side by side, one "straight," the other in blackface, announcing that *The Jazz Singer* would open in New York on October 6. "He not only creates comedy but has an opportunity to do some strong dramatic acting," the magazine said. As if to show that otherwise it was business as usual at Warner Bros., trade publications also reported that *A Dog of the Regiment* "starring Rin Tin Tin" was filming at the Warner studio at the same time as *The Jazz Singer*. George Jessel was also there making *Sailor Izzy Murphy,* and May McAvoy was commuting between soundstages, because she was filming almost simultaneously *The Jazz Singer* and *Slightly Used,* a comedy about a girl who pretends to have a husband so her father will allow her two younger sisters to marry before she does. *Slightly Used* would also open in 1927.

The Jazz Singer wrapped by late September, and on October 1 Warner placed an ad in *Moving Picture World* announcing " 'The Jazz Singer,' Warner Bros Greatest Achievement Completed." (Somewhat ironically, the same issue featured a photograph of Jessel wearing a ship captain's uniform in *Sailor Izzy Murphy*.) In the meantime, Jolson made a quick trip to Chicago so he could be at ringside for the championship boxing rematch between Jack Dempsey and Gene Tunney (won by Tunney in a unanimous decision, but only after he had benefited from the famous "long count," when Dempsey, after knocking Tunney down, was slow to go to a neutral corner).

That evening, a huge poster showing Jolson in blackface could be seen above the glittering marquee of the Warner Theatre on Broadway and Fifty-second Street in Manhattan. "WARNERS SUPREME TRIUMPH," read the legend next to Jolson's image. "Al Jolson in The Jazz Singer With Vitaphone." The price of tickets was $5, an astronomical sum for a movie in those days.

Jolson was also there in the flesh, back from Chicago. In the newsreels he appears amid a milling crowd of politicians and celebrities wearing gowns and top hats in front of the theater, flashbulbs popping, the whole American celebrity culture on full display, for a blockbuster movie about Lower East Side Jews. The movies changed forever that night. So did America.

10

"The cry of my race"

The first image seen by audiences struck the universal theme that Raphaelson envisaged when he wrote "Day of Atonement" nearly a decade before. It's this epigram shown on a title card.

In every living soul, a spirit cries for
expression . . . perhaps this plaintive, wailing song of jazz
is, after all, the misunderstood utterance of a prayer.

It was Raphaelson's original idea that the Jews, having absorbed jazz from the Blacks, had imbued it with the tonality of the Hebrew liturgy and turned it into "primitive and passionate Americanese." The great singers and songwriters—Irving Berlin, Al Jolson, George Gershwin, Sophie Tucker—were "Jews with their roots in the synagogue" who were "expressing in evangelical terms the nature of our chaos."

Raphaelson's view that the Jews had taken possession of jazz seems like an eccentric notion today, in part because the "jazz" of *The Jazz Singer* is not what we usually think of as jazz, namely the music of Jelly Roll Morton, Louis Armstrong, or Wynton Marsalis, in which instruments and voices take turns improvising on a syncopated theme. For Raphaelson, jazz was the music of vaudeville, Broadway, or popular music in general, the kind of

music being written by Irving Berlin, Jerome Kern, and Irving
Caesar. His insight was in seeing the way "raggy time songs," as
Cantor Rabinowitz contemptuously puts it, are spiritually akin
to the Hebrew liturgy, both in their minor key tonality and in
the sense that the suffering of tribes and races lies behind them
both. That's what Jack Robin finds and what Cantor Rabinowitz
doesn't understand—that his son's love of popular music is not a
betrayal, a knife in the heart of a precious tradition, but a kind of
spiritual transference, born from the same deep feeling as the Jewish pleadings with God, just with a different beat. The cantorial
liturgy is not performed in a "raggy time" way but the two genres
emerge from a long, dark experience of oppression, which they've
transformed into soul-stirring, redemptive, prayerlike music.

That idea is encapsulated in that opening caption, and it is followed immediately in the opening frames of the movie (after the
scenes of street life on the Lower East Side), when Cantor Rabinowitz tells a pupil to put more of his soul into his voice. "Sing it
with a sigh," he says (according to the title card). "You are praying
to God, *nu*?" It's present at the end of the Raphaelson play, when
the Broadway producer hears Jack chant Kol Nidre, and immediately calls his colleague to tell him he's just seen "the greatest
ragtime singer in America." It's most explicitly in the famous line
from Mary Dale near the end of the movie when she also hears
Jack sing Kol Nidre, and suddenly she gets it. "He's a jazz singer
singing to his God," she whispers to the producer. And it's present
in a scene in the movie when Mary Dale tells Jack Robin, "You
sing jazz, but it's different—there's a tear in it," the tear being the
hint of supplication, the prayerfulness in Jolson's voice.

From the universalizing theme of the opening epigram,
The Jazz Singer plunges straight into Jewishness, first with the
street scenes of the Lower East Side, filmed by Crosland on the
trip he made to New York for the purpose. Then we're in Can-

tor Rabinowitz's study. The cantor himself, in his dark suit and full rabbinical beard, is identified by the title card as a man who "stubbornly holds to the traditions of his race." The message is already clear: It is the cantor's repudiation of the possibility of anything different that blinds him to the prayerlike meaning of the misunderstood music his misunderstood son yearns to sing. "Stubbornness" signifies the incomplete Americanization of the immigrant generation, which hadn't yet been immersed in Henry Ford's melting pot, its refusal to assimilate.

But Cantor Rabinowitz is not a villain. There's a dignity in his bearing, in his attachment to the tradition, and in his horror that the chain of five generations of Cantor Rabinowitzes will be broken in the Jewish encounter with the freedom of America. Cantor Rabinowitz will never see any commonality between jazz and the Hebrew prayers. To posit such a commonality would seem to him to rationalize spiritual annihilation. For him, to become American is an impossibility; it would be like a Christian missionary in Africa becoming Zulu.

But for the next generation, it was not only tempting, desirable, irresistible to assimilate; it was necessary for full citizenship, for participation in the life of the country, and for economic wellbeing. Because the great paradox of Jewish history is that the place the Jews emigrated from, the Russian Pale of Settlement, with its ghettos, discrimination, blood libels, and pogroms, unwittingly preserved Jewish identity, which itself was a kind of fruit of stubbornness, while the dazzling freedom of America, where there was antisemitism but fewer barriers to success, threatened it with extinction. The threat is something that Cantor Rabinowitz understands; it is what lies behind both his stubbornness and his dignity.

The encounter with America comes next. The scene is a saloon someplace on the Lower East Side, where the thirteen-

year-old Jakie Rabinowitz, played by a very talented young actor
named Bobby Gordon, sings "My Gal Sal" to the café's appreciative customers. Gordon as the young Jakie is very good, a natural, as the young Al Jolson must have been when he was ten or
eleven and sang for tips in saloons and on the streets. The scene
in the café has an appealing brightness and gaiety to it that con-
trasts with the stately gloominess of the Rabinowitz home. The
contrast, moreover, foretells the conflict that portends. Moishe
Yudelson, an Orthodox Jew and a friend of the cantor and his
wife, Sarah, happens to see Jakie performing in the saloon. He
rushes from that festive spot to the solemn Rabinowitz apartment
and tattles on Jakie to the cantor. When Jakie, full of freshness
and good spirits, returns home, he finds his father glowering in
rage, and then, in a scene of Hitchcockian tension, the father drags
the son into his bedroom, where he is unseen, until he emerges a
minute later beaten and humiliated. Jakie runs away from home,
though sometime later we see him sneaking back to the apartment
when his parents are away and stealing a picture of his mother.

The scene shifts to a crowded synagogue, whose ethereal glow
is also a contrast with the gaiety of the saloon. The cantor is in
full regalia surrounded by the boys of the choir, their tallisim, or
prayer shawls, draped over their shoulders and their kippot, skull-
caps, on their heads. The synagogue scenes were filmed inside
the Breed Street Shul on North Breed Street in Los Angeles, an
Orthodox synagogue founded in 1912, and the authentic setting
gives them an authentic feel—the shul's bimah, the raised altar
on which the Torah is read, the procession of Torah scrolls taken
from the ark, the glimmering of the menorah-like candelabra, the
chiaroscuro effect of light and shadow. It's the evening of Yom
Kippur, the holiest moment in the Hebrew calendar. The cantor looks at an empty space on the bimah that had been reserved
for Jakie, who was to have sung the Kol Nidre prayer. The rabbi

whispers something to the cantor, evidently asking where Jakie is, and the cantor's reply appears on a title card: "Now I have no son." And then he sings Kol Nidre, the prayer his son was not there to sing, and as his voice fills the sanctuary, it is saying, here is Jewishness; there, where my son has gone, is not. Fade out.

Ten years later, Jakie is a professional jazz singer named Jack Robin, striving to make it. He sings "Dirty Hands, Dirty Face" in a saloon called Coffee Dan's, a place for new performers to get noticed. When his performance elicits enthusiastic applause, Jack then utters the first bit of synchronized speech ever heard in a full-length feature film. In a melding of an actor and the character he plays, he says what Al Jolson said to audiences during practically every one of his live performances, a variation on the words he pronounces in *A Plantation Act* short,

Wait a minute, wait a minute, you ain't heard nothin' yet. Wait a minute, I tell ya. You ain't heard nothin'. Do you want to hear "Toot, Toot, Tootsie"?

He then sings that song, which is a variation on a common ragtime theme: the sadness of having to travel far from home. According to Jack Warner, Jolson ad-libbed the "wait a minute" line, which is not indicated in the screenplay, though other accounts claiming that the entire scene was planned and rehearsed seem more plausible.

After singing, and receiving enthusiastic applause, Jack meets Mary Dale, played by McAvoy, who'd been seated at a table just as Jolson began to perform. She is small (less than five feet tall), fine-boned, more adorable than classically beautiful. Jack is immediately smitten. In a scene set back in New York that soon follows, Jack's mother, having heard from him—she cherishes his letters—worries that he's fallen for a shiksa, even as his father, "older and more feeble than when we last saw him," the script says, continues to insist, "We have no son!"

Then comes one of the most intrinsically Jewish episodes in the film. Jack, in Chicago where he is in a show, attends a concert of Hebrew and Yiddish music given by Josef Rosenblatt, America's most famous cantor. Outside of certain connoisseur circles, where he is held in reverence, his scratchy 78 rpm recordings listened to today with tears in the eyes, Rosenblatt is hardly known anymore. But his fame in the 1920s when he was at his height extended beyond Jewish communities. Enrico Caruso is reported to have called him the Jewish Caruso. Rosenblatt once gave a recital on the steps of the New York Public Library, after which Caruso went up to him and kissed him. In a famous and revealing episode, Rosenblatt, who gave recitals at Carnegie Hall and all over the country, was offered $1,000 per performance to sing in the Chicago Opera's production of Jacques Fromental Halevy's opera *La Juive,* but, after considerable agonizing (he had a big family and needed the money), he declined, apparently uncomfortable with performing on the same stage as female singers. Instead, Caruso played the role, one of the last in his career.

Rosenblatt was born in 1882 in Russian-controlled Ukraine, and like Jolson and the fictional Cantor Rabinowitz, he came from a long line of cantors. He was a prodigy. At the age of seventeen he was the principal cantor of the largest synagogue in Vienna. He went on tour throughout the Austro-Hungarian Empire before joining the wave of Jewish immigration to America in 1912. There's almost an eerie doppelgänger-like similarity between him and Jolson, four years younger, also a Yiddish-speaking immigrant from the Russian Empire with prodigious musical talent. But Rosenblatt took the road not traveled by Jolson. He was firm—perhaps the word should be stubborn—in the different choice he made between Orthodox tradition and secular success. "I don't want to

be a cantor," the thirteen-year-old Jakie tells Cantor Rabinowitz
in the movie, echoing what the real-life Jolson might have told
his father. "The cantor of the past and the opera star of the future
waged a fierce struggle within me," Rosenblatt told an interviewer
after turning down the operatic role. The conflict, he continued,
ended when a voice whispered in his ear, "Yossele, don't do it."

That refusal, well covered in the press, underlines a certain
irony in Rosenblatt's appearance in the Chicago recital in *The
Jazz Singer,* where he sings "Yahrzeit Candle." It's a lyrical prayer
of remembrance for the dead that Rosenblatt sings mostly in
Yiddish, but with a Hebrew refrain, *yisgadal v'yiskadash,* "glorified and sanctified," the opening of the Mourner's Kaddish, sung
to commemorate deceased close relatives, parents especially, the
prayer that Jolson, with his father, brothers, and sisters recited
on the death of his mother thirty-three years before. It's also the
prayer that a furious father would sing when a son or daughter
married outside of the faith, requiring a kind of funeral rite, a sort
of ultimate expulsion from the fold of the family. The scene is one
of austere beauty. It lasts about two and a half minutes, Rosenblatt with his full rabbinical beard standing primly, stiffly, stodg-
ily onstage wearing his old-fashioned suit, his motionlessness at
the opposite end of the spectrum from the jitterbug gyrations of
Jolson's performances, his song sung in his unforgettably beautiful voice, redolent of the haunting melancholy of the Jewish
liturgy.

Jack Robin takes an aisle seat in the theater, glancing around
him as if nervous to be seen there, looking slightly out of place
in his natty sports jacket and bow tie. But as he listens, a look of
longing (well played by Jolson) comes over his face, the same longing that any son of any cantor chanting the old, almost forgotten
melodies of his people would have felt. It's a look of regret; there's
some guilt in it; that particular prayer would surely have sum-

moned up thoughts in Jack Robin's mind of his father's disown-
ing of him. Critics have talked about a kind of double patricide
in *The Jazz Singer*. The movie itself killed silent films, even as
the character Jack Robin's defiance of his father's wishes for him
is a kind of symbolic patricide. Rosenblatt's song summons up a
third murder, that of the son by the father banishing his wayward
progeny from the family circle, expelling him from the chain of
the generations. From Rosenblatt the scene fades to Jack's father's
synagogue in New York and to Cantor Rabinowitz, resplendent
in his cantorial garb, chanting the same Kaddish that Rosenblatt
was singing. But the effect on Jack Robin is to try to annul these
symbolically homicidal impulses. Listening to Rosenblatt, he
is lured back to the home he'd run away from, which suddenly
seems no longer desiccated and barren; now it is rich and meaningful, but also draped in the darkness of his betrayal of his father
and his father's repudiation of him.

As it happens, Jack gets an opportunity to perform in a new
show on Broadway where Mary Dale will be a featured dancer,
and this enables Jack to return to the Rabinowitz apartment
on the Lower East Side, where he is reunited with his mother.
These scenes are almost embarrassingly oedipal. Jack embraces
his mother, played by the non-Jewish Eugenie Besserer, almost as
a man might embrace his lover. To show her what he'll be doing
in his upcoming Broadway show, he sits at the piano and starts to
sing the Irving Berlin song "Blue Skies," but he interrupts himself
after a few bars for the film's second, longer snippet of synchronized dialogue, when he tells his mother all the things he's going
to do for her if his debut is a success.

> I'd rather please you than anyone I know of. . . . Mama
> darlin', if I'm a success in this show, well, we're gonna
> move from here. Oh yes, we're gonna move up in the

Bronx. A lot of nice green grass up there, and a whole lot of people you know. There's the Ginsbergs, the Guttenbergs, and the Goldbergs. And oh, a whole lot of Bergs. . . . And darling, oh, I'm gonna take you to Coney Island. . . . Yes, you're gonna ride on the shoot-the-chute. Now Mama, Mama, stop now, you're getting kittenish, Mama, listen. I'm gonna sing this like I will if I go on the stage. . . . I'm gonna sing it jazzy. Now get this.

The Americanized son who's made good telling his immigrant mother that he's going to pay her back for her love and sacrifice is, of course, something of a cliché. What makes it different in *The Jazz Singer* is the last word heard on the Vitaphone recording. Cantor Rabinowitz comes into the room, hears Jack playing a "raggy time" song, and peremptorily shouts out his stubborn authority—"Stop!" Jack tries to mollify his father, talking to him now through the title cards. "I came here with a heart full of love, but you don't want to understand," he tells him, and he leaves.

Later, he's back at the theater with Mary Dale. It's a striking scene. As the two talk, Jack smears burnt cork on himself with a practiced hand the way Jolson must have done thousands of times. When he's finished, pulling a nappy wig over his head, the tableau shows a slip of a white girl in her sequined dancer's costume and an imitation Black man looking at each other lovingly, perhaps the first explicit suggestion of interracial love in American film history, even if the Black-looking character is not a Black man, but a Jew looking affectionately at a shiksa.

What follows brings all the confusion in Jack's heart to a point. Jack's mother has sent Yudelson to tell him that his father has fallen ill and to plead with him to sing the next night, Yom Kippur Eve, in the synagogue in his place. But the next night is the Broadway show's opening, and Jack dismisses Yudelson. His big chance is on that very night, and he's not going to spoil it. But the expression on Jack's face alternates between happiness at his looming prospects and sadness at what he knows will be an irrevocable betrayal of his tradition and his family. At first, he tells Mary that his only goal is to do well in the show. "I'm going to put everything I've got into my songs," he says. But as he puts the finishing touches on his makeup, he sees the picture of his mother that he had taken when he ran away from home years before, and we see his resolve melt briefly away, and then return again. "I'd love to sing for my people, but I belong here," he says, and then immediately succumbs to the feeling he had listening to Rosenblatt, and he utters, via the title card, perhaps the most important line in the movie. "But there's really something, after all, in my heart—maybe it's the call of the ages—the cry of my race."

As the scholar Michael Alexander has noted, "That's a very strange thing for a man in blackface to say" given that the race he is referring to is not the Black race but the Jewish one, which, of course, is not a race at all. Jack looks in the mirror and as he does, his blackface image fades away and is replaced by one of his father in the synagogue, resplendent in his cantor's garb, while the soundtrack shifts to an orchestral version of Kol Nidre. Jack turns to Mary. "The songs of Israel are tearing at my heart," he says. His struggle is not over. Suddenly, Jack's mother, escorted by Yudelson, arrives in the dressing room and pleads with Jack to sing Kol Nidre. He tells her he can't, and rushes away when he's called to rehearsal. Unseen by him, his mother listens to his song and accepts his life's choice. "He belongs to the world now," she says.

None of this, certainly none of his mother's flash of insight, was included in Raphaelson's original story or play. There, Jack Robin makes an unambiguous choice, to heed the call of his race, to sing the songs of Israel. "I'm your son," he tells his mother. "I'm the son of my father. And, I'm a cantor, see." Facing his father's

death, Jack reverts to Jakie, making the choice that few Jews in
the real world, like Frederich Meier Weisenfreund, Asa Yoelson,
or Fania Borach, actually did make, or even faced terrible pressure
to make. On questions like marriage, true, the older immigrant
generation that escaped the Russian Pale of Settlement fought for
tribal loyalty. Parents had their sons circumcised and, thirteen
years later, they became Bar Mitzvah, and they sometimes recited
the prayer for the dead when either sons or daughters married
outside of the tribe. But when it came to the possibility of achieving wealth and fame in the New World, the elders didn't generally pull moral guilt trips on their children, insisting on pain of
eternal remorse that, symbolically speaking, they sing Kol Nidre
in shul rather than "Blue Moon" on Broadway.

But in Samson Raphaelson's treatment of the dilemma, the
right choice is the sentimentally unrealistic one of tribal loyalty.
Moreover, it's a morally pure one as Jack Robin makes it, because
he has every reason to believe that in singing Kol Nidre that night
he is wrecking his Broadway career forever. That's the final scene
of the Raphaelson play, Jack's chanting of the Yom Kippur prayer
taking place as the curtain falls. The audience knows that he
hasn't destroyed his Broadway chance, because his producer and
his girlfriend have come to the Rabinowitz home where they hear
him sing Kol Nidre in the nearby shul, and they realize, with
Raphaelson, that it's just another form of jazz. Mary Dale says to
the producer, "He'll be back," and the audience can feel confident
that Jack will find success in show business, sooner or later.

That, with some minor variations, was also the ending of the
original script for the movie version of *The Jazz Singer,* as written
by Cohn. Jack goes home to see his father who is on his deathbed. "My son, I love you," Cantor Rabinowitz says. At first, Jack
makes clear to his mother that he's come to see his father, not
to sing in the synagogue. His mother tells him, "Maybe if you

sing, your pappa will get well"—no moral pressure, no guilt trip
there! Applying the pressure on the other side, the producer, who
has arrived with Mary Dale, warns Jack of the permanent bale-
ful consequences if he doesn't show up at the theater that night.
"You'll queer yourself on Broadway; you'll never get another job,"
he says, and Jack sees the alternatives very clearly—as "a choice
between my career and breaking my mother's heart."

There's a quick return to the theater, where the awaiting audience is told, "There will be no performance this evening," and
that's how we know that Jack has decided for his mother over
his career. When the scene shifts again to the Rabinowitz apartment, the strains of Kol Nidre being sung by Jakie drift from
the nearby synagogue through the open window, allowing Cantor
Rabinowitz to die a happy man. "Mama, we have our son again,"
he says before ascending to his heavenly reward. The chant of the
prayer also moves the producer and Mary Dale, who whispers her
famous line about Jack's "singing to his God."

The original screenplay then closes with Jack in the synagogue,
draped in white robes, a satin skullcap on his head, chanting the
prayer. It is Jolson and Jolson's voice with a tear in it singing not
"Blue Moon" or "Toot, Toot, Tootsie" but the holy Yom Kippur
prayer, and singing it well, his father's lessons of many years before
not forgotten. Jolson could have been a cantor, and he would have
been a worthy rival to the great Rosenblatt.

The notes in Cohn's script then describe the final scene:

> As he comes to the closing notes of the song, the figure of
> the old cantor in his synagogue robes appears on the side
> of the screen very faint and shadowy. . . . There is a smile
> on the face of the old cantor as he slowly raises his hand
> in a blessing. The shadowy figure becomes fainter and

fainter, finally disappearing, leaving Jack standing alone. The music and his figure slowly fade out. THE END.

It's a sweet, sentimental panorama, and a variation on ancient themes: the cantor's forgiveness, the prodigal son's return, the passing of the torch to a new generation. Most of all, it's an affirmation of "eternal Jewishness," in J. Hoberman's phrase; it's Jakie abandoning Jack and becoming Jakie again.

But in the movie version of *The Jazz Singer* it's not the end. Possibly at the insistence of Jack or Sam Warner, or possibly Darryl Zanuck, the producer, a new scene was tacked on. It shows Jack some days later at the Winter Garden, now utterly indistinguishable from the real-life Al Jolson, singing "My Mammy," while in the audience, seated next to a beaming Yudelson, Jack's mother looks on adoringly, a radiant smile on her face. The last thing we see is not Jolson in shul draped in cantorial vestments, standing in the warm glow of Mosaic candelabra, but Jolson in blackface on the very stage where the real Al Jolson became famous, down on one knee, his gloved hands outstretched, not to his God but to his profane audience. He's sung Kol Nidre; now he's back to "My Mammy."

The producers of the movie *The Jazz Singer* made a different choice from that of Raphaelson. They chose Broadway, and in doing so they robbed the movie of its moral urgency. Instead they left the audience with the anodyne happy-ending message that assimilation doesn't have to be an agonizing choice, that you can have it all in America!

11

It Played in Paducah

And it's true, you can have it all in America, or so goes the myth, and the affirmation of that idea was no doubt one reason *The Jazz Singer* was a national sensation. Some of its success was also surely due to Vitaphone, which audiences paid to see out of curiosity. It was the big new thing. But the people at the opening of *The Jazz Singer,* who wildly applauded at the end, didn't watch what we would now think of as a "talkie." For the most part, *The Jazz Singer* played like a standard silent film. The main difference was the six songs sung by Jolson, which were recorded on Vitaphone so the audience could both see him and hear him, though many in that audience had already done that the previous year when they saw *A Plantation Act,* just as they'd seen others in the dozen or so Vitaphone shorts produced by Warner before *The Jazz Singer* was made. Technically speaking, though, *The Jazz Singer* was the first full-length "talkie," earning that historically significant designation because of those two short episodes where Jolson speaks in synchronized sound.

For the rest of the film, the dialogue is mimed onscreen and explained with the same title cards that had been used for the entire history of silent movies. Moreover, when the movie opened, only a very small number of theaters had Vitaphone equipment installed, so especially in the early months of its distribution, many moviegoers saw *The Jazz Singer* the same way they saw other silent films, with musicians in the orchestra pit or onstage next to the screen producing the musical numbers being seen. As the months passed, more and more movie houses installed Vitaphone and showed *The Jazz Singer* with sound. Some showed it initially as a silent movie to satisfy the initial demand, then, sometime later, showed it again with Vitaphone.

Jolson's presence on the screen was also no doubt a part of the movie's crossover success. *A Plantation Act* had made it possible for audiences to see him performing without his actually being there, and now *The Jazz Singer* provided a fuller Jolson experience. "Few men could have approached the task of singing and acting so well as he does in this photoplay," a writer for *The New York Times* said of Jolson after opening night. "His 'voice with a tear' compelled silence, and possibly all that disappointed the people in the packed theater was the fact that they could not call upon him or his image for an encore." *The Jazz Singer* was a critical success as well. The story it told and the themes it explored—tradition versus modernity, father versus son, religion versus secularism, ambition versus filial loyalty—led critics to respond to it favorably. It was the power of Jolson's appeal and the novelty of Vitaphone, but also the eternal triangle represented by the uncompromising father, the wayward son, and the loving mother who tries to bridge the gap between the two. And then there was the you-can-have-it-all-in-America ending that left audiences feeling good. You can almost hear across the decades the collective sigh of relief at Jakie/Jack's narrow escape from the confines of the tradition even as he is able to remain faithful to its beauty.

The previous feature-length Vitaphone movie, *Don Juan*, had a big romantic star, John Barrymore, as its lead. It had synchronized music and sound effects, though no synchronized dialogue, but audiences evidently were not as affected by a swashbuckling adventure story as much as they were by the far more intimate family drama of *The Jazz Singer*.

That the movie was unusually Jewish did not escape notice, and that was generally cast in a favorable light. No doubt for many thousands of people in America, it was their first time hearing the singing of the Hebrew liturgy or glimpsing the exotic interior of an Orthodox synagogue. Millions of gentiles saw the film, and they liked it. The critic for the *Evening Star* in Washington, D.C., refers to "the unusual scenes in the interior of a synagogue, probably never before screened, coupled with the solemnly beautiful music of the cantor and Hebrew choral singers . . . and a certain originality of plot which sets it apart from the average production." The Kol Nidre episode near the end of the film, this unnamed critic wrote, "is one of the most stirring scenes it has been the privilege of this reviewer to witness in any production."

"Al Jolson in 'The Jazz Singer.' Latest Vitaphone to Be Offered Here Thrills Throng at Majestic," was a typical local newspaper headline, this one in *The Times* of Shreveport, Louisiana, which went on to report that "thousands found their anticipation far exceeded by the actual production." The story, the paper continued, "compels attention from the start to the finish. It grips the heart." The paper concludes its summary of the plot this way: "Career or filial love? Love conquers, and Jack Robin, the jazz singer, appears in the synagogue in the vestments of a cantor, his glorious voice—the voice with a tear in it—ringing appealingly and supplicatingly through the sacred edifice."

It was like that all over the country. *The Jazz Singer* "is by far one of the best pictures that has appeared in Paducah," *The Paducah Sun-Democrat* of Kentucky critic said when the movie arrived at the Columbia Theatre there in April. "It is a comedy-drama and there are many smiles and many tears. . . . It is one picture in a million." "This story is intensely appealing and breathes

the spirit of tolerance," someone wrote in *The Richmond Item* in
Richmond, Indiana. A writer in *The Shamekin News Dispatch* in
Shamekin, Pennsylvania: "It is a picture that reaches to the innermost researches of the coldest heart and at the same time brings
new joy into life."

Smalltown Middle America was not surprised at *The Jazz
Singer*'s display of Yiddish exoticism on the screen—this first time
on a national scale that the Jews who invented Hollywood told
their own story to the gentiles—probably because moviegoers had
already been introduced to Jews as ordinary people, rather than
as caricatures, in the Cohens and Kellys movies, and they'd seen
George Jessel on tour in the stage version of the Raphaelson story.
Whatever the reason, the lack of surprise, like Sherlock Holmes's
dog that didn't bark, tells us that Jewishness in America had
already gone a considerable distance toward being unexceptional,
despite the thick residue of classic antisemitism that remained in
the America of the time.

By the 1920s, the Jewish American story had rambled on well
past the world of the Lower East Side. The Jews were literally
almost everywhere, different from other Americans but also more
or less the same. A survey of 1927 showed that there were now Jews
in no fewer than 9,712 towns and rural districts in America, and
a total Jewish population of more than four million. In the 1910s
and 1920s Jewish organizations—including the Hebrew Immigrant Aid Society, B'nai B'rith, and Hadassah, the Women's Zionist Organization of America—had chapters all across the country.
The antisemitism of the time did not stop Jews from succeeding
economically or from becoming, as one historian of the period
has put it, "at home in America."

For example, Shreveport, Louisiana, where the local paper
spoke of the thousands of hearts gripped by the drama, had an
active and well-integrated Jewish population, probably about

2,500 altogether, out of an overall population of 70,000, many of them descendants of German immigrants who arrived before the Civil War. Two mayors of the town had been Jews; there was a Jewish women's organization and two synagogues, both of them dating from the mid-1900s, and a Hebrew school. As in many towns, the movie theaters were owned by Jews, who decades earlier had brought vaudeville to Shreveport and now were bringing Al Jolson and *The Jazz Singer*.

Jews, in other words, were a small minority in Shreveport, and they no doubt retained a tincture of the exotic, and perhaps in churches there were allusions to the stubborn blindness of the Jews to the Light of Christ, but they weren't unfamiliar or foreign anymore. Many of them had been born in other countries, but their American-born children went to school with other children; they spoke unaccented English; they celebrated Thanksgiving and the Fourth of July. Unlike their foreign-born parents and grandparents, they were part of the American whole, and that no doubt helps to explain why the Jewishness of *The Jazz Singer* drew so little astonished notice. That was the case across the country as, from late 1927 through 1928, the Jolson movie played in practically every town in America large enough to have a movie theater, at a time after vaudeville but before television when the movies were by far the most popular form of entertainment in the country. Small-town newspapers, of which there were thousands, reported on *The Jazz Singer* as a major event, but they saw nothing particularly strange about it; few reviewers even bothered to mention that the story was a Jewish one.

"Seldom in the Butte theatrical history has a picture gripped, overpowered, and overwhelmed an audience as *The Jazz Singer* did at the Rialto yesterday," the *Anaconda Standard* of Butte, Montana, critic said when the film played there in May 1928. "What a story! What a cast!"

There had been Jews in Butte since 1875. The mining town's first mayor, one Henry Jacobs, born in Baden-Württemberg, Germany, in 1835 and the proprietor of the H. Jacobs and Co. clothing store, was Jewish. There has been a Jewish cemetery in Butte since 1881; at one point there were three synagogues, two Orthodox, one Reform. Congregation B'nai Israel, which occupies an onion-domed three-story masonry edifice on West Galena Street, served the Jewish community of Butte for 117 years, until, in 2022, it was converted into a cultural center to tell "the stories of all ethnic groups in Butte." There were Jewish saloon keepers, Jewish bakers, Jewish clothing merchants, Jewish lawyers, bankers, and cattle dealers, and there is no history of significant violence against Jews in cowboy Montana. When *The Jazz Singer* came to the Rialto Theater in Butte, it didn't seem odd or outlandish that the movie was about Jews.

The Jews in places like Butte and Paducah, which had a Reform synagogue since 1873, no doubt went to see *The Jazz Singer* and that certainly helped in its commercial success, but they didn't account for all of it, or for the acclaim the movie got. The Jewish population of Shamokin in Pennsylvania coal country in 1919 was 235, which is probably about what it was in 1928 when the movie arrived there at the end of May. The Jewish congregation dated from 1875. The Jews' long presence in the town was large enough for local non-Jews to find them part of the scenery, but not enough to determine the local newspaper's comment about "the innermost reaches of the coldest heart."

And yet, there is something more to be said about the Jewishness of *The Jazz Singer,* the fact that Warner Bros. chose it as the first talkie, and the warm welcome it got across the entire country. The sense of the Jew, in Irving Howe's phrase, "as a stranger to the whole of the western tradition" and therefore "a source of possible infection," hadn't disappeared in the 1920s, or even today.

The immutable strangeness of Jews had been reflected over many decades in their theatrical representations, from Shylock to Private Izzy Murphy. But *The Jazz Singer* made Jews and Jewishness less strange. Samson Raphaelson in this sense was right when he said he was reaching for something universal when he wrote his story "Day of Atonement." The Jewishness of the story was to him almost incidental. Audiences saw something of themselves in the saga of Cantor Rabinowitz, Jakie Rabinowitz/Jack Robin, and Sarah Rabinowitz. When they watched Al Jolson watch Yossele Rosenblatt chanting in Hebrew and Yiddish, they were both, Jolson and the moviegoers, hearing the original voice with a tear in it, the voice rooted in age-old Jewish suffering, the voice with the tragic sense that, mingled with Black voices also with tears in them, created much of American music in the twentieth century. Jewish observers at the time perfectly understood this. "Is there any incongruity between this Jewish boy with his face painted like a southern Negro singing in the Negro dialect," a writer in the Yiddish-language *Morgen Journal* wrote. "No, there is not. Indeed I detected again and again the minor key of Jewish music, the wail of the hazan, the cry of a people who have suffered."

It's hard to calculate in this sense whether *The Jazz Singer* illustrated the Jewish assimilation to America or the American assimilation to the Jews. Certainly the movie and its favorable reception was a major step in the Judaization of the American culture, an antecedent to the Jewish comics of the 1940s and 1950s—Milton Berle, Jack Benny, and Sid Caesar among the first—the spectacular success of *Fiddler on the Roof* and *Funny Girl,* the plays of Neil Simon, Gilda Radner on *Saturday Night Live,* television shows like *Seinfeld,* movies like Woody Allen's. It didn't start with *The Jazz Singer.* But the essential idea goes back to Raphaelson's notion of jazz as prayer, which itself is linked to the idea, as Neal Gabler put it, that "Judaism somehow fructifies show business" in a way that the goyim couldn't, for the simple reason that the goyim have been too privileged or perhaps too complacent in their majoritarian status to possess the fructifying awareness of collective outsiderness. "After centuries of persecution," Gabler writes, "Jews feel more. So, of course, do Blacks, for much the same reason." The artist is always the person outside with his nose pressed to the glass as he or she gazes at the self-unaware society of those Thomas Mann called the blond blue-eyed people. That's what Mary Dale understands in her supremely insightful snatch of dialogue. "You sing jazz, but it's different." By singing it in blackface the Jew Jolson doubled his outsiderness. He sang it "different," and in so doing he sublimated the Black and Jewish experience of persecution and made it American.

* * *

The Black press also praised *The Jazz Singer*. A *New York Amsterdam News* writer recounted the opening of the movie at the Lafayette Theatre on Seventh Avenue in Harlem, calling Jolson "one of the world's greatest performers" and the movie "one of the greatest pictures ever produced and said to relate the fascinating biography of Al Jolson himself." Like many other theaters, the Lafayette first showed the movie before it was equipped with Vitaphone, presumably because it sensed the demand for it and didn't want to postpone it until it could provide the full audio experience. The theater engaged a singer, Willie Jackson, to sing Jolson's jazz numbers and a cantor—the *New York Amsterdam News* identifies him as Cantor Silverbush—for Kol Nidre. One of the first Black theaters to show the movie with Vitaphone was the Royal Theatre in Atlantic City, New Jersey, which prompted a writer for *The Pittsburgh Courier* to say "'The Jazz Singer' is a stirring mother-love tale that contains many a tear and a laugh."

"Jew, Gentile, and Negro alike packed the house to overflowing," another *Courier* writer said a couple of weeks later. "This epic screen version of racial inclination offers one of the greatest lessons of modern times." The *Courier* provides a quick summary of the plot, including the Jolson character's decision to sing "Kol Nidre, the synagogue's sacred prayer," before going back to the stage, and provides the "lesson" it referred to earlier: "a lesson of sacrifice to his race could not but drive home the point that Negroes need the same sterling qualities." When the movie played with Vitaphone at the Republic Theatre in Washington, D.C., the critic for *The Washington Tribune,* also a Black paper, practically exulted over its brilliance. "Seen it? Heard it? If not, you'd better, because if you miss it, you'll miss the treat of your life. So don't fail to see Al Jolson in *The Jazz Singer* now playing the Republic Theater. . . . Each performance of *The Jazz Singer* rouses the audience to wild outbursts of enthusiasm, expressed by tears, laughter, and cheers. It is unique. Tremendous. Unforgettable."

All of this, it should be remembered, is being said about a movie one of whose conspicuous elements, Jolson in blackface, would now be unacceptable. Indeed, there are two Jolsons in the film and blackface is what distinguishes them. The Jolson playing Jack Robin, the aspiring vaudeville and Broadway singer, puts on blackface in his performances. The Jolson of Jakie Rabinowitz singing Kol Nidre in his father's shul does not. "Blackface and Jewish history pull in opposite directions," the historian Irving Saposnik has written. Blackface in *The Jazz Singer* is the physical embodiment of Jack's breaking of the generational chain. He's changed his name and his skin color, such that when his mother comes to see him at the theater to plead with him to come home and sing the Kol Nidre, she doesn't recognize him at first—"Jakie, this ain't you," she says.

* * *

Over the years, Jews have had a lot to say about *The Jazz Singer,* starting with Raphaelson himself, who hated it as only the originator of an idea can hate the watered-down, popularized form it takes when it becomes mass entertainment. A couple of years before the movie, as we've seen, he'd been angry at Jessel for wanting to insert "slick and smooth little vaudeville jokes" into his play. "It was a matter of taste," he said, and it was in that spirit that he found the movie not serious, its jagged edges filed smooth. Jolson moreover didn't come across on the screen the way he came across when he performed onstage, Raphaelson felt. He was "a terrific comedian, and a lousy actor," Raphaelson said years later. "It was embarrassing, a dreadful picture; I've seen few worse." He continued:

> The picture opened with East Side shots. Then I saw this cantor. They "refined" him. . . . His whiskers were beautifully combed, as if he had been to a beauty parlor. And the mother was made just too spotlessly clean, as though she were demonstrating stoves or refrigerators. The whole damned thing—the dialogue, whatever they had taken from my innocent play—was either distorted or broken up. I had a simple, corny, well-felt little melodrama, and they made an ill-felt, silly, maudlin, badly-timed thing of it.

But Raphaelson also admitted to being a snob in his young years, or, as he put it, looking back with the wisdom of his older age, "I was very superior about movies . . . I was an intellectual, and I felt about them the way probably I would feel about radio soap operas now, or pulp magazine stories." He doesn't complain specifically about the tacked-on Winter Garden scene wherein Jolson sings "My Mammy" while his mother beams in the audience, but others among the Jewish detractors of the movie did. Jessel, speaking of the brief time when he assumed he would play the lead role in the movie, read the script and told the Warner brothers he wouldn't do it with the Winter Garden ending. "Money or no money, I would not do this version," he wrote later. It's possible that Jessel is confusing things, since the original Cohn script, which is presumably the one he would have been shown, didn't have the Winter Garden ending. He may have been talking after he'd seen the film, not when he was shown the script. It's also possible, indeed likely, that there were some sour grapes in Jessel's complaint, built on his belief that he'd been robbed of the role of his life.

Still, Jessel's objections to the final scene of the movie were echoed by others, who voiced the opinion that Jolson's return to the theater at the end sapped the Kol Nidre scene in the synagogue of its meaning. The movie, this criticism went, portrays the intractable dilemma of modern Judaism, the impossibility of being loyal to the faith and modern at the same time, and then trivializes it.

"The jazz singer in the final scene is not drawn toward his God because of his belief in Him, but sings in the synagogue mainly as a concession to his mother, and then goes back to the stage sacrificing his traditions for its sake," an unnamed rabbi in South Bend, Indiana, complained to the local newspaper. "It should have ended in the synagogue."

But most Jewish commentators seem hardly to have noticed, very likely because they understood that, while it was nice to see personal sacrifice for the sake of tradition portrayed on the screen, most of them would have made the same choice as Jack Robin; they would have made their gesture to the ancestors in the synagogue and then gone to the Winter Garden and sung "My Mammy." They also loved *The Jazz Singer* because it was a Jewish story told sympathetically, and it was a national sensation that legitimized Jewish life in America. We're speaking here of second-generation Jews who may have learned Yiddish from their parents at home but probably didn't know how to read or write it and, in this sense, belonged more to Jack Robin's generation than to his father's. And *The Jazz Singer*, in telling Al Jolson's story, gave standing to *their* stories also. They were happy to see a member of their assimilating generation portrayed in a hit movie "full of nobility, gentleness of feeling, and possessing a love of humanity," as a critic for *The Sentinel,* the main Jewish paper in Chicago, put it.

The paper was reporting on the movie's arrival at the 1,300-seat Garrick Theatre, where *The Jazz Singer* was "the most profit-able and successful engagement ever played by a motion picture in Chicago." At one showing, twenty prominent ministers attended the movie as guests of the Warners and the Shuberts (who owned the Garrick), so it was doing well as a vehicle for interfaith under-standing. "The home life of a Jewish family is depicted with rare fidelity while the scenes in the synagogue with Jolson chanting songs of his fathers never fails [*sic*] to electrify the audience," a critic for the paper said.

That was the main Jewish response, repeated in the Jewish press, English and Yiddish, across the country. "A photoplay of especial interest and pride to the Jewish race," the *B'nai B'rith Messenger* said, announcing the imminent arrival of the movie, starring "Al Jolson, the world's greatest entertainer." An organi-zation like B'nai B'rith was acutely aware of social antisemitism, of Henry Ford and *The Dearborn Independent,* of the conviction that "the Jews" controlled the levers of finance (a notion avidly propagated by Ford's newspaper); they knew about exclusion, quotas, formal and informal, that Jews needn't apply to private clubs, that there was a stereotype that would never really die. They were certainly well aware of the blatantly racist and antisemitic movement to curtail immigration that had been building for decades, motivated by the terror, fanned by a prominent group of racial purity theorists and eugenicists, that the hordes of allegedly small, dark people from eastern and central Europe were a genetic threat to the supposedly Nordic character of what these theorists called "native Americans," those of good "Colonial stock." This theory was given its fullest expression in a 1916 book, *The Passing of the Great Race or the Racial Basis of European History,* by one Madison Grant, a socially well-connected nature conservationist and writer, who warned that "the Slovak, the Italian, the Syrian, and the Jew" would bring about "the destruction of the best human strains." This "chauvinistic nationalism," as a Jewish leader of the time called it, triumphed during the presidency of Warren G. Harding, when Congress passed the Johnson-Reed Act of 1924 that established such strict quotas on new arrivals as to put an effective stop to immigration from eastern and southern Europe. Jews in this situation craved toleration and acceptance, even a bit of admiration. Jolson, it's safe to say, along with figures like Louis Brandeis and Albert Einstein, played something of the role for Jewish kids that baseball players like Hank Greenberg and Sandy Koufax played for later generations. Jolson gave a fraternal Jewish organization like the B'nai B'rith a kind of reflected glory.

The Yiddish press picked up on that theme. The review of *The Jazz Singer* in the *Forverts,* one of the two or three most widely read of the Yiddish-language papers, recounts the story of an "American boy" who inherited his father's "cantorial voice" and his "cantorial heart," but not his father's "understanding of Jewishness and of life in general." But even though he sings in cabarets and on the streets instead of in the synagogue, he does it "with the same ardor, with the same fire, with the same heart and overall with the same soul and melancholy as his father who sings prayers in a synagogue," and that is what gave the movie its universal appeal. "The heart and the fire and the melancholy that he pours into his songs elicits the same reaction from the American audience as his father's prayers elicited from the Jewish audience."

Rabbis, also fully aware of the animosity against Jews in the first decades of the century, had a good deal to say about the movie and about several related topics—how it showed, for example, "the vast abyss that separates the elders from the younger generation of Jews in America." The comment was by Edgar F. Magnin, a son of the founder of I. Magnin, the San Francisco department store, who was chief rabbi of the Wilshire Boulevard Temple in Los Angeles for sixty-nine years, close both spiritually and geographically to Hollywood. The worship of the immigrant generation "is a product of the ghetto," he said, "based upon a philosophy of isolation," while the younger generation "has all it can do to hold its own in the opposing battle with athletics, the pursuit of pleasure, dancing, theatricals, free thinking, and the struggle to advance materially."

"Vain, deluding joys," the rabbi might have said, echoing the poet Milton, when he contrasted "the seriousness and solemnity that attach to an old-fashioned Jewish home . . . [and] the stage in all its glamour and illusion." That sounds like wistfulness for the old ways, which, it's a safe bet, Rabbi Magnin's Wilshire Boulevard Reform congregation did not closely follow, but in fact it's a lead-in to a kind of panegyric about the unity of the new Jewishness and jazz, which Raphaelson would have liked. The latter was "inherited from the Negro," Rabbi Magnin wrote, and was "born of persecution and monotony." It's "the wailing of a people sad and broken," which is why "the Jew writes jazz and interprets it so well."

"Can it be possible," the rabbi concludes, "that jazz is the prayer of those who have lost their God, seeking a new one in rhythmic forgetfulness?"

Magnin's essay sums up a kind of ambivalence. It's as if he can't quite make up his mind whether he actually liked the message of *The Jazz Singer* or not, and so he tries, like the movie itself, to have it both ways—the theater is "glamour and illusion," which seems to translate into something shallow, without the "seriousness and solemnity of the old Jewish home," and jazz is "the prayer of those who have lost their God." But is to substitute jazz for God good for the cause of Jewish identity and acceptance?

Writing later in the same publication, the *B'nai B'rith Messenger,* Herman Lissauer, another prominent California Reform rabbi, saw jazz and Judaism not in heartwarming harmony but in conflict. Jazz as a modern style of life (the sort of life led by the real-life Al Jolson) was not a solution to the challenge of assimilation, and in this sense, *The Jazz Singer* was both good for the Jews and bad for them. It was good as "an unexampled means to educate the non-Jewish masses out of their misconceptions of the Jew." But the jazz life is not the way to go, the rabbi said. The son's life in *The Jazz Singer* is "superficial"; it's a life "without deep currents," and, moreover, a life "symbolized by jazz music, which is a pitiful expression of immaturity, longing, sensuality, and cheap sentimentality," by no means, it would seem, a desirable new form of prayer for assimilating Jews.

A few months before the movie came out, Lissauer left his San Francisco congregation to become chief rabbi at the much larger Temple Emanu-El in Los Angeles, where he said his goal was "to create a synthesis of Judaism with the spirit of America."

Exactly what he meant by that wasn't clear, but after less than two years, he fought out in an awkwardly public way his own conflict between customary belief and modernity. "I cannot believe in the personal God of traditional religion," he wrote in a circular to his synagogue membership, and when his statement caused consternation among some of those members, he resigned. The issue for him was Jewish survival, which he believed would not be ensured by clinging to unscientific ideas, or, as he rather directly put it, "a belief in the supernatural." But Lissauer agreed with Rabbi Magnin that the jazz life, meaning assimilated, secular life in the fast lane, was not a viable alternative. The real choice for modern American Jews wasn't an either-or one, Broadway or a Lower East Side shul, but a sensible adaptation. It was to participate fully in public life while retaining a moderate, reformed Jewishness for the private sphere.

"Will the Jew in America be able to continue his tradition here?" Lissauer asked in his essay on *The Jazz Singer.* "Will his children be Jews in spirit, or will they first be jazz singers and then cease altogether to be Jews? No one knows the answer."

Now, a century later, we do know the answer. *The Jazz Singer* was a way to be Jewish in America and to turn the Jewish experience into American culture. Later came Sid Caesar's *Your Show of Shows, Fiddler on the Roof* onstage and as a movie, Mel Brooks and *The Producers,* Neil Simon's *The Sunshine Boys* and *Brighton Beach Memoirs,* Woody Allen, Gilda Radner, Jerry Seinfeld, and others. Two conditions needed to be met for the Jewish experience to become part of the American experience. First, the Jews had to engage in the hard bargain of life in the outside-the-Pale that was America, not to engage in self-erasure but to break sufficiently with the customs, manners, and sometimes the people of the past so as to blend in, so that their experience could reach even "the coldest heart." Second, America had to be ready to give space to

Jewish stories and sensibilities. *The Jazz Singer* in this sense was part of a larger transformation that is difficult to imagine happening on anything like the American scale in any other country. *The Jazz Singer* was a landmark event in this transformation. It was at the beginning of something that has perhaps ebbed and flowed, but it has never stopped, and never will.

12

Stars Crossing

There's no record that Jolson knew Damon Runyon, the reporter and short-story writer whose subject was . . . well, the Runyonesque world of New York, Broadway, and its Hollywood affiliate—the showgirls, the gamblers, the cops, the gangsters, the bootleggers, the newspaper hacks and gossip columnists, not to mention the actors, songwriters, and singers who inhabited the theaters, the clubs, the speakeasies, the in-crowd restaurants. It would seem almost certain that Runyon and Jolson ran into each other at places like the Stork Club where Jolson was known to sit with Walter Winchell, who was close to Runyon. The two men had a certain foreignness, an outsiderness in common: Runyon, born in 1880, was, by coincidence, from Manhattan, that is, Manhattan, Kansas, then he moved as a child to Pueblo, Colorado, neither quite as far as Seredzius but worlds away from New York nonetheless. He dropped out of school in the fourth grade, became a sports reporter for various newspapers, and then hit it big as a chronicler of the guys-and-dolls demimonde of New York. Whether he and Jolson knew each other or not, there was at least one time when Jolson played a role that could well have come straight from a Runyon short story.

In 1933 at a prizefight at the Hollywood American Legion Stadium, Jolson hit Winchell hard enough to knock him down. There's some dispute over exactly the punches thrown. Winchell later claimed, not very persuasively, that the man who struck him was someone other than Jolson, hired for the purpose. "There were two of them; two guys hit me," Winchell said. But newspapers, which, needless to say, gave lavish coverage to the incident, quoted a policeman, one Lieutenant "Lefty" James, testifying that Jolson faced Winchell from the front and delivered his blows "very, very fast." According to some accounts, Winchell's wife, June, added a bit of Keystone Cops to the scene, taking off her shoe and trying to hit Jolson on the head, but she hit a Warner executive, Hall Wallis, instead. In another version of the story, which Jolson probably told to his first biographer, Pearl Sieben, he saw Winchell at ringside and pounded him on the back of the neck, just to "show his friendship," after which people, misunderstanding what had happened, rushed between the two men to deter further fisticuffs. But that contradicts what Jolson told reporters at the time, namely: "I just up and popped him. I hit him several times, and I know I knocked him down at least twice. . . . He had it coming to him."

The altercation outside the ring at the Hollywood stadium wouldn't have been the only time Jolson resorted to his fists. His brother, Harry, as we saw, talked about Jolson's scrappiness when he was a boy in Seredzius, and there was that time in St. Louis when Jolson decked a man who'd called him a kike. On another occasion, he got into a fight with a man at the Cocoanut Grove in the Ambassador Hotel in Los Angeles after Jolson heard the man making derogatory comments about Jews. "I didn't like the music," Jolson said later, and he punched him.

It was the incident with Winchell, however, that had the Runyonesque elements. It took place during Jolson's post–*Jazz Singer* period, mostly as an actor in a series of Warner Bros. films. While *The Jazz Singer* was playing to sold-out movie theaters, Jolson went to Los Angeles to film *The Singing Fool*, which, like

The Jazz Singer, was a semi-talkie, with Vitaphone to record Jolson's songs. Jolson plays a blackface minstrel who has a son, whom he calls Sonny Boy, whom he loses when his fickle, gold-digging wife leaves him. The story is "cleverly and shrewdly pictured," Mordaunt Hall, *The New York Times* movie critic, wrote when the film appeared later that year, but the chief interest is "Mr. Jolson's inimitable singing . . . One waits after hearing a selection, hoping for another, and one is not in the least disappointed." *The Singing Fool* grossed $5 million in a year and a half, even more than *The Jazz Singer.* It was the first Jolson movie to open at the Winter Garden, where the most expensive tickets, $11, were embossed with a silhouette of Jolson for customers to keep as souvenirs. It led Warner Bros. to offer Jolson another contract—three movies, $500,000 for each. For a few years, he appeared only onscreen.

While filming on *The Singing Fool* was suspended for a time, Jolson went to Chicago, where he caught a performance of the musical *Sidewalks of New York,* and got his first glimpse of a chorus girl who went by the name Ruby Keeler (birth name: Ethel Hilda Keeler). After the show he went backstage to meet her, much to her astonishment, it was later reported, she something of a nobody, Jolson one of the biggest stars in Hollywood. Keeler was from Nova Scotia but was brought up in New York, the daughter of an Irish truck driver. She studied tap dancing and started her stage career at thirteen in George M. Cohan's *The Rise of Rosie O'Reilly,* and she clearly had something special, an impish, coquettish charm, a good singing voice, and an acrobatic ability (though, while she was good, she wasn't a topflight tap dancer; there was a heaviness to her step and she had a tendency to look at her feet).

She was Jolson's type, small (five foot three, 105 pounds), adorable, a shiksa, a showgirl, and barely legal, eighteen years old to Jolson's forty-two. In a development that could have been portrayed in one of the Cohen and Kelly movies, Jolson was smitten by Ruby, and when the latter went to Los Angeles for a West Coast show, the former was at the train station to meet her. A hot, gift- and flower-rich pursuit followed—a diamond-studded cigarette case, a lynx fur, many dozens of long-stemmed roses crammed in vases in Keeler's dressing room, and then, finally, a five-carat diamond ring.

If Jolson thought Keeler was an innocent, an ingenue, he was mistaken. There was something very fresh about her—"sweet and appealing" were the words often used by critics to describe her—but she was well acquainted with show business in all of its Runyonesque shades of gray: the speakeasies, the gossip columnists, the hustlers, the late nights and late mornings, the guys of social prominence who were also gangsters. Ruby's special gangster was Johnny "Irish" Costello, a sort of fixer for a mobster prominent in bootleg liquors. Sieben, probably echoing what Jolson had told her, says Ruby and Johnny were just friends, a notion somewhat belied by the fact that she was known as "Costello's girl." When she was in California sitting in her dressing room amid the bouquets of long-stemmed roses, she'd call Johnny in New York and complain about Jolson's overbearing attentions, and yet she doesn't seem to have done much to discourage those attentions. After a few months, seemingly out of the blue, she decided that she'd fallen in love with Jolson and wanted to marry him. She was in Washington, D.C., at the time, and asked her agent, Bill Grady, to break the news to "Johnny."

"The word [of the impending marriage] was very quick," the memoirist Jim Bishop, a friend of Grady's, writes. "It hummed along Broadway faster than heat lightning and then it burst its bonds and hit Chicago," where Costello was. Costello, or so Bishop's version of the story goes, called Jolson who was at the Winter Garden for the opening of *Singing Fool,* telling him to get on a train to Chicago right away, suggesting that it was for his own protection, presumably against friends of Costello who might go after Jolson for his theft of "Costello's girl." Jolson, unsure of whether he should go to the police or accept Costello's invitation, went to Chicago. Other accounts of this incident are similar, except in them Jolson met Costello in New York. Wherever the meeting took place, Costello told Jolson he'd heard that he'd beaten his first wife, which, if Henrietta Keller's divorce court testimony is to be believed, was true. Costello wasn't opposed to Keeler marrying Jolson, but he wanted to be sure that the same thing wouldn't happen to her, and he warned Jolson of consequences if it did. Jolson swore to treat Keeler well. At Costello's urging, he also gave her $1 million as a sort of prenuptial gift, a kind of sign of his good faith and security for Keeler if things went bad. He and Costello parted on cordial terms.

It might seem strange that a gangster like Costello would give up his girl so easily, but there are several accounts of this, including one by Bishop and another by Grady, saying that he really did. Maybe he wasn't so deeply in love in the first place, and had plenty of alternatives. Maybe he enjoyed being Keeler's magnanimous but protective ex, a kind of godfather.

If Costello was a gentleman rogue, others were not so nice. Word of Jolson's $1 million gift to Keeler spread fast, according to Bishop, and when another prominent gangster, Jack "Legs" Diamond, heard of it, he reached Jolson by phone at the Winter Garden and tried to shake him down for $50,000 by morning—or else. At this point another Runyonesque character comes into the picture, Mark Hellinger, a Jew from the Lower East Side, a gossip columnist, and future movie producer (for whom a theater on Fifty-first Street was once named). Hellinger, then a columnist for the New York *Daily News,* was one of those people who knew everybody—actors, showgirls, agents, and mobsters. He was close to Jolson, close enough so that when Jolson and Keeler got married in a civil ceremony in Westchester on September 21, 1928, not only was Hellinger present but he was also one of the two male friends who accompanied the newlyweds on their honeymoon trip to Europe (a sign that when it came down to it, Jolson preferred the company of men, or at least that the company of one woman was never enough).

Jolson, very nervous about Diamond's attempt at extortion, found Hellinger at a nightclub and informed him of the situation. Hellinger knew the bootleg gangster that Diamond worked for and called him. The next morning, Diamond called Jolson and told him he'd been "only kidding." "Nobody's going to hurt you, Jolson, least of all me," he said. On a related occasion, related by his friend and accompanist Harry Akst, the scrappy, streetwise Jolson replaced the one nervous about gangland threats. Akst was in Jolson's hotel room one night when a phone call from "a gangster" came in, warning Jolson to "lay off Ruby Keeler, or else."

"Listen, you sonuvabitch," Jolson said, according to Akst. "Get this: I'm leaving the Ritz Towers in exactly eight minutes. I'm walking down Park Avenue to Fifty-first Street. Then I'm turning west and walking on the north side of Fifty-first to Seventh Avenue, and then I'm going through the stage door of the Winter Garden. Take your best shot." Then Jolson hung up.

How does this relate to Jolson's belligerence toward Walter Winchell? Five years into the marriage, Keeler, now a Warner Bros. movie star in her own right, saw an article by Louella Parsons, whose syndicated Hollywood gossip column was read by twenty million people. According to Parsons, Winchell had written a script for Universal Studios called *Broadway Thru a Keyhole,* about a gangster who, to protect his girlfriend during a gang war, sends her to Florida, where she falls in love with a popular singer. The gangster, hurt and jealous at first, accepts the girl's love for the singer, and when she is kidnapped by a rival gang, he rescues her.

Keeler was convinced, with good reason, that the script was based on her, Jolson, and Costello, and she didn't like it. "Keeler cried for days after learning the nature of the projected story," the newspapers reported, quoting Jolson. When Keeler saw Winchell going to his seat at the Hollywood Legion Stadium, the crying started again, and that's when Jolson "just up and popped him."

According to Goldman, there was another possible instigating factor for Jolson's fury at Winchell, which, in light of Jolson's role in *The Jazz Singer,* has a certain irony to it. In 1930, Winchell had scolded Jolson for working on the Jewish high holidays. Jolson, an inordinately sensitive man, was hurt by Winchell's criticism. Perhaps he felt guilty, knowing that his deceased mother would also have disapproved, as, no doubt, did his father. The insult of three years earlier may not have been the proximate cause of Jolson's aggression, but it may have been festering and played a role. In any case, he responded to it by declining some performance offers that would have involved working on Rosh Hashanah and Yom Kippur. Many Jews, who are otherwise nonobservant, go to the synagogue and fast on Yom Kippur; or if they don't, they feel uneasy, that they've let their side down. That's what the fraught expression on Jolson's face conveys when he hears Cantor Rosenblatt sing "Yahrzeit Licht" in *The Jazz Singer,* and it seems likely that the nonfiction Jolson felt the same way.

As for *Broadway Thru a Keyhole,* Winchell ended up the winner of the bout. "Swell publicity for the picture I wrote," he told the press after the Jolson dustup. Warner Bros., which was also Keeler's and Jolson's studio, bought the movie rights to the play for a reported $500,000, and the film opened in New York with a traffic-stopping gala on November 2, 1933. The gossip columns continued to speculate on whether it told a true story or not, about Jolson, Keeler, and Costello. Surely it did, but there's no record that Jolson or Keeler made any further comment.

* * *

They were both busy with other things. After Keeler's marriage to Jolson, she played in three Warner musical comedy movies, *42nd Street, Footlight Parade,* and *Gold Diggers of 1933,* appearing in duets with James Cagney and Dick Powell. Newspapers reported on her marriage with Jolson as an entirely happy affair. "Ruby Keeler is very much in love with Al Jolson," the gossip columnist for the New York *Daily News,* Sydney Skolsky, wrote. "She doesn't make a move without his okay. She does everything he says." In fact, things were tense from the beginning, as Jolson repeated with Keeler the pattern of his earlier marriages—infatuation and a full-court-press courtship followed by possessiveness, attempts at control, then a progressive loss of interest.

Keeler must have sensed something peculiar when Jolson brought two male friends along as companions on their honeymoon. Skolsky said in his column on the marriage that Keeler was learning to eat "Jewish food" and had learned a few words of "Jewish," but they were already arguing on the honeymoon when Jolson, always needing to be in control, insisted that Keeler eat a fish dish that she didn't want.

When the honeymoon was over, Keeler began performing in *Whoopee!,* a Florenz Ziegfeld review with Eddie Cantor in the lead role. Four days after the show opened in Pittsburgh, Jolson, who was in Los Angeles negotiating a new movie deal with Warner Bros., called Keeler and insisted that she join him in California, saying he was sick. "Honey I need ya," Cantor, who was with Keeler at the time, quotes Jolson as saying. "I'll give ya all the money in the world, you come on back to your daddy, honey."

Keeler left Pittsburgh right away, abandoning Ziegfeld, Cantor, and *Whoopee!*, eventually missing its New York premier. It was a remarkable display of loyalty to her new husband, but to her surprise, when she got to Los Angeles, she found Jolson in perfectly good health.

It's possible that Jolson was simply exercising what he saw as his husbandly rights regarding the nineteen-year-old Keeler, or perhaps he didn't like the idea that she might become as big a star as he. Or, as some in the press speculated at the time, Jolson had second thoughts about Keeler playing in *Whoopee!* because of Cantor, whom Jolson saw as his chief rival—"good friends and competitors," as Cantor put it. "These two great comedians regard everything else in life as funny except each other," a writer for the *San Francisco Examiner* said in a long report on Keeler's abrupt departure from Pittsburgh. Four years earlier, when Jolson was on tour in Chicago with *Big Boy,* he'd become obsessed with the resounding success Cantor was having in *Kid Boots,* which was playing in New York at a theater across the street from the Winter Garden, Jolson's usual venue. Jolson told the Shuberts that Cantor was "stealing his public"; he wanted to leave *Big Boy* right away and open in a rival show at the Winter Garden to divert Cantor's audience to himself.

The story is credible. The Shuberts refused Jolson's demand, whereupon Jolson left Chicago anyway. Arriving in Florida, reporters asked him why. "The Shuberts," he replied, wielding a clever verbal scalpel. "They messed everything up; that's why they're called the Messrs Shubert."

But there's another version of the story of Keeler's departure from *Whoopee!* It is that Cantor, in an ad-libbed moment in the show, couldn't resist poking fun at her for her recent marriage to Jolson. At the end of the show, "with an expression of exaggerated longing, Cantor gazed at Ruby and crooned 'Mammy' at her in imitation of his rival," one press account said. The audience, getting the joke, "snickered, causing an angry flush under Ms. Keeler's makeup, which, in turn, made the audience roar, sending the curtain down on a gleeful comedian and a furious dancer." In other words, it wasn't so much Jolson demanding Keeler's presence as Keeler being unable to take a joke at Jolson's expense. In that light, her fury at Winchell and Jolson's response seem all that much more understandable.

* * *

By the time Jolson confronted Winchell, he was declining into a kind of middle-level celebrity, which he struggled against, striving to remain at the center of things, the only place where Al Jolson experienced happiness. Very few people in any walk of life, outside perhaps of president-for-life dictators and the leaders of personality cults, sustain the kind of dominance that Jolson enjoyed in his musical comedy heyday, and losing a bit of his sheen wasn't unexpected, as the culture changed, producing new, younger stars who eclipsed him. One of those new stars was Ruby Keeler, whose fast-ascending line crossed Jolson's slow-descending one as the 1930s progressed. There's a bit of *Sister Carrie* in the relationship between the two. As in Theodore Dreiser's novel, the talented, much younger actress emerges from the shadows her middle-aged husband had cast her in. Jolson by no means became the broken, homeless wreck of a husband in *Sister Carrie,* but he became kind of ordinary in the show business scheme of things, like an athlete past his prime.

In the years after *The Jazz Singer* and *The Singing Fool,* Jolson stuck with movies—*Say It with Songs* in 1929, *Mammy* in 1930, a filmed version of *Big Boy* in 1931. That year, Jolson returned to the stage in *Wonder Bar,* based on an Austrian musical that takes place in a Parisian nightclub, a kind of predecessor to *Cabaret,* though not as pungently atmospheric. The play opened in New York and then played in fifty cities over six months; it was mostly a success but a modest one, not like Jolson's earlier shows. In 1933, he made another movie, *Hallelujah, I'm a Bum,* a critical and commercial dud. After that, Jolson agreed to cancel his contract with United Artists, which would have paid him $500,000 for each of three additional films. It probably didn't improve this highly competitive man's mood to know that Keeler at the same time was in the midst of making the three movies she did for Warner Bros. at the height of her success.

By 1932, Jolson had switched to the hot new entertainment medium, radio, as his principal vehicle. The first such venture was a half-hour program on Friday nights that he did in 1932 on NBC. The last was a series of seventy-one Kraft Music Hall broadcasts also on NBC that he did from 1947 to 1949. Besides that, he was a frequent guest on other people's radio programs—including those of Rudy Vallee, Bob Hope, and Jack Benny. He received poor reviews as well as enthusiastic ones. The consensus was that the full Jolson experience could only be enjoyed live and in person, and that he didn't convey the entirety of his magnetic talent when he could only be heard and not seen. Radio, in addition, was encouraging a new, cooler, more intimate, microphoned style of singing, illustrated by crooners like Bing Crosby, which made Jolson's more declamatory, oratory-like, belt-it-out style seem kind of middle-aged, like Jolson himself.

He didn't set box-office records in his radio appearances, though they helped keep him on the scene, and every once in a while he got back in the spotlight—as in "Jolson's back!" the headline that greeted *Hold On to Your Hats,* a musical comedy in which he starred in 1941. "He's a little heavier about the middle and there is a touch of gray at his temples," the *Boston Post* said.

"But the thundering vitality which has always been his trade mark is undiminished." He would probably have done well at that point to stick with live theatrical performances with the Shuberts, since the movies too, where he had been a pioneer, were moving beyond him. "The movies were growing up," Sieben wrote, "and Al's type of talent—his stock in trade—was too maudlin, too corny for an audience that was growing in sophistication." On the radio, Jolson always played more or less the same character, likable and clever, but innocuous, psychologically thin. In the movies he was up against the likes of Fred Astaire, Basil Rathbone, Gary Cooper, Clark Gable, Charles Boyer, Spencer Tracy, Edward G. Robinson, and Humphrey Bogart, not to mention the old Yiddish-theater actor Paul Muni who, like most of these others, was playing intellectually complex, emotionally rich, psychologically deep characters in films like *The Story of Louis Pasteur* and *The Life of Emile Zola*. Jolson, who was never a powerful dramatic actor and never tried to be one, always seemed like a talented amateur onscreen, and he simply couldn't compete. Yet he was driven to keep trying, even as he was unable to change. The numbers that got the most enthusiastic responses on the radio were the old songs from the 1920s and earlier, "My Mammy," "Swanee," "Rockabye Your Baby with a Dixie Melody." Harry Von Tilzer, Irving Berlin, and Irving Caesar no longer wrote songs hoping that Al Jolson would pick them up. Blackface was, happily, fading away. Jolson remained well enough liked and in demand, but he was now a figure of nostalgia, like the players who show up for old-timers day at baseball stadiums.

During the 1930s, when he wasn't working, he spent whole afternoons at the racetrack, evenings at the fights. He and Keeler built a house on five acres in the San Fernando Valley north of Los Angeles where he had a separate apartment, but their relationship soured, first slowly, then more quickly, the sourness fueled

by Jolson's possessiveness and egotistical resentment, his pride in
his wife's celebrity vitiated by his cranky suspicion that the girl
he'd married when she was a starstruck nineteen-year-old nobody
was surpassing him. "He wasn't jealous of her accomplishments,"
Sieben writes, putting this in the best possible light, "but he was
fearful of what life would be like if he toppled from his pinna-
cle. . . . Al could not envision a future devoid of the plaudits of
the crowd." As we've seen, those plaudits were becoming fewer
and farther between.

When he was fifty, he and Keeler adopted a baby boy, naming him Al Jolson, Jr., a departure from Ashkenazi Jewish custom,
which doesn't favor naming children after living relatives. But,
while being a father was something new and meaningful to Jolson, he had learned little from his failed marriages. He and Keeler
were apart months at a time. Frequently, Jolson would urgently
summon Keeler to his side, saying he needed her, always address-
ing her as "baby" this and "baby" that, an ersatz intimacy mas-
querading as affection. Keeler would return, and after a day or
two, Jolson would ignore her.

Ruby began seeing John Lowe, a wealthy real estate dealer,
and on October 30, 1939, she filed for divorce in Los Angeles, saying in her two-page deposition: "Since said marriage, defendant
has treated plaintiff with extreme cruelty and has caused plaintiff grievous mental and physical suffering thereby." Jolson agreed
to a settlement but continued to try to get Keeler to change her
mind. "The romance is definitely over, but the melody lingers
on," wrote a *Los Angeles Times* reporter after spotting Jolson and
Keeler together at dinner in February. Asked by the reporter if
they were getting back together, Jolson said, "I'd give my life if
it were true," but when he asked Keeler the same question, she
"looked away and made no comment."

A year after their separation, at the end of 1940, a Los Angeles judge granted Keeler her divorce, giving her custody of Al Jr., who had no further relationship with Al Sr., and a weekly payment from Jolson of $400, plus a lump sum of $50,000 if she ever remarried. Even then, from time to time, Jolson would invite Keeler to evenings out, but she never allowed herself to be alone with him again.

Keeler had signed a contract to perform in the new musical comedy *Hold On to Your Hats,* agreeing to stay with the production as long as it lasted in theaters. After her contract was signed, Jolson bought 80 percent of the show, meaning that Keeler suddenly found herself working for the man from whom she was separated on the grounds of "extreme cruelty." The show went on, with Jolson starring in it and Keeler playing her part. The press reported on Jolson doing what he usually did when he was trying to gain, or regain, a woman's heart—showered Keeler with "flowers, gifts, and reconciliation attempts"—but also continued to do the kind of thing that most upset Keeler, which was to turn their private life into a kind of public performance, with Jolson the star. When the two were onstage together in *Hold On to Your Hats,* he would ad-lib comments about their former married life, until, after a show in Chicago, Keeler asked to be relieved of her contractual obligations and to leave. She complained about Jolson's onstage off-script remarks and that Jolson's constant criticism of her gave her an inferiority complex. After a day's hesitation, Jolson agreed to release Keeler from the contract.

13

The Final Decade

Despite Al Jolson's disappointments, his third failed marriage, the distressing sense that he was in the winter of his career, he lived a hectic final decade, and even enjoyed an impressive comeback, both personally and professionally. Jolson performed for troops during both World War II and the Korean War, following a grueling schedule that would have sorely tested the endurance of a man twenty years younger and demonstrating a patriotism that seems almost old-fashioned by today's standards. He continued to appear on the radio, usually as a kind of old-timer, joining with other celebrities of his generation to tell jokes, sing the old familiar songs, and talk in a kind of good-old-fellow style about bygone days.

At the age of fifty-six when America got into World War II, Jolson could have stayed at home or just made token appearances. But he was far too driven a man for halfway measures. He wrote a letter to Stephen Early, President Roosevelt's press secretary, expressing his "urge to serve my country in the only field I know—amusement." He started in January 1942, shortly after Pearl Harbor and the declarations of war against Germany and Japan, going to various stateside army camps, sometimes doing several shows a day, performing in all before sixty thousand servicemen and -women. He flew to an air base near Seattle, then on to Fairbanks, Nome, and Anchorage, Alaska, where in one single day he did nine hour-long performances. In New York, he called the mothers, wives, and girlfriends of some of the soldiers he'd met on his tour.

Others, of course, also entertained troops during the war— Bob Hope most famously—but there was an avidity to Jolson's effort, a zeal that sets him apart. He wanted to do something good, something virtuous, to show gratitude to the adopted country that had generously hosted his remarkable career. Jolson never seems to have spoken of it, but perhaps he knew that on September 4, 1941, most of the Jewish population of Seredzius, Lithuania, was murdered by the Nazis, 198 people in all. Even if he didn't know that specifically, he certainly knew that the Jewish life he'd lived in the Russian Empire had been annihilated, never to be restored. But for the lucky fact of his departure, he would have been murdered by the banks of the Niemen River rather than feted on the shores of the Pacific, and the war gave him a chance to repay his good fortune.

And so he trucked on. After Alaska, he and Akst went on a three-week tour of Trinidad, Curaçao, and Aruba and then to Panama, after which he, along with Merle Oberon, the actress, and Patricia Morison, a singer, flew to England and did shows in London, Dublin, Belfast, Limerick, and Glasgow, among other places.

In 1943, he was entertaining troops again, traveling to British Guiana (since 1966, the independent nation of Guyana), to Belem, Natal, and Recife, Brazil, where he was billeted with soldiers, sleeping on a cot covered with a mosquito net, getting up at five A.M. to travel to the next destination. He and Akst went to Dakar, then to Marrakech, Casablanca, Oran, and Algiers, where he was invited into Dwight Eisenhower's headquarters. From there he went to Tunisia, then across the Mediterranean to Sicily, where he fell ill and had to go home for some rest and rehabilitation. Akst, in an account he wrote a few months after Jolson's death, recounts that when the two of them arrived back home from Europe, Akst was calling his wife from their hotel in Miami when he heard Jolson weeping in the next room.

"'What's the matter, Al?'" Akst asked him. "He was sitting there with his head in his hands. 'You've got someone to come back to,' he choked. 'What have I got? Not a soul in the world cares whether I live or die.'"

Soon, Jolson and Akst traveled by station wagon to perform for wounded soldiers, some very seriously, at hospitals across the South, one of which was the Eastman Annex in Hot Springs, Arkansas. It was while onstage there that he noticed Erle Chenault Galbraith, a nurse, and, in Jolson style, went to talk to her after the show. He was fifty-eight; she was twenty and pretty. In the meantime, Jolson was diagnosed with malaria, and in January 1945 he lost two ribs and most of a lung in an operation that saved his life. As soon as he'd recovered, he proposed to Erle, and on March 24, 1945, the two were married in a civil ceremony in Quartzite, Arizona, and went on to adopt two children, a boy named Asa Albert Jolson, Jr., in 1947, and a girl, Alicia, in 1950. Erle seems to have made Jolson happier than he'd ever been before.

It was when he got back to the United States that he began the negotiations, first with Warner, then with Columbia Pictures, for *The Jolson Story*, selling his life rights to Columbia for a percentage of the film plus $10,000 for recording the songs. It would be an enormous box-office sensation, the fifth-biggest-grossing film of the year, selling nearly fifty million tickets, which means that one-third of the entire American population at the time saw the movie. *The Jolson Story* was part of an ongoing series of Hollywood biopics about historical figures in music, including George Gershwin, Cole Porter, Frédéric Chopin, and George M. Cohan, in which the music mostly took precedence over the life.

A producer at Columbia Pictures proposed it to him, and Jolson readily agreed, wanting to play himself. But according to Harry Akst, he looked in the mirror one day and realized that what others were hesitating to tell him openly was true, that he was too old. Instead, Columbia Pictures hired Larry Parks, a young actor who looked a bit like the young Jolson, though larger framed, more classically, square-jawedly handsome, and a flowery pink in complexion compared to Jolson's more sallow Mediterranean hue. Parks played Jolson in the spoken part of the script, but Jolson recorded the songs and Parks lip-synched them onscreen, while mimicking Jolson's characteristic moves and gestures, playing in blackface as Jolson himself did, even though by 1946, blackface, like minstrelsy in general, had pretty much disappeared from American entertainment.

"The Biography of a Voice" was the headline on a two-page pictorial feature on the movie in *The New York Times*. The idea was that Jolson, having been performing since the early years of the twentieth century, embodied the entire modern history of popular music, from the minstrel era to the jazz era, with ragtime, musical comedy, and movies in between. "Through those years, the Jolson ways became institutions—the dynamic prance, the clapped hands, the outstretched arms," the text read. "It looks suspiciously as though the picture that moves is just an adjunct of the behind the scenes phonograph," the *Times* critic Bosley Crowther wrote in an otherwise favorable review of the movie. "What happens on the screen might as easily be told in a series of slides. . . . All this absurd contrivance, mind you, just to sell Mr. Jolson's songs again."

Crowther was right. Except for the music, *The Jolson Story* is a hackneyed, almost immorally untruthful exercise in mythmaking. The opening scenes are reasonably faithful to Jolson's life, though the Lithuanian period is absent. Jolson is Asa Yoelson, the son of a bearded Orthodox cantor, played by the Austrian-born actor Ludwig Donath, a Jew who escaped Europe after the Anschluss, Germany's annexation of Austria in 1938. Young Asa is a preternaturally talented boy who yearns to sing on the stage, and he does, eventually becoming a great star, first in vaudeville, then on Broadway, performing in blackface, but, in contrast to Jolson's real-life father, his movie father quickly accepts his son's choice and becomes his biggest fan. The Jolson of *The Jolson Story* is an only child, his older brother, Harry, and his two sisters missing in the movie, along with most of the other pungent elements of his actual biography. The entire generational conflict that pre-occupied the real Jolson and inspired *The Jazz Singer* is absent. So is Jolson's dead mother; in *The Jolson Story,* she is very much alive, economically and socially transformed into an upper-middle-class matron wearing colorful fashionable dresses and feathered hats, the only suggestion that she's Jewish being her vaguely East Euro-pean accent. Early on, there's a scene in the synagogue in which the young Jolson sings in the choir directed by his cantor father, but that's pretty much it as far as Jewishness is concerned. A scene indicated in the script showed Parks as Jolson at an elegant the-atrical cocktail party. When asked to sing a song, he agrees, but it's something, he says, you probably won't understand. He goes to the piano and sings "A Cantor on Sabbath," which is redo-lent of Yiddishkeit and shows that the real Jolson hadn't forgotten the language of his ancestors. But that scene was not included in the final cut. It's available on YouTube.

Jolson's first two wives have also been eliminated from *The Jolson Story,* so his first marriage is the one with Ruby Keeler, except that his wife in the film is named Julie Benson; Keeler refused to allow her name to be used. Julie is played by Evelyn Keyes, most known for her portrayal of Suellen O'Hara in *Gone with the Wind.* When she meets Mr. and Mrs. Yoelson, there isn't even a trace of concern over the fact that she's a shiksa. She is instantly embraced. The real Moshe Yoelson, who died at the age of eighty, just a few months before the making of the movie, must have rolled over in his freshly dug grave.

Insofar as there is a plot to *The Jolson Story,* it follows the dissolution of the Jolson-Benson marriage, not because Al keeps her out of his life but because Julie wants a quiet, simple retirement in the country and bans Al from performing. He tries to adapt to a life lived in an easy chair in front of the fireplace rather than on the stage. One night, however, Jolson's parents come for a visit, and after celebrating Cantor Yoelson's birthday, they all go to a nightclub. Jolson is recognized and asked to sing, something he's given up, like a smoker trying to stay off cigarettes. But he reluctantly agrees to do just one number, and then, in response to the demand, he sings another, and then he can't stop himself. He keeps singing for his rapturous audience, and Julie, having seen that her husband's true love is not her but performing, quietly tiptoes out of the nightclub and out of the marriage.

It's hardly a searing psychological study. "It becomes boring," the *Los Angeles Times* critic said of the love story, "even as it is unbelievable." The breakup depicted in *The Jolson Story* bore hardly any resemblance to the Jolson-Keeler divorce, of course, but the kernel of truth it contained is one of the things that makes the movie almost unbearable. The Jolson in the movie is rude, manipulative, overbearing, controlling, relentless, and obnoxiously self-assured, all of that without the redeeming charm and boyish enthusiasm of the real Jolson. He's blinded by his own ambition and desires. He doesn't listen. He swats away the feelings and yearnings of people close to him like so many mosquitoes. He substitutes a kind of jocular casualness for real connection, and he always gets what he wants. The other characters in the movie seem oblivious to these objectionable qualities, as if not noticing a bad smell in the room that's conspicuous to everybody else.

The real Jolson also seemed oblivious to the obnoxious elements of his onscreen depiction. He loved *The Jolson Story*, no doubt because it put him center stage again after his years as a kind of favorite uncle, but perhaps also because the fabricated story of his life felt better to him than his real life ever did. There was no death of his mother when he was nine, no perpetually disapproving father. The Hollywood father celebrates his son's success as a popular singer, joyously following the reviews of his shows. He goes to the lavish estate that Jolson has built in the San Fernando Valley where he waltzes with Mrs. Yoelson while Al sings "The Anniversary Song" (which reached number sixteen on the pop charts in 1947).

Oh how we danced on the night we were wed
We vowed our true love, though a word wasn't said.

Because the film was a commercial success, Columbia Pictures made a sequel, *Jolson Sings Again,* advertised as "the most eagerly awaited event in the history of motion pictures," which might seem absurdly hyperbolic except that it wasn't far from the truth. It was the highest-grossing film of 1949. The *New York Times* critic, moreover, declared it "at least twice as good" as *The Jolson Story.* "There is only one voice like Jolson's, and it's good to be hearing it again," his review said. The movie picks up the story after Jolson's wife has left him. At first, he slides into the decadent fast life of horse races, the fights, and the nightclubs that Jolson actually did lead after his divorce from Ruby Keeler, though the film only hints briefly at the affairs with the succession of showgirls that Jolson actually had. When World War II breaks out,

Jolson does in the movie what he did in real life, volunteering to sing for the troops, following such an exhausting schedule that he falls sick and loses a lung. But he meets a nurse named Ellen Clark, a stand-in for Erle Galbraith, whom he marries.

Jolson's courtship of Erle, a.k.a. Ellen Clark, is enacted in *Jolson Sings Again,* but mainly the sequel to *The Jolson Story* is the story of *The Jolson Story.* The Plot: As Jolson's stage career flags, somebody proposes a movie based on his life. Jolson is too old to play himself, so a young actor—and here Larry Parks plays himself—is brought on to incarnate him on the screen and to lip-synch his songs. On opening night, Jolson is too nervous to sit in the theater, so he roams the lobby, as he did during the real opening of *The Jolson Story* three years before, popping sedatives and peering from time to time into the screening room. The happy ending is the newspaper clippings declaring the movie a smash hit.

* * *

In 1950, when Jolson was happily married and the new father of two small children, he ventured out again to entertain American soldiers, this time in Korea. As soon as the war broke out, he volunteered to go into action, and when informed that there was no money available to cover the costs of his travels, he offered to cover the expenses out of his own pocket. He was sixty-four years old and had recently lost a lung, but that special Jolsonian zeal took over. Akst, who again accompanied him on the trip, playing a piano they called the purple cow (because it was painted purple), wrote later that "the trip fitted in somewhere in the strange and the puzzling complexities of the Jolson ego." Akst speculates that Jolson had been bruised by Columbia's decision to have somebody more youthful play him in *The Jolson Story;* it was "concrete evidence that he was no longer young." "So now Korea!" Akst writes. "He'd show them!"

But there was also the same tremendous moral commitment that Jolson showed as he traveled the Western Hemisphere during World War II, the successful immigrant's compulsion to give back to the country that had given him wealth, fame, and freedom. Jolson and Akst left from Los Angeles on September 11, 1950, flying overnight on a Boeing Stratocruiser to Honolulu, then on to Wake Island, where engine trouble forced them to spend the night sleeping in a damp, drafty Quonset hut in upper bunks so as to avoid the rats scurrying below. They arrived in Tokyo after another long flight, both suffering from colds and coughs. Jolson went straight to an army hospital before checking into his hotel. A young army doctor looked at his throat and whispered to another doctor, "This man can't sing," to which Jolson replied, "Listen, son, I gotta sing," after which Jolson was installed in what Akst calls a cabinet where he wrapped his head in a Turkish towel and breathed mentholated steam.

In *Jolson Sings Again,* Jolson worries that he's too much of a has-been to appeal to the nineteen- and twenty-year-old soldiers who will be his audience in Japan and Korea, but he needn't have worried. The first show was at a Tokyo army hospital, where he was introduced as "the world's greatest entertainer." He came bounding across a courtyard in his loose-fitting fatigues to take the microphone. With Akst playing the purple cow, he sang "Swanee," "April Showers," and other songs from the Jolson repertoire to hundreds of cheering men massed in a semicircle around him or on surrounding balconies. He and Akst spent several days in Japan, Jolson shuttling back and forth between the Imperial Hotel and the hospital steam room, flying to bases outside the

Tokyo-Yokohama area, singing on makeshift stages outside or inside airplane hangars, writing notes to Akst on a pad instead of talking to him in a constant effort to save his voice.

After Japan, they flew to Pusan, in the very southeast corner of Korea, where the Americans had made a last stand to avoid being pushed off the peninsula altogether. As Akst remembered the trip, it was " 'Rock-a-bye Your Baby with a Dixie Melody' to guys in battle dress with rifles and bazookas in their hands," some of them leaving in the middle of a song when they were called to the front line. Photographs show Jolson in his fatigues standing on a makeshift stage, Akst sitting next to him at the piano. They could hear what they thought was a rifle drill in the distance, but it wasn't a drill, they were told; it was North Korean snipers. "Don't worry, Al," someone told him. "They're lousy shots." Jolson warmed up the crowd with a few jokes. "I don't know why I'm here," he said. "I'm old enough to know better, you know. Going on forty-nine, you don't have to run around." A roar of laughter followed that, then came the usual songs and the usual lusty cheers.

They went by jeep and helicopter to various locations along the front, Jolson and Akst doing forty-two shows in sixteen days on their Asia tour, Jolson breathing in that mentholated steam whenever he could and constantly gargling Dobell's solution (sodium borate, sodium bicarbonate, glycerin, and phenol) to protect his vocal cords. At a lunch, General W. B. Kean, commander of the Twenty-fifth Division, noticed that Jolson looked worn-out and asked him if he didn't think he'd already done enough for the boys. Jolson's reply sounds almost too good to be true, but Akst, who was there, is emphatic. "How could anybody do enough for them?" Jolson said. When he returned to Japan for shows in another half-dozen places, he visited Kean's son, who'd been wounded by an antipersonnel mine and was in an army hos-

pital in Osaka; then he managed to get a call through to the soldier's father to tell him he'd shaken the boy's hand and his grip
was strong. The day before leaving for the States, Jolson and Akst
were invited to the living quarters of Commander in Chief Douglas MacArthur in Tokyo (this was before Truman removed him
from his command for insubordination). The Jewish boy from
Lithuania sat at the piano and sang for two hours to the American
Caesar and his wife. When he got back to California, he bragged
that he'd had two hours with MacArthur; Truman, he said, only
had one.

On their last day in Tokyo, Akst and Jolson were invited to
dinner by General Paul B. Kelly, the surprise event of the evening
being a chorus of geisha girls who sang "April Showers," one of
Jolson's signature numbers, and "You Are My Sunshine." Before
leaving the country, Jolson appeared by telephone on the gossip
columnist Louella Parsons's radio show. "The mud and dust are
unbelievable," he told her. "I've played in hospital wards for boys
with torn and twisted bodies. I did one show for three thousand
men on a stage built over a swimming pool, and they loved it.
What a ham I am." And then this: "Do me a favor, honey, and
don't fail me in this. Tell all the Bob Hopes, the Jack Bennys, Bing
Crosby, Danny Thomas, Tony Martin, Eddie Cantor, George Jessel, and many others, if they don't come to Korea to entertain
these kids immediately and do their part, well, they'll be sorry for
the rest of their lives."

Jolson left Tokyo on September 23, 1950, carrying pearl neck-
laces that he'd bought in Tokyo for Erle and Akst's wife. During
a stopover in Hawaii, he called the Tripler Hospital in Honolulu and squeezed in a quick visit to wounded servicemen there.
Arriving in Los Angeles, he came down the airplane ramp, and
while the news cameras flashed he got on his knees and kissed the
ground. "Every time I come home from one of these trips," he told

a reporter, "I always look up my last income tax return to make sure I paid enough."

Erle was there with little Asa, and the next day they went to Palm Springs. When they got back a few days later, as Akst remembered it, Jolson seemed rejuvenated after the arduous efforts of their Asian trip. He was brimming with excitement over new possibilities. There was a guest appearance coming up on Bing Crosby's radio show. Some producers were asking him to star in a picture about American actors and singers entertaining American troops in far-flung and dangerous places. A bit more than two weeks after his return, he went with Akst for a boxing match at the Olympic Stadium, where he complained about indigestion. Akst chastised him for eating Spanish food. But he liked Spanish food, Jolson replied.

The next day, Jolson went to a cardiologist who told him not to "do any more Koreas." The day after that, a second cardiologist told him what he wanted to hear. Only a few months before, he and his heart had passed a test for a $1 million life insurance policy, and, the doctor now told him, his heart hadn't changed much since then. But the doctor gave him the name of a cardiologist in San Francisco, where Jolson was going with Akst the next day, just in case. On October 27, the two flew there for some meetings about his appearance with Crosby. When they passed Magnin's Department Store on the way to town from the airport, Jolson said something about going there for some shopping the next day.

He and Akst checked into the St. Francis Hotel, then went to dinner at Tarantino's, a restaurant on Fisherman's Wharf, where both of them noted the usual buzz that accompanied Jolson's presence almost everyplace he went. Back at the hotel, Jolson went to his bedroom for some rest, but soon he asked Martin Fried, a pianist and conductor who was helping to orchestrate some songs, to go downstairs and get some bicarbonate of soda. When Akst went in to see him, Jolson was tapping his chest and saying he had indigestion.

They called for the hotel doctor, who was out but would come to the suite when he got back. They called the cardiologist who had been recommended to Jolson. While they were waiting, Fried arrived with the bicarbonate of soda, which failed to make Jolson feel better.

"Harry, I'm not going to last," he said.

A hotel nurse arrived, took his pulse, rubbed his back, and assured Akst that Jolson was not having a heart attack. At ten P.M., both the hotel doctor and the cardiologist arrived. Jolson expressed some embarrassment at having two doctors there over a case of indigestion.

Akst and Fried looked on as the doctors asked some questions. What had he been doing? What had he eaten? "Oh . . . oh . . . I'm going," Jolson said, sinking back on his pillow, closing his eyes. His heart was failing. The hotel doctor put a stethoscope to his chest, listened for a minute, and announced to the cardiologist, "He's dead."

14

The Afterlife

During the Jews' long sojourn in the Russian Empire, there was virtually no possibility for them to give up their Jewishness in exchange for integration into the life of Russia, though there were exceptions: Jews who went to the university, Jews who lived in Moscow, Jews who became revolutionaries, like Leon Trotsky, even Jews who married out of the faith. But for the vast majority of Jews in Russia and in the territories of its empire, Poland, Ukraine, Latvia, and Lithuania, restricted to the Pale of Settlement as they were, there was little choice and therefore rarely any jazz-singer-like dilemmas.

But in the Western world, and especially in America, the choices were vast and bewildering, producing dilemmas like the one portrayed by *The Jazz Singer* of 1927. The film, moreover, has had a prolonged afterlife. Since the Jolson original, there have been three remakes plus a radio drama, all of them motivated by commercial interests but all of them testifying to continuing Jewish ambivalence, to the inner Jewish turmoil. Each of the remakes was cast from the same mold, each of them centering on the conflict between father and son, tradition and modernity. But each of them is also embedded in its own time and in that way reflects the history of the Jews in America, from Lower East Side poverty to American prosperity, even as the residue of Jewishness adheres.

In the broadest sense, the various iterations of *The Jazz Singer* represent the habit of American Jews always to look at themselves looking at themselves in America, nervous about their status in a Christian-majority country, eager to achieve full engagement, searching for the balance between their ancient rites and the limits of the possible.

The first remake came at the end of 1952, twenty-five years after the original movie, just two years after Jolson's death. Things were different. For one, the Holocaust had shocked the world, awakening it to the danger of racial hatreds while also reminding the Jews of their vulnerability, in the unaltered fact that in some way the world is always out to get them, but also imbuing them with a knowledge of their good fortune to have been in America when the European horror was unfolding. The Jews who stayed in the former Russian Empire had been slaughtered while the Jews in America remained safe—except for those who had been soldiers in the United States Army. Two years after the end of the war, Hollywood dramatized antisemitism with the aforementioned movie *Gentlemen's Agreement,* in which Gregory Peck plays a journalist who pretends to be Jewish to investigate the ancient hatred directly. *Gentleman's Agreement* was a reminder of the persistence of antisemitism even in America. In fact, despite that, the Jews had done well in the twenty-seven years since *The Jazz Singer* played all over the country to rave reviews. Jews in the cultural sphere were enjoying a success that would have been dreamlike to their Pale of Settlement ancestors, not to mention their contemporaries who were slaughtered in Hitler's death factories. True, there remained in a corner of the public mind an association of Jews with Communism, an old trope dating to the Bolshevik Revolution, fanned into flames by Father Coughlin, the radio demagogue, implicit in the anti-Communist hysteria

of Senator Joe McCarthy of Wisconsin, given life by the espio-
nage trial and execution of Julius and Ethel Rosenberg for passing
nuclear secrets to the Russians. They were executed in 1953.

But if the Jewish unease over these events stuck like burrs in
their collective mind, there is none of it in the 1952 version of *The
Jazz Singer,* which portrays Jews as prosperous and assimilated,
having long escaped the ghetto and entered into the American
mainstream. If there was still a worry about their acceptance into
American life, if they still suffered from slights and insults, or
if they worried about how they appeared to the gentile majority, this worry is conspicuous by its absence from the film. The
opening shot shows the sky and stars; then, as the camera descends,
a Star of David appears before a signboard for Temple Sinai in
Philadelphia, "founded in 1790," looms into view. Inside the synagogue, impeccably dressed men and women—sitting together,
not apart, as they would in an Orthodox synagogue—listen to a
Hebrew prayer in a choral rendition. These are in no way the former shtetl Jews of the immigrant ghetto. These are, symbolically
speaking, *Mayflower* Jews, Daughters of the American Revolution
Jews, WASPy Jews, assimilated Jews, happy Jews, the products
more of aristocratic privilege than religious persecution.

The lead role is played by Danny Thomas, who looked a bit
like a Jewish stereotype with his dark features and prominent
nose, though he was a Maronite Christian of Lebanese origin
(born Amos Muzyad Yaqoob Kairouz) and thus the first gentile
to play this quintessentially Jewish role. His character is called
Jerry Golding, a less ethnically craggy name than Jakie Rabinowitz, smooth enough so that he doesn't need to change it to
make it more publicly digestible in the way that Jakie did, and, for
that matter, the way thousands of real-life Jews did, Asa Yoelson
among them.

Jerry is first seen getting out of a taxi wearing an American army uniform. He's coming home from service in the Korean War, which has two meanings, not difficult to fathom. First, it's a throwback to *Abie's Irish Rose,* when the Jewish boy is depicted, not as the usual slope-shouldered stranger in a strange land but as a tall, handsome soldier coming home from purple-hearted service in World War I. Second, it reaffirms Jewish patriotism at a McCarthyite time when it was sometimes questioned, including in 1952, just a few years after the establishment of a Jewish national homeland in Israel. Jerry's father is Cantor Golding who, like Cantor Rabinowitz in the 1927 *The Jazz Singer,* comes from a long line of cantors, but in Golding's case not a line reaching into the Pale of Settlement but, like Temple Sinai itself, all the way to Philadelphia, 1790. It's as if the immigrant origins of the Jews has been replaced by an all-American ancestry, as if the shtetl, Yiddish, foreign accents, and foreign ways never existed.

There were of course Jews in colonial-era Philadelphia, German émigrés as well as Sephardic Jews who came from England and the Netherlands, to which they'd gone after their expulsion from Spain in 1492. In 1775, the Jewish population was about 300 people, about 1 percent of the total in British America. The first congregation wasn't Temple Sinai—but Mikveh Israel, dedicated in 1782 in the midst of the War of Independence. There doesn't appear to have been a Temple Sinai in Philadelphia, but there is one in Los Angeles where the synagogue scenes were filmed. Among the congregants at Mikveh Israel was Haym Salomon, the financier of the Continental Congress, born in Poland to a Sephardic family that emigrated to New York in 1775. Decades later, Philadelphia, like other major American cities, took in a portion of the great *Ostjuden* immigration. Still, the Goldings live not like the Rabinowitzes in a gloomy Lower East Side tenement, but in a richly appointed, wood-paneled home more appropriate, as one scholar has noted, for a college president than a synagogue cantor. The most conspicuous meaning of the remake in this sense is its reflection of Jewish prosperity, even if most Philadelphia Jews still did not live amid quite the soignée opulence enjoyed by the Goldings.

The director was Michael Curtiz, born in Budapest in 1886, who had become well-known in film circles in Europe. In 1926, Warner Bros. invited him to Hollywood, where over the next three decades he directed dozens of movies for the studio, most famously *Casablanca*. His *The Jazz Singer* is certainly not one of his great works. The Warners made it to mark the twenty-fifth anniversary of the Jolson original, but if the material spareness of the original helped to give it some of its authentic, emotional power, it's the very taken-for-granted sumptuousness of the 1952 copy that makes it feel ersatz and emotionally stripped. As the film historian Robert Carringer put it, "It is little more than an outer shell enclosing material whose fundamental terms are not in conflict but rather affluence and adjustment."

The remake reduces the father to blandness. His cantorial style is a bit like his home, decorative but innocuous, stripped of the quality of longing, the lacerating, tragic tone of the tradition of Yossele Rosenblatt. He wants his son to replace him as cantor of Temple Sinai, but his objections to Jerry's refusal to do that are more perfunctory than deeply felt. As for Jerry himself, he pursues his ambition, but he's foiled when the big-time producers hardly notice him, despite the efforts of his girlfriend, played by Peggy Lee, to get him attention. The highest he reaches is to sing in a radio commercial for soap powder. Defeated, chastened, he returns home and accepts his fate, to be the seventh in the long line of Golding cantors at Temple Sinai. His girlfriend leaves as a result. "I have no right to take this away from you," she says,

gesturing at the splendid decor. But Jerry can't get Broadway out
of his mind. "Help me remove from my heart this grand desire
that calls me away," he pleads to God, kneeling in front of the ark
in the synagogue.

The temptations have been reversed. In the Jolson original it's
the music of the ancestors, sung in concert by Josef Rosenblatt,
that haunts Jack Robin and draws him home from his modern life.
For Jerry Golding, it's popular tunes like "Living the Life I Love"
that tempt him away from the tradition. When he announces his
intention of not being a cantor after all, his father runs to the
same sanctuary where Jerry had made his unanswered prayer,
rips open the curtains to the ark, and in front of the holy Torah
says Kaddish, the prayer for the dead, over his son. But Cantor
Golding seems more troubled by embarrassment—because he'd
proudly announced to his synagogue board of directors that Jerry
would take his place—than by the fact that Jerry doesn't want to
be a cantor.

In any case, the prayer doesn't come off as serious, because
Cantor Golding is too moderate, colorless, clean-shaven a figure
to impart a genuine sense of emotional devastation. Despite himself, he can't help but keep track of Jerry, who in the meantime
has been reunited with his girlfriend and is working hard to make
it in show business, which he does with little explanation for his
sudden success. The night of a big Broadway opening, he gets a
call from Philadelphia. His father is at death's door. He is called
to come home right away. There's no agony here over a lost opportunity, no terrible decision—do I go home and destroy my career
or do I betray my family for the sake of my worldly ambition? He
just tells a stagehand to get his understudy ready and then leaves
for the train station.

When he gets back to the Philly mansion, it's not the son who
begs forgiveness but the father. "I had no right to be so posses-

sive of my son," Cantor Golding says, seemingly on his deathbed. "Now I want him back, the way he wants to be back." The lesson of the movie has nothing to do with the son's obligations to his father, and hence to his tribe, his ancestors, his tradition; the lesson is the father's obligation to the son to respect his autonomy, his separateness, his American freedom to break from his ancestors and from their traditions. Jerry does make a filial gesture. It's Yom Kippur eve, and he sings Kol Nidre in shul in place of his sick father. The camera, inverting the opening shots, pans upward to the synagogue dome, and then the scene fades to the happy ending. Jerry is on a theater stage and, in an echo of Jolson's "My Mammy," sings a lullaby in honor of his mother, who is in the audience, not alone, but with his father, who has miraculously recovered and is rapturous over his son's success.

"It is a well-dressed, well-mounted show and its principals' hearts are in the right place," the *New York Times* reviewer commented generously, "but it is nothing new or especially exciting." In the original, the son returned to the tradition believing he had left his career behind. In the 1952 version, the absence of conundrum that lurks behind the facade of Americanization robs the story of its dramatic power. We're left with the simple story of a young man who, after some struggle, makes it in America, just as millions of others did in the 1950s.

* * *

Seven years later a television version starring Jerry Lewis played on NBC. It's kind of a CliffsNotes version of the original, stripped down by necessity because of its one-hour playing time. It's different in one important respect from the Danny Thomas version. In the latter, blackface has been eliminated; in the former, Lewis, famous at the time as a slapstick comedian in partnership with the singer Dean Martin, adopts a kind of disguised blackface, a suggestion of blackface without actual blackface. It's clownface instead. The scene in the 1927 version in which Jolson stares at his blackface image in a mirror and thinks of his father in the synagogue has been changed so that now Lewis looks at himself with a red nose and a white painted face around exaggerated lips. Lewis, a political liberal, would never have appeared in blackface, which, in any case, had gone out of fashion by the late 1950s. But, as Vincent Brook, the UCLA film historian puts it, Lewis was "evoking if not mimicking, Jolson's blackface performance style." He "uncannily manages to conjoin the sacred and the theatrical and to convey . . . American Jews' irremediable difference."

The Lewis version, which was performed live in front of a studio audience, evokes and mimics the 1927 version in other ways as well, most importantly in the conflict between the cantor father and the popular entertainer son. There's the doting Jewish mother (played by Molly Picon, a onetime star of the Yiddish theater) eager to mediate between the two men in her life, and the shiksa girlfriend. Lewis pleads with the father by drawing a parallel between cantorial singing and stand-up comedy, echoing Raphaelson's parallel between the Jewish liturgy and jazz as forms of prayer. "What I've done takes ability, to create laughter," Lewis's character says. The father, played by Eduard Franz, reprising his 1952 role as the father/cantor, replies, "But who will be left to remember and recall the heartbreaks of our people if our young ones move away from their roots and their heritage?"

Good question. But while subsequent Jewish history provided at least a partial answer—namely that Jewish identity would survive and even flourish in America—the movie offers no resolution. As in the Danny Thomas version, the father and son reconcile, with the father coming to understand, "I don't have

the right to change you to my tradition." This scene takes place
with Lewis in clownface, which he wears when he visits his father
on his sickbed and also when, inevitably, he chants Kol Nidre in
his father's shul. The idea seems to have to do with the duality
of American-Jewish life, or perhaps it's a kind of you-can-have-
it-all reassurance; you can be Jewish, sing the holiest prayer in
the liturgy, the prayer of eternal Jewishness, and be anything else
you want to be at the same time, though to watch the Jerry Lewis
version today, the clownface just comes across as a snippet of slapstick. It's Rudolf the red-nosed cantor, as one commentator has
quipped. But in this version that's where things end, Bozo, having gotten his father's blessing to be Bozo, pleading with God
to forgive us our sins. There's no final "Mammy" act with mom
and dad watching happily in the audience. It was too inevitable
to bother with. Nobody would believe anymore that there was a
Hobson's choice to be made between being a cantor and being a
popular entertainer, any more than there was between being Jewish and being American.

By the time the Jerry Lewis version of *The Jazz Singer* came
along in 1959, the Jewish presence in entertainment was so nearly
hegemonic as to make any anguish over the matter seem contrived
and implausible—even if in real life Jews from deeply Orthodox
families did agonize over their secular choices. During the 1930s
and 1940s, Jewish characters and topics had faded away from both
stage and screen and they were absent entirely from early television. But after World War II, they came roaring back. Now Milton Berle (born Mendel Berlinger) was "Mr. Television," having
more or less taken over from Jolson as America's most famous
performer—his Tuesday night television show captured 97 percent of the television audience. To a great extent the "golden age
of television" was the Jewish age of television, as evidenced by the
prominence of Sid Caesar's *Your Show of Shows,* George Burns's

The George Burns and Gracie Allen Show, the Groucho Marx
quiz show, Jack Benny, Jerry Lewis himself, and others. Under
the circumstances, nobody would have supposed that there was
anything incompatible between show business and synagogue
business; by the late 1950s, it was established that in America you
can indeed have it all.

* * *

In the fall of 1972, CBS canceled its hit new show of that
year, *Bridget Loves Bernie,* when some rabbis protested against it
on the grounds that it depicted intermarriage in a favorable light.
The accusation was certainly factual. The twenty-four half-hour
episodes told the story of a handsome Jewish taxi driver and aspiring playwright, Bernie Steinberg, and an Irish Catholic teacher,
Bridget Fitzgerald, who enjoy a happy married life, batting away
the objections of their families like so many Ping-Pong balls. The
show, which was an updated version of *Abie's Irish Rose* of fifty
years earlier, was lighthearted, irresistibly adorable, and funny,
even as its trivialization of religious tradition and family continu-
ity was almost boundless. "This is the sort of thing that religious
Jews consider anathema," said one rabbi cited in the newspaper
articles about the protest. The program treats intermarriage "in
a cavalier, cute, condoning fashion, and deals with its inevitable
problems as though they're instantly, easily solvable."

   The actor who played Bernie, David Birney, was not Jewish. The actress Meredith Baxter, who played Bridget, was herself
twice divorced. After CBS canceled the show, the two married
each other, and then split up. The owner of CBS, William Paley,
the son of Jewish immigrants from Ukraine who had become rich
in the cigar business, was himself famously married to a non-
Jewish socialite. When he died in 1990, he was buried in an Epis-

copal cemetery. In other words, the real-life personnel of the show embodied its fictitious characters in their disregard of identity and tradition.

But in a way that was the rabbis' point in their protest. When, half a century earlier, the Cohen and Kelly movies were depicting Jewish boys marrying Catholic girls, the intermarriage rates were so low that the movies touched no collective nerve. But by the 1970s, some 40 percent of Jews were marrying non-Jews, which in its way showed the power of assimilation to threaten long-term Jewish survival, and this, not surprisingly, caused alarm among the rabbis.

In response to studies showing the high intermarriage rates, an intermarriage crisis conference convened in New York, where the phenomenon was called, with some panic-driven hyperbole, a "second Holocaust." Judaism had survived three thousand years of persecutions, forced conversions, pogroms, and the Holocaust, but would it survive American freedom? It was an urgent question.

Given this context, it's not surprising that when *The Jazz Singer* was remade yet again in 1980, eight years after *Bridget Loves Bernie* was canceled, the story now centered much less around the theme of generational conflict or tradition versus modernity as it did around the question of intermarriage. The slick, glittery new production starred the rock 'n' roll star Neil Diamond, who wrote three songs for the movie, all of which became hit singles. Diamond plays Jess Robin, born Rabinovitch, who leaves his job as a Hebrew school teacher to seek stardom in Hollywood. He's married to a mousy, sexless fellow Hebrew school teacher who comes to L.A., hates the tinselly non-Jewishness of it all, and slips away. They are divorced, after which Jess marries the shiksa love of his life, the talent agent he'd met who believed in him and who fosters his rock-star career. When Cantor Rabinovitch, played by a very sorrowful looking Laurence Olivier who speaks in a heavy

Yiddish accent (!), shows up at their beach cottage and learns that Jess has left his wife and married a shiksa, he announces, "I have no son," and, following the Jewish funeral rite, tears his clothes.

It's an "outmoded story," the *New York Times* critic said, and certainly by 1980 the elements of the story that are left over from the Jolson version are so tired and predictable as to have lost whatever emotive power was left after the other remakes. The Diamond version contained updating elements: The opening scene shows the Statue of Liberty while Diamond sings "Coming to America" and images of multicultural New York flash on the screen. Jess Robin's best friends are Black; when he's not giving Bar Mitzvah lessons in shul, he's singing with them in their band and shares their ambition to make it as musicians. Jess wears blackface because his Black musician friends insist that he black up so that a Black audience in a club they perform in will think he's Black and thus, presumably, authentic, and when an audience member notices the fakery, a brawl ensues. It's nonsense, but the blackface element seems to be in there as a kind of 1980s racial virtue signaling, perhaps a way to preempt a reaction to Jolson's use of blackface in the 1927 original. By the 1970s, it was more common in white liberal circles to have Black friends. During the one-year run of *Bridget Loves Bernie* eight years earlier, Bernie's best friend and the best man at their wedding is also Black, and a musician. There is no mother in the Neil Diamond version; she's died of what his father calls "terrorism," though whether that means at the hands of the Nazis or somebody else is not clear. In any case, she doesn't seem to be in Jess's thoughts.

But, as in all four versions of *The Jazz Singer,* there is the love interest—non-Jewish in three of the productions—who falls for the cantor's son and enables his non-cantorial career. And there is always the father who falls sick, the reconciliation between him and his son, who proceeds to sing Kol Nidre in place of the sick

father. In the Neil Diamond version, this is followed by a nation-
ally televised concert, with Jess's newly recovered father sitting
side by side with Jess's shiksa wife applauding in the audience.

Like the other versions, this one reflects a change in the collective conscience, both Jewish and gentile. Despite Laurence Olivier's chagrin at his son's divorce and remarriage, there's no longer
much in the way of conflict between an old way of life, which has
disappeared anyway, and a new one. The Jewish story of this final
iteration of *The Jazz Singer* has become a variation on the American dream story. Will Neil Diamond make it in California? The
movie in this sense is less in the spirit of the original Jolson version
and more in that of another classic movie remade four times since
its original production in 1937, *A Star Is Born,* about a sublimely
talented woman (Judy Garland and Barbra Streisand in the 1954
and 1976 versions, respectively) who surmounts various obstacles
to achieve stardom.

The four productions of *The Jazz Singer* reveal the transformation of the Jewish story, or the ascendance of one aspect of
that story over another, the generational conflict replaced by the
making-it drama. Still, the theme of Jewish generational conflict
persists as a theme in the popular culture. The year after the Neil
Diamond version, the movie of Chaim Potok's novel *The Chosen*
depicted the questing son of a Hasidic rabbi who wants to study
psychology at Columbia University. In 2000 came *Keeping the
Faith,* directed by Ben Stiller, a variation on the eternal triangle,
wherein a rabbi and a priest are in love with the same non-Jewish
woman, so that for each of them in their separate, religiously
grounded reason, the love is illicit and must be kept secret. More
recently still was the Netflix streaming series *Unorthodox,* the
story of an Orthodox woman in Brooklyn who escapes a soulless
marriage to go to Berlin of all places, where she falls for a German

man even as emissaries from the betrayed Brooklyn community try to force her to return to the fold.

But the most celebrated product of the theme of generational difference after *The Jazz Singer* was *Fiddler on the Roof,* one of the biggest hits of American theatrical history, a kind of apotheosis of the Jewish story beloved by Americans of all types, religions, and colors. Opening in 1964, it became the longest-running show to play on Broadway, until it was supplanted by *The Phantom of the Opera.* Even today, it remains among the productions most commonly produced in American high schools across the country. *Fiddler* in this sense recapitulated *The Jazz Singer* in its universal appeal. It did so also in its main theme. Like *The Jazz Singer,* it's a new-generation/old-generation comedy, but the focus shifts from a son to three daughters, each of whom makes a choice of love disapproved of by the father, the lovable Tevye. The father learns to live with two of these acts of defiance, but when the third daughter commits the ultimate desecration of the tradition by falling in love with a Russian boy, the father disowns her, seemingly irrevocably. But like *The Jazz Singer,* the mass culture version of the story sweetens its original harshness, in part by sentimentalizing the shtetl (critics like Irving Howe and Philip Roth called it shtetl kitsch), endowing it most of all with beautiful music and song. *Fiddler* in this sense reproduces the scenes of cantorial singing in *The Jazz Singer* when, for the first time, non-Jews were introduced to the haunting loveliness of Yiddishkeit. In the case of *Fiddler,* it's the ethereal, minor-key loveliness of the Sabbath prayers. But the sweetening of the story comes also with some tampering with the harshness and bleakness of Sholem Aleichem's original. In the Yiddish stories about Tevye the Milkman, Tevye ends up alone after the pogrom, his family scattered, destroyed. *Fiddler,* by contrast, ends like *The Jazz Singer* did, with a kind of you-can-have-it-all-in-America hopefulness. Tevye hints at a willingness to forgive the wayward daughter once they're all settled into new lives in the New World.

This is the price the uncompromising original pays to popular entertainment. This is what happens when, in the words of one writer, there is an amalgam of "Yiddish source material with American razzmatazz." Generational conflict makes for a good story with universal appeal, but for Jewish fathers to be depicted as the symbolic murderers of their wayward children, that's a step too far.

The softening was in this sense necessary for the secularized Jewish culture to flourish in non-Jewish America, and flourish it did. *The Jazz Singer* wasn't the very beginning of the Judaization of the American culture, but it was the moment when that Judaization got mass approval and met with huge commercial success. Since then, the world of popular entertainment has been largely dominated by two groups, the Blacks and the Jews, each with their history of enslavement and persecution, each endowed with the outsider sensibility that gave their songs, plays, and movies their edge. The roots of one were in the Russian Pale of Settlement, the other in slavery and Jim Crow. It's not a coincidence. It's America.

Epilogue

They were all there for the funeral at Temple Israel on Hollywood Boulevard—Erle, the children, and the old Hillcrest Country Club fraternity, Cantor, Jessel, Winchell, Benny, and others while some twenty thousand onlookers gathered outside. The temple itself, dedicated only two years before, was the synagogue of the stars. The congregation was founded in 1926 and initially held services in a former church on Ivar Street before moving to its new building on Hollywood Boulevard in 1948. Later, it was where Eddie Fisher sang Kol Nidre, Elizabeth Taylor converted to Judaism, Bob Dylan attended a Passover seder, and Martin Luther King, Jr., spoke in 1965. It's not clear whether Jolson ever attended services or, indeed, ever set foot in the building when he was alive, but he always knew he was a Jew and never wished to be something else. And now he lay in state in a blue suit and a tallis while his fellow vaudevillians delivered eulogies, attesting to the greatness of the man they called "the king."

"Jolie brought more joy to more people than any other man alive," Eddie Cantor intoned. Walter Winchell: "The Jolson story epitomizes the American story in the grand tradition." George Jessel, America's toastmaster, plunged directly to the heart of the matter, attributing to Jolson nothing less than a grand rejuvenation of the Jews.

For in 1910, the Jewish people who emigrated to America
were a sad lot. . . . Men of thirty-five seemed to take on
the attitude of their fathers and grandfathers. They walked
with stooped shoulders. When they sang, they sang with
lament in their hearts and their voices, as if they were
pleading for help from above. . . .

And the actors, even the great ones, came on the stage
also playing characters like their fathers . . . monologists
with beards and shabby clothing telling humorous stories
that had a tear behind them. Likewise did this happen in
legitimate theater . . . in plays bewailing the misfortunes
that had happened to the Jews.

Then there came on the scene a young man vibrantly
pulsating with life and courage, who marched on the stage
head high, like a Roman emperor, with a gaiety that was
militant, uninhibited, and unafraid that told the world
that the Jew did not only have to sing in sorrow. . . .

Jolson is the happiest portrait that can ever be painted
about an American of the Jewish faith.

A year later, Jolson's remains were moved to a memorial built
by Erle at a reported cost of $76,000 at the Hillside Memorial
Park, where, since 1941, Hollywood Jews have gone for their final
resting place. It's an audacious edifice, some might say pretentious, the kind of thing Chinese emperors might have had done
for themselves if they were into neoclassical Greek architecture.
The architect was Paul R. Williams, who built homes for Frank
Sinatra, Lucille Ball, Lon Chaney, and numerous other celebrities,
and was the first Black architect to be inducted into the American
Institute of Architecture's College of Fellows. The main struc-
ture is a seventy-foot-tall, open-air marble rotunda held up by
six pillars. A mosaic beneath the dome shows Moses amid clouds

holding on to a shard of the tablets of the Ten Commandments. The inscription reads: "The man raised on high, the sweet singer of Israel." Beneath is a Pharaonic sarcophagus holding Jolson's remains. A fountain cascades downward toward Centinela Avenue, because Jolson told Erle he wanted to be buried near a waterfall. The traffic-choked San Diego Freeway looms beyond.

It's perhaps a suitable monument for the world's greatest entertainer. When Jessel spoke of Jolson marking the end of the era of Jewish American sorrow and the beginning of a great American Jewish renaissance, he captured the historical meaning of the man and his life. Jolson, lying inside his Greco-Roman temple, heralded the greatest era of Jewish history since the destruction of the Second Temple by the Romans in 70 A.D.

That's a grand statement, but a true one. Jolson's life from Lithuanian shtetl to the Hillside Memorial Park illustrates the trajectory that Russian immigration in general took, if more modestly. Two conditions were necessary for Jolson and the Jews to arrive at their destination: talent and freedom. Jews like Jolson had the one; America gave them the other.

Acknowledgments

I've always felt from the beginning of my work on this book that it would be a kind of homecoming for me, a secular Jew who's written on many topics over the years but relatively rarely on Jewish ones. I should in that sense acknowledge my father, Herbert Bernstein, with whom, growing up in a small town in Connecticut, I used to listen to the scratchy 78 rpm recordings of Cantor Josef Rosenblatt. It was my father's example, his gentle prodding, and his storytelling skills (his Yiddish recitations of famous children's tales were always the highlight of our Passover seders) that informed my own Jewish identity. I have tried (though without the Yiddish storytelling) to be a similar kind of father to my son, Elias, to keep him linked to the chain of the generations. Whether I have succeeded in that, or will succeed, is now up to him, but I see my prodding of him, like my father's prodding of me, as a kind of duty gladly owed to my Pale of Settlement ancestors. I see my turn to a Jewish topic in similar terms. Like Al Jolson, Jews like us wander off, and then we come home, or, at least, many of us do. I am not a believer in the idea that our ancestors look down on us from on high, checking to see if we carry on their heritage. But fathers live on in their sons, as my father does in me, and as I hope to do in Elias, even as he will go his own way, as did I.

As usual, my friend and editor Jon Segal was an indispensable partner in this project, starting from the COVID-era phone con-

versation during which I first broached the idea. Literally within
minutes he had conveyed the notion to Altie Karper, the legendary editor in chief of Schocken Books, and literally within hours
I knew what my next book would be. I am grateful to them both,
to the indispensable Sarah Perrin, Muriel Jorgenson, Nicholas
Latimer, Isabel Ribeiro, and the others at Knopf and Schocken who
played a role. My thanks also go to Kathy Robbins, my intrepid
agent, not of years but of decades, who never wavers either in her
criticism or her praise, both of which were important in this book.
Catherine Talese did her usual great job finding the photographs
that adorn the text. I benefited also from my conversations with
Andy Bachman, my rabbi, and from the members of the study
group he leads, and of which I am lucky to be a member, not to
mention my Friday breakfast compatriots, Mark Federman, Gary
Shaffer, David Abramson, and Michael Whiteman. I'm grateful
to Carol Korn-Bursztyn and Alberto Bursztyn for their interest in
this project and their precious gift of old Jolson recordings. I've
had conversations with David Margolick, Kati Marton, Clémence
Boulouque, Vince Bielski, Edward Jay Epstein, David Denby,
Carlin Romano, and Jeremy Dauber that have been informative,
reassuring, and motivational. I'm grateful to Sandra Chiritescu
for her research into the Yiddish press and her deft translations.
My thanks also to the staff of the Columbia University archives
for their help with the Raphaelson papers, and to Sylvia Wang,
the archivist at the Shubert Archive in New York who unearthed
material, especially the Jolson–J.J. Shubert correspondence, that I
didn't even know existed.

Most books build on previous work, and *Only in America*
is by no means an exception. Among the books that were especially helpful to me were Herbert G. Goldman, *Jolson: The Legend
Comes to Life;* Neal Gabler, *An Empire of Their Own: How the
Jews Invented Hollywood;* Foster Hirsch, *The Boys from Syracuse:*

The Shuberts' Theatrical Empire; Harvey Erdman, *Staging the Jew: The Performance of an American Ethnicity, 1860–1920;* and Michael Alexander, *Jazz Age Jews.* Other books and articles are referenced in the Notes.

Finally, as always, there's Zhongmei, my wife, who comes from her own rich tradition, who loves Judaism, and who helps in more ways than she knows. She is always there with her love, support, and sometimes forbearance. I couldn't do a thing without her.

Notes

Preface

xi   "There was nobody as good as Jolson": George Burns, *Playboy* interview, June 1978.

xi   "To call him the biggest hunk": Cantor eulogy, available online at https://jolsonville.net/eulogies/by-eddie-cantor/.

1. The Risky Dreams of the Fathers

4   "gentle and tolerant folk": Harry Jolson, *Mistah Jolson* (Hollywood, Calif.: House-Warven, 1951), Kindle edition, location 271.

5   One of these sons was Asa's father: Harry Jolson, *Saturday Evening Post,* December 7, 1929.

5   "embodies the paradox of the Jewish artist": J. Hoberman, *Bridge of Light: Yiddish Film Between Two Worlds* (Philadelphia: Temple University Press, 1995), 258.

6   "with elaborate ceremony and great feasting": Jolson, *Saturday Evening Post.*

6   "he'll be a great cantor": Jolson, *Mistah,* location 48.

7   "through wide-open spaces": Jolson, *Mistah,* location 395.

7   "ragged kingdom": Irving Howe, *World of Our Fathers: The Journey of the East European Jews to America and the Life They Found and Made* (New York: Harcourt Brace Jovanovich, 1976), 8.

8   "was governed by the Law": Jolson, *Mistah,* location 154.

9   he chanted the traditional four questions: Jolson, *Mistah,* location 190.

9   "but the law is inexorable": Jolson, *Mistah,* location 119.

9   stored in straw for the summer: Jolson, *Mistah,* location 202.

10   "satisfied with a career": Jolson, *Mistah,* location 271.

12   "radically different from the one in which they lived": Howe, *World of Our Fathers*, 24.

13   First to go: Jolson, *Mistah*, location 283.

13   "Off you go to America": Jolson, *Mistah*, location 294.

15   "the magic word, 'Come!' ": Jolson, *Mistah*, location 318.

15   "after thrilling rides": Jolson, *Mistah*, location 348.

15   "a terrible ship": Pearl Sieben, *The Immortal Jolson: His Life and Times* (New York: Frederick Fell, 1962), Kindle edition, location 65.

2. The Fraught Triumphs of the Sons

16   The club was started: Hillcrest Country Club website: https://www.hcc-la.com/THE_CLUB/GENERAL_INFORMATION/HISTORY.

18   "with its dark and smelly houses": Irving Howe, *World of Our Fathers: The Journey of the East European Jews to America and the Life They Found and Made* (New York: Harcourt Brace Jovanovich, 1976), 96.

19   "I would stand in the narrow space": Anne Borden, "Sophie Tucker," in *The Shalvi/Hyman Encyclopedia of Jewish Women*, https://jwa.org/encyclopedia/article/tucker-sophie.

20   "We'd put hats down": George Burns, *Playboy* interview.

20   "We had to laugh": Eddie Cantor, *Take My Life*, with Jane Kesner Ardmore (Garden City, N.Y.: Doubleday, 1957), 13.

21   when the Yoelsons' ship arrived: Herbert G. Goldman, *Jolson: The Legend Comes to Life* (New York: Oxford University Press, 1988), 12.

22   first experienced American life: Samuel J. Rosenberg, "4½ St. SW: It's Full of Memories," *The Washington Post*, February 7, 1985, https://www.ostns.org/history.

22   shops at street level and living quarters upstairs: https://www.washingtonpost.com/archive/local/1985/02/07/4-12-st-sw-its-full-of-memories/e1781367-4e4f-4722-b470-4b2511a6dab3/.

23   "This is Harry and my name is Al": Pearl Sieben, *The Immortal Jolson: His Life and Times* (New York: Frederick Fell, 1962), Kindle edition, location 114.

23   "the spirit of freedom and unrest": Harry Jolson, *Mistah Jolson* (Hollywood, Calif.: House-Warven, 1951), Kindle edition, location 390.

23   "crazy old buildings": Jacob Riis, *How the Other Half Lives: Studies Among the Tenements of New York* (New York: Hill and Wang, 1957), 10.

23   "enslaved [the Jews] in bondage": Riis, *How the Other Half Lives*, 78.

24   three times a day: Jolson, *Mistah*, location 404.

3. Street Singers

25   That's where Harry and Al went to sing: Harry Jolson, *Mistah Jolson* (Hollywood, Calif.: House-Warven, 1951), Kindle edition, location 423.

26   knife throwers, and acrobats: Pearl Sieben, *The Immortal Jolson: His Life and Times* (New York: Frederick Fell, 1962), Kindle edition, location 144.

27   "Waaaaatamelons / Red to the rind": Sieben, *The Immortal Jolson*, location 434.

28   a $10 gold coin: Sieben, *The Immortal Jolson*, location 500.

28   "the rough young savages": Jacob Riis, *How the Other Half Lives: Studies Among the Tenements of New York* (New York: Hill and Wang, 1957), 136.

29   "out through the swinging doors": Jolson, *Mistah Jolson*, location 571.

30   "a messenger of the congregation": Quoted in J. Hoberman, *Bridge of Light: Yiddish Film Between Two Worlds* (Philadelphia: Temple University Press, 1995), 257–58.

31   half of the people working in entertainment: Harley Erdman, *Staging the Jew: The Performance of an American Ethnicity, 1860–1920* (New Brunswick, N.J.: Rutgers University Press, 1997), 96.

31   "strangers to soap and water": Irving Howe, *World of Our Fathers: The Journey of the East European Jews to America and the Life They Found and Made* (New York: Harcourt Brace Jovanovich, 1976), 395–96.

31   "The journalism of those years": Howe, *World of Our Fathers*.

32   the Theatrical Syndicate: Erdman, *Staging the Jew*, 93–94.

32   the Shubert Organization: Foster Hirsch, *The Boys from Syracuse: The Shuberts' Theatrical Empire* (Carbondale: Southern Illinois University Press, 1998), 4–6.

32   William Morris, Vaudeville Agent: Frank Rose, *The Agency: William Morris and the Hidden History of Show Business* (New York: HarperBusiness, 1995), 2–7.

32   the lure of "the theater trade": *Variety*, December 22, 1905.

33   gave his consent: Herbert G. Goldman, *Jolson: The Legend Comes to Life* (New York: Oxford University Press, 1988), 25.

34   "a peculiar dread of loneliness": Goldman, *Jolson*, 27.

34   a stout Irishman: Goldman, *Jolson*, 27.

34   "One time I hit a jackass": Jolson, *Mistah*, location 765.

35   "a grotesque figure": Daniel Appleby, "Hebrew Acts in British Music Halls: The Career of Julian Rose," *Jewish Historical Studies* 52, no. 1 (2020): 167–96.

35   "Jewish comedians were all the rage": Cited in Appleby, "Hebrew
      Acts in British Music Halls."

35   the most famous of them was Julian Rose: Appleby, "Hebrew Acts in
      British Music Halls."

36   "Oy, vey I gedt troubles": Cited in Appleby, "Hebrew Acts in British
      Music Halls."

37   (burned down that morning): Jolson, *Mistah,* location 924.

37   "Finally the solution came": *Washington Herald,* November 16, 1928,
      quoted in Charles Musser, "Why Did Negroes Love Al Jolson and
      The Jazz Singer: Melodrama, Blackface, and Cosmopolitan The-
      atrical Culture," *Film History: An International Journal,* 23, no. 2
      (2011): 207.

38   "The nervous, monotoned, self-conscious kid": Goldman, *Jolson,* 36.

4. A POWER BEYOND HIMSELF

39   "months of the bitterest disappointment": Quoted in Michael Alex-
      ander, *Jazz Age Jews* (Princeton, N.J.: Princeton University Press,
      2001), 138.

39   "the aroma of beans and coffee": Harry Akst, "The Jolson Nobody
      Knew," *Cosmopolitan* 30 (February 1951): 106–7.

40   "Everything he touches": Quoted in Herbert G. Goldman, *Jolson:
      The Legend Comes to Life* (New York: Oxford University Press,
      1988), 87.

40   "a laugh producer of the first class": *Oakland Tribune* (CA), Octo-
      ber 13, 1906.

40   "as they've never been entertained before": *Reading Times* (PA),
      October 30, 1917.

41   "wowed by a blackface singer": Frank Rose, *The Agency: William
      Morris and the Hidden History of Show Business* (New York: Harper-
      Business, 1995), 24.

42   "split open the conventions": Irving Howe, *World of Our Fathers: The
      Journey of the East European Jews to America and the Life They Found
      and Made* (New York: Harcourt Brace Jovanovich, 1976), 566.

42   "a genuine emotional effect": Gilbert Seldes, *The Seven Lively Arts*
      (reprint, Good Press, 2022. Originally published by Harper and
      Brothers in 1924), 156.

43   they "bring something to America": Seldes, *The Seven Lively Arts,*
      160.

44   "applause and laughter": *The Butte Daily Post,* June 25, 2006.

45   "very pronounced Scandinavian features": Goldman, *Jolson,* 43.

45   "until he had exhausted his repertoire": *Minneapolis Star Tribune*, May 7, 2007.

45   "the greatest monologist in the business": *El Paso Star Times*, March 6, 1907.

45   Jolson laid him out with a punch: Goldman, *Jolson*, 51.

46   "one that was the equal of Al Jolson": *Oakland Star Tribune*, October 10, 2007.

46   "His stories are new": *Knoxville Sentinel*, March 2, 1908.

46   to take the Little Rock example: *Arkansas Democrat*, April 9, 1908.

47   "Why should I save money?": Harry Jolson, *Mistah Jolson* (Hollywood, Calif.: House-Warven, 1951), Kindle edition, location 1160.

47   "I always thought [Al] was a little crazy": Jolson, *Mistah*.

48   "If you want to talk": Pearl Sieben, *The Immortal Jolson: His Life and Times* (New York: Frederick Fell, 1962), Kindle edition, location 680.

48   didn't come back until dawn: Sieben, *The Immortal Jolson*, location 717.

49   "a riot of appreciation": Goldman, *Jolson*, 56.

49   "If those three dollar seats": Goldman, *Jolson*, 90.

49   "Let me say hello": *Bombo* script, Shubert Archive.

49   "Jolson and all his kind": *The American Magazine* 69 (November–April 1910–11).

50   "there will be bigger opportunities": Sieben, *The Immortal Jolson*, location 751.

50   "roughneck sort of egalitarianism": Howe, *World of Our Fathers*, 557.

51   "a coarse hunger for success": Howe, *World of Our Fathers*, 557.

52   where he distributed programs to patrons: Foster Hirsch, *The Boys from Syracuse: The Shuberts' Theatrical Empire* (Carbondale: Southern Illinois University Press, 1998), 9–17.

53   a forty-year rental: Hirsch, *The Boys from Syracuse*, 81.

54   "a very flashy toy": *The New York Times*, March 21, 1911.

54   "Lots of brave folks": Sieben, *The Immortal Jolson*, location 777.

55   "Basically, J.J. would present": Hirsch, *The Boys from Syracuse*, 85.

55   a five-year contract: Goldman, *Jolson*, 74.

56   "the scalawag servant": Seldes, *The Seven Lively Arts*, 160.

56   "shares private jokes": Goldman, *Jolson*, 69.

57   "Jolson now had all the trappings": Goldman, *Jolson*, 95.

57   15 to 25 percent . . . of gross receipts: Goldman, *Jolson*, 95.

58   "He sang in California": Burns, *Playboy* interview.

58   "a duck hitting water": Quoted in Goldman, *Jolson*, 81.

59   "They seemed very much alike": Samson Raphaelson, oral history interview, Columbia University Libraries, 1959.

59   "To have heard Al Jolson sing": Seldes, *The Seven Lively Arts*, 157.
59   "he sang and talked": *The New York Times*, March 22, 1926.
60   "Jolson was unobtainable": Raphaelson, oral history.

5. The Good Story

62   "all I knew were Jewish kids": Samson Raphaelson, oral history inter-
      view, Columbia University Libraries, 1959.
63   "I thought it would have universal appeal": Raphaelson, oral history.
66   "I shall never forget the first five minutes": Raphaelson, oral history.
68   "Yiddish folk tunes and black melodies": Irving Howe, *World of Our
      Fathers: The Journey of the East European Jews to America and the
      Life They Found and Made* (New York: Harcourt Brace Jovanovich,
      1976), 563.
68   "Put Yiddish and black together": Cited in Howe, *World of Our
      Fathers*, 563.
68   "the sobbing crack in his voice": Saul Jay Singer, "Caruso's Favorite
      Chazzan," *The Jewish Press*, December 1, 2021.
68   "I decided to put it in a story": Pearl Sieben, *The Immortal Jolson:
      His Life and Times* (New York: Frederick Fell, 1962), Kindle edition,
      location 1383.
69   "You didn't come to the show": Sieben, *The Immortal Jolson: His Life
      and Times,* location 895–908; Herbert G. Goldman, *Jolson: The Leg-
      end Comes to Life* (New York: Oxford University Press, 1988), 86.
      The verbatim quotes in the Sieben account, which Sieben probably
      got from Jolson, are somewhat longer than in the Goldman version,
      which seems to have trimmed them, but both end with Cantor Yoel-
      son telling his son, "I was singing for God."
71   "to fuse these people who come to us": John Higham, *Strangers in
      the Land: Patterns of American Nativism, 1860–1925* (New Brunswick:
      Rutgers University Press, revised ed., 2002), 238–39.
71   the Ford English School: Higham, *Strangers,* 247–48.

6. Different and the Same

73   "both rare and touching": William Saroyan, Foreword to George
      Jessel, *So Help Me: The Autobiography of George Jessel* (New York:
      Random House, 1943), reprint by Kessinger's Legacy Reprints (The
      World Publishing Company).
73   "Jessel held court": George Burns, *Playboy* interview.

73   "they all *listen* to Georgie": Eddie Cantor, *Take My Life,* with Jane
      Kesner Ardmore (Garden City, N.Y.: Doubleday, 1957), 84.

73   "toastmaster at his own *briss*": "The Friars Club Roast Georgie Jessel
      1948," https://www.youtube.com/watch?v=NUdl6bofqTA.

74   "If it was not for their divorce": *Daily News* (New York), July 2, 1926.

74   "I ran back to tell Jessel": Burns, *Playboy* interview.

75   "the heart throb of 116th Street": George Jessel, *The World I Lived In*
      (Chicago: Henry Regnery, 1975), 6.

75   They "jumped from the Beacon Theater": Jessel, *The World I Lived
      In,* 21.

76   "Prince Al tore his heart out": Jessel, *The World I Lived In,* 39.

76   "Hello mother": "George Jessel and Molly Picon Classic Jewish
      Comedy 1980," YouTube, https://www.youtube.com/watch?v=ZBa
      Onf5bKGc.

77   "as a great dramatic actor": Samson Raphaelson, oral history inter-
      view, Columbia University Libraries, 1959.

78   "He was there with Mary Lewis": Raphaelson, oral history.

78   "Like most young authors": Jessel, *The World I Lived In,* 57.

78   "this agonizing, aspiring kid": Raphaelson, oral history.

79   "It killed me": Raphaelson, oral history.

80   "One of the most powerful dramas": *Wisconsin State Journal,* Octo-
      ber 26, 1926.

80   "great dramatic triumph": *The Lathrop Optimist* (Kansas City, MO),
      December 30, 1926.

80   "orthodoxy whose pull and tug": *Chicago Tribune,* October 5, 1926.

80   "It is a near and yet far cry": *Daily News* (New York), September 16,
      1925.

81   "a thousand ministers": *The New York Times,* February 1, 1926.

81   "sermons in every city we played": Jessel, *The World I Lived In,* 58.

81   "the deepest emotions and highest inspirations": *The Modern View*
      (St. Louis), March 11, 1926.

81   "the traditions of the Hebrews in a serious vein": *The Wisconsin Jew-
      ish Chronicle,* December 24, 1926.

82   "The mother pleads": *The Modern View* (St. Louis), March 11, 1926.

83   "the Jew came to be noticed": Harley Erdman, *Staging the Jew: The
      Performance of an American Ethnicity, 1860–1920* (New Brunswick,
      N.J.: Rutgers University Press, 1997), 8.

83   "a regular feature in vaudeville": Erdman, *Staging the Jew,* 102.

83   fast-talking Jew or the world-weary, pathetic Jew: Erdman, *Staging
      the Jew,* 102.

83   "Well, I guess Abe's lucky, now he's married": Erdman, *Staging the Jew*, 165.

84   "He carries his exaggeration": *The New York Times*, May 6, 1894.

84   "'Solomon,' 'Levi,' or 'Moses'": Erdman, *Staging the Jew*, 84.

85   "always faithful to his roots": Erdman, *Staging the Jew*, 109.

86   "generous, sympathetic, and far-seeing": *The New York Times*, September 14, 1920.

87   "for performers to parody": Erdman, *Staging the Jew*, 150. Erdman cites Paul Antoine Distler, "The Rise and Fall of the Racial Comics in American Vaudeville," PhD dissertation, Tulane University, 1963, 188.

88   "about as low": Cited in *The New York Times*, May 11, 2022.

90   "a dignified fourth cousin": *The New York Times*, November 10, 1926.

7. From Lithuania to "Alabammy"

92   "I don't think you are treating me": Jolson to J.J. Shubert, May 27, 1912, Shubert Archive.

94   "they could never deny": Irving Saposnik, "Jolson, Judy, and Jewish Memory," *Judaism: A Quarterly Journal of Jewish Life and Thought*, 50, no. 4 (2001): 411.

95   where his mother's grave was: Pearl Sieben, *The Immortal Jolson: His Life and Times* (New York: Frederick Fell, 1962), Kindle edition, location 933.

96   "Many a night I saw him in the wings": Harry Akst, "The Jolson Nobody Knew," *Cosmopolitan* 30 (February 1951), 106.

96   "There was no conversation": Samson Raphaelson, oral history interview, Columbia University Libraries, 1959.

96   Stagehands knew to keep the water running: Herbert G. Goldman, *Jolson: The Legend Comes to Life* (New York: Oxford University Press, 1988), 95.

97   "Every performance varies": J.J. Shubert to Jolson, November 29, 1913.

98   "I know your condition": J.J. Shubert to Jolson, November 6, 1915.

98   "I know there are many thousands": Jolson to J.J. Shubert, March 17, 1917.

98   "You know that is impossible": J.J. Shubert to Jolson, March 19, 1917.

99   "Am trying to arrange": J.J. Shubert to Jolson, September 21, 1917.

99   113 different cities and towns: Goldman, *Jolson*, 240–42.

99   "Now JJ, there is no use": Jolson to J.J. Shubert, October 12, 1917.

100   He turned it down: *Variety*, April 7, 1926.

101   giving her a black eye: Goldman, *Jolson,* 99.

101   "He had virtually no 'love affairs' ": Goldman, *Jolson,* 168.

101   "There was always a girl with him": Goldman, *Jolson,* 168.

101   the occasional slap across the face: Goldman, *Jolson,* 137.

102   "It's all right to say": *Variety,* July 9, 1913.

105   "to actually identify with the struggles of real African Americans": Marc Aronson, "The Complicated Mix of Racism and Envy Behind Blackface," *The Washington Post,* July 22, 2018.

105   the only white man: Goldman, *Jolson,* 58.

106   "He was so sore about that story": Goldman, *Jolson,* 171.

107   "There's a lot of prejudice": Jolson to J.J. Shubert, October 4/5, 1911.

107   "he hotly presented his resignation": *Variety,* May 19, 1926.

108   Jolson sang a solo at her funeral: *The Pittsburgh Courier,* November 12, 1927, January 21, 1928.

108   something called the Al Jolson Silver Loving Cup: *The Pittsburgh Courier,* April 25, 1925.

108   "intellectual, cultured, and spiritual side of the Negro": *New York Amsterdam News,* December 30, 1925.

110   "an allegiance with the white Protestant majority": Nic Sammond, quoted in Seth Abromovitch, "Blackface and Hollywood: From Al Jolson to Judy Garland to Dave Chappelle," *The Hollywood Reporter,* February 12, 2019.

110   "appropriative identification": Michael Rogin, *Blackface, White Noise: Jewish Immigrants in the Hollywood Melting Pot* (Berkeley: University of California Press, 1998), 18.

110   "condensing into a single figure": *Rogin, Blackface, White Noise,* 5.

110   "the Jew becomes white": Matthew Frye Jacobson, *Whiteness of a Different Color: European Immigrants and the Alchemy of Race* (Cambridge: Harvard University Press, 1998), 105.

110   "I have had the dream": Hanif Abdurraqib, *A Little Devil in America: Notes in Praise of Black Performance* (New York: Random House, 2021), 77.

111   "Thus blacks were taught": Thomas Cripps, *Slow Fade to Black: The Negro in American Film, 1900–1942* (New York: Oxford University Press, 1977), 253.

113   "Al and the Jubilee singers": *The New York Times,* September 26, 1925.

113   spirituals, being revived and presented: Musser, "Why Did Negroes Love Al Jolson and *The Jazz Singer*?: Melodrama, Blackface and Cosmopolitan Theater Culture," *Film History: An International Journal,* 23, no. 2 (2011): 209–10.

113   "an entertaining melange": *Democrat and Chronicle* (Rochester, N.Y.), July 26, 1925.

114   "A Jew using blackface": Musser, "Why Did Negroes Love Al Jolson and *The Jazz Singer?*" 137.

114   Robeson, the celebrated performer: Jonathan D. Karp, "Performing Black-Jewish Symbiosis: The 'Hassidic Chant' of Paul Robeson," *American Jewish History*, vol. 91 no. 1, 2003, p. 54. Project MUSE, https://doi.org/10.1353/ajh.2004.0032.

115   "African-Americans gained the mainstream stage": Lynn Abbott and Doug Seroff, *Ragged but Right: Black Traveling Shows, "Coon Songs," and the Dark Pathway to Blues and Jazz* (Jackson: University Press of Mississippi, 2012), 12.

116   *As I caution all white dandies:* John Strausbaugh, *Black Like You: Blackface, Whiteface, Insult & Imitation in American Popular Culture* (New York: Jeremy P. Tarcher/Penguin, 2006), 78.

116   the main prototypes of American history: Strausbaugh, *Black Like You,* 26.

117   "various other brands of broadly played ethnic stereotypes": Strausbaugh, *Black Like You,* 131.

118   "the Negro is yet unrivaled": *New York Amsterdam News,* August 9, 1924.

118   "IMPOSTERS STEAL RACE MATERIAL": *The Pittsburgh Courier,* May 10, 1930.

118   "trying to talk southern": *New York Amsterdam News,* February 3, 1926.

118   "When you realize that Al Jolson": *The Chicago Defender,* November 6, 1920.

119   "as a Gothic horror tale": Cripps, *Slow Fade to Black,* 41.

119   "demanded censorship of racial slander": Cripps, *Slow Fade to Black,* 42.

119   "Undoubtedly one of the greatest": *New York Amsterdam News,* July 3, 1929.

8. WARNER BROS. TAKES A CHANCE

120   "The fact is we were barely breathing": Jack L. Warner, *My First Hundred Years in Hollywood: An Autobiography* (Kindle edition, Graymalkin Media, 2017), Chapter 9.

121   attenuated in the order of their birth: Neal Gabler, *An Empire of Their Own: How the Jews Invented Hollywood* (New York: Crown, 1988), 125.

121   wanted to get rid of it: Gabler, *An Empire of Their Own*, 124–25.
122   "rather a dim speck": Gabler, *An Empire of Their Own*, 131.
122   "Our new studio": Warner, *My First Hundred Years*, 93.
122   "we would have closed up the lot": Warner, *My First Hundred Years*, 113.
122   "I can hear your brother": *Daily News* (New York), August 22, 1926.
124   "the cinema abhorred silence": Scott Eyman, *The Speed of Sound: Hollywood and the Talkie Revolution, 1926–1930* (New York: Simon & Schuster, 1997), 25–26.
124   "the foremost employers of musicians": Eyman, *The Speed of Sound*, 26.
126   "If it can talk, it can sing": Eyman, *The Speed of Sound*, 70.
126   an exclusive license for the sound process: Gabler, *An Empire of Their Own*, 137.
126   eventually settling on Vitaphone: Warner, *My First Hundred Years*, 140.
126   Sam moved the whole operation: Warner, *My First Hundred Years*, 141.
127   "A marvelous device": *The New York Times*, October 7, 1926.
128   "Armageddon was at hand": Warner, *My First Hundred Years*, 142–43.
129   sailed to Europe: Herbert G. Goldman, *Jolson: The Legend Comes to Life* (New York: Oxford University Press, 1988), 129.
129   "rotten" in his screen test: *The New York Times*, September 20, 1926.
130   "the conquest of ubiquity": Paul Valéry, "The Conquest of Ubiquity," 1928, essay available online at: https://codepen.io/andyhullinger/full/BooKgB.

9. "A HIGHLY UNLIKELY PROSPECT FOR IMMORTALITY"

131   gone off to the gentiles: Ted Merwin, *In Their Own Image: New York Jews in Jazz Age Popular Culture* (New Brunswick, N.J.: Rutgers University Press, 2006), 65.
133   he took them to a kosher restaurant: George Jessel, *The World I Lived In* (Chicago: Henry Regnery, 1975), 17.
133   she "testified to the romanticization of the ghetto": Merwin, *In Their Own Image*, 46–47.
135   "I couldn't even get Jack or Darryl on the telephone": Jessel, *The World I Lived In*, 67.
136   Jolson quickly agreed: Jack L. Warner, *My First Hundred Years in Hollywood: An Autobiography* (Kindle edition, Graymalkin Media, 2017), 147.
136   "Jessel was a vaudeville comedian": Robert L. Carringer, ed., *The Jazz Singer* (Madison: University of Wisconsin Press, 1979), 17.

137   "familiar racial character comedy": *Motion Picture World,* September 10, 1927.

139   a perniciously progressive influence: Kevin Brownlow, *Behind the Mask of Innocence: Sex, Violence, Crime: Films of Social Conscience in the Silent Era* (New York: Alfred A. Knopf, 1990), xv–xxvi.

139   "is it any wonder": Brownlow, *Behind the Mask of Innocence,* 381.

140   "a very unusual choice": Neal Gabler, *An Empire of Their Own: How the Jews Invented Hollywood* (New York: Crown, 1988), 139.

140   "for the sake of racial tolerance": Gabler, *An Empire of Their Own,* 140.

141   "a highly personal dramatization": Gabler, *An Empire of Their Own,* 141.

142   "they all refused to use English": Brownlow, *Behind the Mask of Innocence,* 419.

143   scenes outside the Winter Garden: Pearl Sieben, *The Immortal Jolson: His Life and Times* (New York: Frederick Fell, 1962), Kindle edition, location 1462.

143   "an opportunity to do some strong dramatic acting": *Motion Picture World,* September 24, 1927.

10. "The cry of my race"

151   "The cantor of the past": David Olivestone, "Standing Room Only: The Remarkable Career of Cantor Yossele Rosenblatt," *Jewish Action,* Fall 2003, https://d1ydyrae2d92wn.cloudfront.net/publications/ja/5764/5764fall/YOSSELER.PDF.

154   "That's a very strange thing": Michael Alexander, lecture at USC, May 7, 2008, https://www.youtube.com/watch?v=OdQNENWj1Pw.

157   "eternal Jewishness": J. Hoberman, "My Songs Mean as Much to My Audience as Yours Do to Your Congregation," *London Review of Books* 18, no. 14 (July 1996).

11. It Played in Paducah

159   "Few men": *The New York Times,* October 7, 1927.

160   "the unusual scenes": *Evening Star* (Washington, D.C.), February 6, 1928.

160   "thousands found their anticipation": *The Times* (Shreveport, La.), September 1, 1928.

160   "by far one of the best": *The Paducah Sun-Democrat* (KY), April 30, 1928.

160   "This story is intensely appealing": *The Richmond (Ind.) Item,* October 7, 1928.

161   "the innermost researches": *The Shamekin (Pa.) News Dispatch,* May 31, 1928.

161   A survey of 1927: The Jacob Rader Marcus Center of the American Jewish Archives, "Timeline in American Jewish History," https://www.americanjewisharchives.org/educational-resources/timeline/.

161   "at home in America": Deborah Dash Moore, cited in Jonathan D. Sarna, "That Other Time Jews Were Hated in America," *The Forward,* November 15, 2016.

161   Shreveport . . . well-integrated Jewish population: "Shreveport, Louisiana," *Encyclopedia of Southern Jewish Communities—Shreveport, Louisiana,* https://www.isjl.org/louisiana-shreveport-encyclopedia .html.

162   "Seldom in the Butte theatrical history": *The Anaconda Standard* (Butte, Mont.), May 21, 1928. Butte Jews, Jewish Museum of the American West, http://www.jmaw.org/jacobs-jewish-butte/.

163   "the stories of all ethnic groups": John Emeigh, "Historic Butte Synagogue Being Converted into Cultural Center," KXLF Butte, rettps://www.kxlf.com/news/local-news/historic-butte-synagogue-being -converted-into-cultural-center.

163   Paducah, which had a Reform synagogue: "Temple Israel, Paducah, Kentucky," http://templeisraelky.com/.

164   "Is there any incongruity": *Morgen Journal,* cited in Michael Alexander, lecture at USC, May 7, 2008.

165   "Judaism somehow": Neal Gabler, *An Empire of Their Own: How the Jews Invented Hollywood* (New York: Crown, 1988), 144.

165   "one of the greatest pictures ever produced": *New York Amsterdam News,* May 2, 1928.

166   "many a tear and a laugh": *The Pittsburgh Courier,* June 16, 1928.

166   "Jew, Gentile, and Negro": *The Pittsburgh Courier,* June 30, 1928.

166   "Seen it? Heard it?": *The Washington Tribune,* April 13, 1928, cited in Musser, "Why Did Negroes Love Al Jolson and *The Jazz Singer,*" 206.

166   "Blackface and Jewish history": Irving Saposnik, "Jolson, Judy, and Jewish Memory," *Judaism: A Quarterly Journal of Jewish Life and Thought* 50, no. 4 (2001): 412.

167   "a terrific comedian": Samson Raphaelson, oral history interview, Columbia University Libraries, 1959.

168   "I was very superior about movies": Raphaelson, oral history.

168   "Money or no money": Jessel, *The World I Lived In,* 67.

168   "ended in the synagogue": *South Bend (Ind.) Tribune,* May 13, 1928.

169   "full of nobility": *The Sentinel* (Jewish weekly in Chicago), Febru-
       ary 17, 1928.

169   "The home life of a Jewish family": *The Sentinel* (Jewish weekly in
       Chicago), March 2, 1928.

169   "A photoplay of especial interest": *B'nai B'rith Messenger,* Decem-
       ber 16, 1927.

170   "the Slovak, the Italian, the Syrian, and the Jew": Madison Grant,
       The Passing of the Great Race, or the Racial Basis of European History
       (New York: Scribner, 1916), 5, 82.

170   "chauvinistic nationalism": Sarna, "That Other Time Jews Were
       Hated in America."

171   "understanding of Jewishness": *Forverts,* October 11, 1927. Translated
       from the Yiddish by Sandra Chiritescu.

171   Rabbi Magnin wrote: *B'nai B'rith Messenger,* December 16, 1927.

172   Herman Lissauer: *B'nai B'rith Messenger,* January 20, 1928.

172   "to create a synthesis": Jewish Telegraph Agency, February 4, 1927.

                              12. STARS CROSSING

176   "There were two of them": *Los Angeles Times,* July 23, 1933.

176   she hit a Warner executive: Neal Gabler, *An Empire of Their
       Own: How the Jews Invented Hollywood* (New York: Crown, 1988),
       177.

176   to deter further fisticuffs: Pearl Sieben, *The Immortal Jolson: His Life
       and Times* (New York: Frederick Fell, 1962), Kindle edition, location
       1787.

176   "I just up and popped him": *Buffalo Evening News,* July 22, 1933.

176   "I didn't like the music": Herbert G. Goldman, *Jolson: The Legend
       Comes to Life* (New York: Oxford University Press, 1988), 186.

177   "cleverly and shrewdly pictured": *The New York Times,* Septem-
       ber 20, 1928.

177   one of the biggest stars in Hollywood: *Daily News* (New York),
       July 17, 1933.

178   "The word [of the impending marriage] was very quick": Jim Bishop,
       The Mark Hellinger Story: A Biography of Broadway and Hollywood
       (Whitefish, Mont.: Literary Licensing LLC, 2012), Kindle edition,
       Book 3.

179   Wherever the meeting took place: Neal Gabler, *Winchell: Gossip,
       Power, and the Culture of Celebrity* (New York: Alfred A. Knopf,
       1994), 177.

179   Costello wasn't opposed: Billy Grady, *The Irish Peacock: The Con-*

fessions of a Legendary Talent Agent (New Rochelle, N.Y.: Arlington House, 1972), 66.

180   "Nobody's going to hurt you": Bishop, *The Mark Hellinger Story,* 155–56; Herbert G. Goldman, *Jolson: The Legend Comes to Life* (New York: Oxford University Press, 1988), 162–63.

180   "lay off Ruby Keeler, or else": Akst, "The Jolson Nobody Knew," 35.

180   Winchell had written a script: Gabler, *Winchell,* 176.

181   "Keeler cried for days": *Oakland Tribune,* July 22, 1933.

181   Winchell had scolded Jolson: Goldman, *Jolson,* 215.

181   "Swell publicity for the picture I wrote": Goldman, *Jolson,* 215.

182   "Keeler is very much in love": *Daily News* (New York), July 17, 1933.

182   insisted that Keeler eat a fish dish: Goldman, *Jolson,* 183.

182   "Honey I need ya": Eddie Cantor, *Take My Life* (Garden City, N.Y.: Doubleday & Company. Inc., 1957), 90.

183   she found Jolson in perfectly good health: Goldman, *Jolson,* 186.

183   "good friends and competitors": Cantor, *Take My Life,* 88.

183   "These two great comedians": *San Francisco Examiner,* December 16, 1928.

183   "stealing his public": *San Francisco Examiner,* December 16, 1928.

183   "They messed everything up": *San Francisco Examiner,* December 16, 1928.

183   "with an expression of exaggerated longing": *San Francisco Examiner,* December 16, 1928.

185   "He's a little heavier": Cited in Goldman, *Jolson,* 251.

186   "The movies were growing up": Sieben, *The Immortal Jolson,* location 2025.

187   "He wasn't jealous": Sieben, *The Immortal Jolson,* location 1953.

187   "Since said marriage": *Los Angeles Times,* October 31, 1939.

187   "The romance is definitely over": *Los Angeles Times,* February 14, 1940.

13. The Final Decade

189   "the only field I know—amusement": Cited in Herbert G. Goldman, *Jolson: The Legend Comes to Life* (New York: Oxford University Press, 1988), 254.

190   he called the mothers, wives, and girlfriends: Goldman, *Jolson,* 257.

191   " 'What's the matter, Al?' ": Harry Akst, "The Jolson Nobody Knew," *Cosmopolitan* 30 (February 1951), 110.

191   the two were married: Goldman, *Jolson,* 266–73.

192   he looked in the mirror: Akst, "The Jolson Nobody Knew," 111.

192   "The Biography of a Voice": *The New York Times,* October 13, 1946.
192   "What happens on the screen": *The New York Times,* October 13, 1946.
194   "It becomes boring": *Los Angeles Times,* November 8, 1946.
195   "at least twice as good": *The New York Times,* August 18, 1949.
196   "the trip fitted in": Akst, "The Jolson Nobody Knew."
197   "Listen, son, I gotta sing": Akst, "The Jolson Nobody Knew."
198   it was " 'Rock-a-bye Your Baby' ": Akst, "The Jolson Nobody Knew."
198   "How could anybody do enough for them?": Akst, "The Jolson Nobody Knew."
199   "The mud and dust": Akst, "The Jolson Nobody Knew."
201   "Harry, I'm not going to last": Akst, "The Jolson Nobody Knew."
201   "Oh . . . oh . . . I'm going": Akst, "The Jolson Nobody Knew."

14. THE AFTERLIFE

205   where the synagogue scenes were filmed: Robert L. Carringer, ed., *The Jazz Singer* (Madison: University of Wisconsin Press, 1979), 30.
206   a college president: Carringer, *The Jazz Singer,* 30.
206   "It is little more than an outer shell": Carringer, *The Jazz Singer,* 31.
208   "It is a well-dressed, well-mounted show": *The New York Times,* January 14, 1953.
209   "evoking if not mimicking": Vincent Brook, "The Four *Jazz Singers:* Mapping the Jewish Assimilation Narrative," *Journal of Modern Jewish Studies* 10, no. 3 (2011): 401–20.
210   Rudolf the red-nosed cantor: Cited in Brook, "The Four *Jazz Singers.*"
211   "This is the sort of thing": *The New York Times,* February 7, 1973.
212   an intermarriage crisis conference: *The Forward,* May 12, 2021.
216   "American razzmatazz": Jenna Weissman Joselit, "Fiddler on the Roof Distorted Sholem Aleichem," *The New Republic,* June 7, 2014.

EPILOGUE

217   "Jolie brought more joy": quotes from other funeral eulogies online at: https://jolsonville.net/eulogies/by-george-jessel/.

Index

Abbott, Lynn, 115
Abdurraqib, Hanif, 110–111
Abie's Irish Rose (Nichols), 88–90, 139,
  205, 211
Academy Awards, 123
Adorno, Theodor, 19
Akst, Harry, 39–40, 96, 180, 190–191,
  192, 196–199, 200–201
Al Jolson Silver Loving Cup, 108, 112
Aleichem, Sholem, 30–31, 215
Alexander, Michael, 154
Alexander II, Czar, 4, 12
Alexander III, Czar, 4, 12
"Alexander's Ragtime Band," 65
Allen, Woody, 164, 173
Allison, Bessie, 117–118
American Horse Exchange, 50, 52
American Institute of Architecture's
  College of Fellows, 218
American Magazine, The, 49–50
Anaconda Standard (Butte, Montana),
  162
Anderson, Garland, 108
"Anniversary Song, The," 195
Anti-Defamation League of B'nai
  B'rith, 87, 103
antisemitism
  in America, xii, xiv–xv, 16, 18, 31–32
  awareness of, 169–170
  Gentlemen's Agreement and, 203
  lack of impact of, 161

pervasiveness of, 140
  in Russia, xiii, 3, 4
  stereotypes and, 87
Anti-Stage Ridicule Committee, 87
Appearances, 108–109
"April Showers," 197, 199
Aqueduct Racetrack, 129
Armstrong, Louis, 42, 58, 104, 145
Arnold, Matthew, 65
Arnshteyn, Mark, 5
Ashamed of Parents, 122
Astaire, Fred, 186
Auctioneer, The (Warfield), 85

Babe Comes Home, 122
Baker, Josephine, 106
Barrymore, John, 127, 138, 139–140,
  159
Barrymore, Lionel, 138
Baxter, Meredith, 211
Beacon Theater, 75
Beeler, Aggie, 33–34
Behler, Agnes, 33–34
Belasco, David, 108–109
Bell Labs, 123, 125
Bell Telephone, 123
Bell Theatre, 46
Belle Paree, La, 53–54, 55
Benchley, Robert, 88
Benny, Jack, 16, 164, 185, 211, 217
Berkeley, Busby, 132

Berle, Milton, 32, 59, 164, 210
Berlin, Irving
  "Alexander's Ragtime Band"
    and, 65
  "Blue Skies" and, 152
  Cantor on, 21
  Jolson's later career and, 186
  legacy of, 57
  plantation South and, 93, 117
  Raphaelson and, 145, 146
  Tin Pan Alley and, 36, 41
Bernhardt, Sarah, xiii
Bernstein, Herschel, xiii–xiv
Bernstein, Louis, 48
Besserer, Eugenie, 152
Big Boy, 56–57, 100, 111–114, 136, 183,
    184
Bijou Theatre, 33
Biltmore country club, 107
"Bird in a Gilded Cage," 48
Birnbaum, Nathan (George Burns),
    17, 20
Birney, David, 211
Birth of a Nation, 119, 128
Bishop, Jim, 178, 179
Black entertainers, 103–106, 107–108,
    115
Black Magic, 129
blackface
  in Big Boy, 111–114
  clownface as replacement for, 209,
    210
  decline in use of, 186
  Dockstader and, 47
  Gus (character) and, 56, 66, 111–112,
    113–115, 134
  in The Jazz Singer, 94, 143, 144, 153,
    157, 165, 166
  in The Jolson Story, 192
  Jolson's early use of, 37–38, 55–56
  overview of use of, 109–115, 116–118
  pervasiveness of Jolson's use of, 67,
    102

  in A Plantation Act, 128
  in Robinson Crusoe, Jr., 66
  in The Singing Fool, 177
  version of The Jazz Singer from 1980
    and, 213
  in Wonder Bar, 132
  in Ziegfeld Follies, 104
Blake, Eubie, 42, 105–106
"Blue Skies," 152
Blum, Léon, xiii
B'nai B'rith, 161, 170
B'nai B'rith Messenger, 169, 172
Bogart, Humphrey, 186
Bombo, 49, 56, 95, 100, 105, 114–115, 132
Borach, Fania, 155
Boston Post, 185–186
Bow, Clara, 138
Boyer, Charles, 186
Brace, Charles L., 28
Brandeis, Louis, 50–51, 170
Brice, Fanny, 19–20, 42–43, 59, 75,
    104, 116, 133
Bridget Loves Bernie, 211, 212
Brighton Beach Memoirs, 173
Broadway, 50–51
Broadway Thru a Keyhole, 180–182
Brook, Vincent, 209
Brooks, Louise, 138
Brooks, Mel, 173
Brooks, Shelton, 104–105
Brown, Clare, xiv
Brownlow, Kevin, 138–139, 142
Buffalo Bill, Jr., 137
Burns, George, xi, 16–17, 20, 32, 58,
    73, 74, 210–211
Bush Leaguer, The, 138
Byers, Peewee, 77–78

Cabaret, 185
Caesar, Irving, 41, 117, 146, 186
Caesar, Sid, 164, 173, 210
Cagney, James, 182
Cahan, Abraham, 18

Cantor, Asa, 6
Cantor, Charlie, 13
Cantor, Eddie
  background of, 20
  ethnic caricature and, 116, 118
  at Hillcrest Country Club, 16, 73,
    217
  The Jazz Singer and, 135
  Jessel and, 73, 75
  Jolson and, xi–xii, 59, 133
  Keeler and, 182–184
  marriage of, 44
  name of, 17
Cantor, Naomi (mother), 6, 13–15,
  22, 24
"Cantor on the Sabbath, A"
  ("Khasndl Oyf Shabbos"), 132,
  134, 193
Carringer, Robert, 206
Caruso, Enrico, 58, 150
Casablanca, 206
Celeste, Grace, 34
Century Theatre, 134
Chaney, Lon, 138
Chaplin, Charlie, 32, 35, 55, 75, 124,
  130
Chaplin, Syd, 138
Chicago Defender, The, 117, 118
Chicago Tribune, 80
Children's Aid Society, 28
Chopin, Frédéric, 191
Chosen, The (Potok), 214
Circle, The (Maugham), 61
Clancy's Kosher Wedding, 137
Clef Club, 108, 112
Cocoanut Grove, 176
Cohan, George M., 177, 191
Cohens and Kellys in Paris, The, 88
Cohens and Kellys in Trouble, The, 88
Cohens and Kellys series, 137, 161, 212
Cohn, Alfred A., 137, 155, 156–157, 168
Cohn, Harry, 96
College, 138

Columbia Pictures, 191–192, 195
Columbia Theatre (Paducah,
  Kentucky), 160
"Coming to America," 213
Communism, 203–204
condenser microphones, 125
conquest of ubiquity, 130
conscription, 4–5
Cooper, Gary, 186
Costello, Johnny "Irish," 178–179,
  181–182
Cotton Club, 105
Coughlin, Charles, 89, 203
Courtney, Florence, 74
Cripps, Thomas, 112, 119
Crosby, Bing, 185, 200
Crosland, Alan, 142, 143, 146
Cross, Will, 46
Crowther, Bosley, 192
culture industry, 19
Curtis, M. B., 84
Curtiz, Michael, 206

Dancing Around, 55, 69
"Day of Atonement" (Raphaelson),
  61–65, 69–72, 77–78, 134, 164.
  See also *Jazz Singer, The*
Dearborn Independent, The, xii, 140,
  170
Delmar, Ethel, 101
Delmonico's, 44
DeMille, Cecil B., 137, 138
Dempsey, Jack, 144
Desired Woman, The, 138
Deslys, Gaby, 55
Diamond, Jack "Legs," 179–180
Diamond, Neil, 212–214
Dickens, Charles, 83
Dillon, William, 49
"Dirty Hands, Dirty Face," 149
Disraeli, Benjamin, xiii
Dixie Duo, 106
Dockstader, Lew, 47, 49

Dog of the Regiment, A, 138, 143
Don Juan, 127–128, 139–140, 159
Donath, Ludwig, 193
Dooley, James Francis, 38
Dr. Wu, 138
Dreiser, Theodore, 184
Dumont, 46
Dylan, Bob, 217

Early, Stephen, 189
Eastman Annex, 191
Edison, Thomas, 124–125
education, 7, 20
Edwards, Gus, 75
Edwards, Lou, 75
Eichelbaum, Pearl Leah, 120–121
Einstein, Albert, 170
Eisenhower, Dwight, 190
El Paso Times, 45
Elman, Mischa, 127
emigration, 12–13
Endeavor Talent Agency, 32
Erdman, Harley, 82–83, 85
ethnic caricature, 35–36
Evening Star (Washington, D.C.), 160
Eversole, William, 33
Everybody's Magazine, 61, 134
Eyman, Scott, 124

Fairbanks, Douglas, 124, 138
Fiddler on the Roof, 4, 164, 173,
    215–216
Fields, W. C., 138
Fisher, Eddie, 217
Fletcher, J. S., 61
Flippen, Jay C., 118
Footlight Parade, 182
Ford, Henry, xii, 71, 140, 147, 170
Ford English School, 71
Fortune Hunter, The, 138
42nd Street, 182
Forverts, 18, 170–171
Foster, Stephen, 25, 93

Franz, Eduard, 209
Freud, Sigmund, xiii
Friars Club, 44, 73
Fried, Martin, 200–201
Fu Manchu, 138
Funny Girl, 19–20, 164

Gable, Clark, 186
Gabler, Neal, 121, 122, 140, 141, 165
Gaieties, 76, 77
Galbraith, Erle Chenault, 191, 196,
    199–200, 217, 218, 219
Garbo, Greta, 138
Garland, Judy, 214
Garrick Theatre, 169
Gentlemen's Agreement, 141, 203
George Burns and Gracie Allen Show,
    The, 17, 211
Gerry, Elbridge Thomas, 28
Gerry Society, 28, 29, 75
Gershwin, George, 36, 41, 57, 68, 93,
    117, 145, 191
Gish, Lillian, 138
"Go Down Moses," 111–112, 113–114
"Goin' to Heaven on a Mule," 132
Gold Diggers of 1933, 182
Goldberg, Isaac, 68
Goldman, Emma, 18
Goldman, Herbert G., 38, 45, 55–57,
    99, 101, 105, 135, 181
Goldman Sachs, 125–126
Goldwyn, Samuel, 16
Gone with the Wind, 193
Gordon, Bobby, 148
Gordon, Max, 77–78
Grady, Bill, 178
Grant, Madison, 170
Great Train Robbery, The, 121
Green, Joseph, 142
Greenberg, Hank, 170
Griffith, D. W., 119, 128–129
Gus (character), 56, 66, 111–112,
    113–115, 134

Hadassah, 161
Halevy, Jacques Fromental, 150
Hall, Mordaunt, 127, 177
Hallelujah, I'm a Bum, 185
Hammerstein's Victoria Theatre,
  47–48
Harding, Warren G., 170
Harlem/Harlem Renaissance, 103,
  105, 108, 113, 165
Harris Theater, 80
Harry Von Tilzer Music Publishing
  Company, 48–49
Hartford Courant, 106
Hasidism, 11
Haskalah, 10–11, 12
"Heat Wave," 105
"Hebrew and the Cadet, The," 34–35,
  37, 133
Hebrew Immigrant Aid Society, 161
Hecht, Ben, 132
Hellinger, Mark, 179–180
"Hello Mother," 76
Hesselman, Meyer, 5
Hillcrest Country Club, 16, 44, 73, 217
Hills of Kentucky, 138
Hillside Memorial Park, 218
"Hip Hip Hypnotize Me," 48, 49
Hirsch, Foster, 55
His People, 137
Hitchcock, Alfred, 62, 137
Hoberman, J., 5–6, 157
Hoffman, Aaron, 86
Hold On to Your Hats, 185–186, 188
Hollywood American Legion
  Stadium, 175–176, 181
Hollywood Express, The, 55
Holocaust, 203
Holtz, Lou, 59
Hope, Bob, 73, 185, 190
Houdini, Harry, 42, 57
Howe, Irving, 7, 12, 32, 42, 50, 51, 68,
  163, 215
"Humoresque" (Dvořák), 127

"I Want a Girl Just Like the Girl
  Who Married Dear Old Dad,"
  48–49
immigration, xii, 12–13, 170
Imperial Theatre, 74
Imperial Trio, 75
intermarriage, 87–88, 211–212
International Al Jolson Society, 58
intertitles, 124, 127, 158

Jackson, Willie, 165
Jacobs, Henry, 163
Jacobson, Matthew Frye, 110
James, "Lefty," 176
Jaws of Steel, 138
jazz, 145–146, 172
Jazz Singer, The
  Black press on, 165–167
  casting and filming of, 142–143
  description of, 145–157
  as exception regarding movie
    topics, 139
  impact of, 173–174
  iterations of, 202–203, 214
  Jessel and, 16, 74, 77, 78–80,
    134–135
  Jolson and, 54, 77–78, 81, 110, 120,
    130, 132, 134, 135–136, 143, 144,
    145, 159
  Jolson in, 94, 130
  making of, 60, 120, 122–123, 137
  opening of, 145–148
  Raphaelson and, 58–59, 62
  reviews of, 80–82, 160–162, 165–166,
    168–169, 170–171
  as risk for Warners, 139–140
  success of, 158–164
  television version of, 208–211
  themes of, xii, 91
  uniqueness of, xiii
  version of from 1952, 204–208
  version of from 1980, 212–214
Jeffries, James J., 102

Jessel, George
  background of, 74–76
  on Broadway, 75–77
  fame of, 73–74
  Izzy Murphy movies and, 88,
    90–91, 137, 143
  The Jazz Singer and, 134–135, 136,
    140
  in *The Jazz Singer* (stage version),
    16, 77, 78–80
  Jolson and, 43, 59, 133
  Jolson's death and, 217–218, 219
  name of, 17
  Raphaelson and, 167
  response to movie, 168
  silent films and, 74, 124
  in stage version, 161
Jessel's Troubles, 77
Jessop, George H., 84, 85
Jewish high holidays, working on, 181
"Jewish question," 11–12
Jim Crow, 102, 105
Jim Crow (character), 116
"Joelson Brothers, The," 34–35
Johnson, Jack, 101–102
Johnson-Reed Act (1924), 170
Jolson, Al
  arrival of in America, 21
  biopic about, 191–195
  birth of, 3, 6
  in blackface, 37–38, 55–56, 66, 67,
    94, 109–115, 116–117, 118, 128, 132,
    143, 144, 153, 157, 165, 166, 177,
    192
  comedy routine and, 34–35, 37–38
  discrimination and, 106–107
  early film work of, 128–130
  education of, 7–8
  family and childhood of, 3–15
  first marriage of, 45–46, 100–101
  first solo performance of, 47–48
  funeral for, 217
  greediness of, 95–96

  growing fame/reputation of, 39–42,
    47–50
  Hillcrest Country Club and, 16
  insecurities of, 96, 98
  The Jazz Singer and, 54, 77–78, 81,
    94, 110, 120, 130, 132, 134, 135–136,
    143, 144, 145, 159
  Jessel and, 76, 135
  on Johnson-Jeffries fight, 102
  Keeler and, 177–184, 186–188
  during Korean War, 196–200
  memorial for, 218–219
  Morris and, 32
  in New York, 28–29
  plantation South and, 92–95
  post–*Jazz Singer* films of, 176–177,
    184–185
  radio and, 185–186, 189
  Raphaelson and, 66–67, 68, 77–78,
    167–168
  reputation of, xi–xii
  reviews of, 45, 46, 54–55
  Seldes on, 42–43
  Shuberts and, 53–57, 92, 96–99
  at St. Mary's, 29–30
  success of, 57–59
  teen years of, 26–27
  time off requests from, 98–100
  on vaudeville circuit, 44–47
  in Washington, D.C., 22–23,
    25–27, 33
  Winchell and, 175–176
  during World War II, 189–191,
    195–196
Jolson, Al, Jr., 187, 188
Jolson, Asa Albert, Jr., 191
Jolson, Alicia, 191
Jolson, Harry. *See* Yoelson, Hirsch
  "Harry" (brother)
Jolson Sings Again, 195–196, 197
Jolson Story, The, 191–195, 197
Jolson's 59th Street Theater, 95
Juive, La (Halevy), 150

Kafka, Franz, vii
Kaye, Danny, 16, 17
Kean, W. B., 198
Keaton, Buster, 138
Keeler, Ruby, 177–184, 185, 186–188,
    193, 195
Keeney Theatre, 38
Keeping the Faith, 214
Keller, Henrietta, 45–46, 47, 48, 50,
    100–101, 179
Kelly, Paul B., 199
Kern, Jerome, 53, 146
Keyes, Evelyn, 193
"Khasndl Oyf Shabbos" ("A Cantor
    on the Sabbath"), 132, 134,
    193
Kid Boots, 183
Kid Kabaret, 75
Kinetophone, 124–125
kinetoscopes, 121
King, Martin Luther, Jr., 217
King of Kings, 138
Klein, Arthur, 47, 48
Knoxville Sentinel, 46
Korean War, 189, 196–200
Kosher Kitty Kelly, 88
Koufax, Sandy, 170
Kraft Music Hall, 185
Ku Klux Klan, 89, 102, 128, 140

Laemmle, Carl, 137
Lafayette Theatre, 165
Lamb, Arthur A., 48
Lang, Fritz, 137
Lansky, Meyer, 18, 21
Lasky, Jesse, 41
Lastfogel, Abraham, 32
Lathrop Optimist, The, 80
Leaves of Grass (Whitman), vii
Lee, Peggy, 206
Lefty Louie, 21
Leroy's, 105
Letter to the Father (Kafka), vii

Levinshteyn-Strashunsky, Yoel-
    David, 5
Levinsky (character), 36, 83–84
Levinson, Nathan, 123
Levy, Isaac, 22
Lew Dockstader's Minstrels, 47, 49
Lewis, Al, 77
Lewis, Jerry, 208–211
Lewis, Mary, 78
Life of Emile Zola, The, 186
Lissauer, Herman, 172–173
Little Devil in America, A
    (Abdurraqib), 110–111
"Little of Everything, A," 37–38, 44,
    133
"Living the Life I Love," 207
Lloyd, Harold, 138
Los Angeles Times, 187, 194
loudspeakers, electrical, 125
Lowe, John, 187
Lower East Side Jews, 51
Lubitsch, Ernst, 62
Luciano, Lucky, 18
lynchings, 102

MacArthur, Douglas, 199
Magnin, Edgar F., 171–172, 173
Main, Walter L., 29
Majestic, 129
"Mammy," 65
Mammy, 184
Mammy's Boy, 129
Mann, Thomas, 165
Marsalis, Wynton, 145
Martin, Dean, 209
Marx, Julius "Groucho," 16–17, 20, 75,
    114, 211
Marx Brothers, 32, 42
Maugham, W. Somerset, 61
Mayer, Louis B., 16
Mayhew, Stella, 53
McAvoy, May, 138, 142, 143, 149
McCarthy, Joe, 204

"Meine Yiddishe Mama," 94–95
melting pot, concept of, 71, 91
Mendelssohn, Moses, 12
*Mendicant's Son, or, the Jew of
    Southwark, The* (Stirling), 83
Merchant of Venice (Shakespeare),
    82–83
Merwin, Ted, 133
Metropolis, 137
Metropolitan Opera House,
    126–127
mezuzah, 8
military service, 4–5
Mills, Florence, 106, 107–108, 109
Milton, John, 171
minstrelsy, 56–57, 111, 115–116
Modern View, The, 81, 82
Moore, Fred E., 34
Morgen Journal, 164
Morison, Patricia, 190
Morris, William, 19, 32, 41
Morris, William, Jr., 32
Morton, Jelly Roll, 145
Moving Picture World, 137, 142–143
Muni, Paul (Frederich Meier
    Weisenfreund), 131–132, 134, 155,
    186
Murnau, F. W., 137
Musser, Charles, 113, 114
"My Gal Sal," 148
"My Mammy," 94–95, 110, 157,
    168–169, 186
"My Old New Hampshire Home," 48
"Mystery of Ravensdale Court, The"
    (Fletcher), 61
Mystery of the Louvre, The, 138

NAACP, 103, 119
names, changes in, 17
NBC radio shows, 185
Negro Actors' Guild, 107
New York & Philadelphia Telephone
    and Telegraph Company, 35

New York Amsterdam News, 108, 117,
    118, 119, 165
New York *Daily News,* 74, 80, 179, 182
New York Evening World, The, 40
New York Philharmonic, 127
New York Society for the Prevention
    of Cruelty to Children (Gerry
    Society), 28, 29, 75
New York Times, The
    on *The Auctioneer,* 85
    on *Big Boy,* 112–113
    on Curtis, 84
    on *Don Juan,* 127
    on *The Jazz Singer,* 159, 177
    on *The Jazz Singer* remakes, 208, 213
    on *The Jazz Singer* (stage
        version), 81
    on *Jolson Sings Again,* 195
    on *The Jolson Story,* 192
    on *La Belle Paree,* 54
    on *Private Izzy Murphy,* 90
    on *Welcome Stranger,* 86
    on Winter Garden show, 59
Newsboys' Lodging House, 28
Nichols, Anne, 88, 89

Oakland Tribune, 40
Oberon, Merle, 190
O'Brien, Ray, 101
"Oh How I Laugh When I Think
    How I Cried About You," 76
Oland, Warner, 142–143
"Old Folks Back Home, The," 93
Oliver Twist (Dickens), 83
Olivier, Laurence, 212–213, 214
Olympic Stadium, 200
One-Round Hogan, 138
Ostjuden, 17–18, 205

Paducah Sun-Democrat (Kentucky),
    160
Pale of Settlement, xiii, xv, 3–4, 93,
    147, 155, 202

Paley, William, 211–212
Palmer, Joe, 37, 41, 44, 133
Parks, Larry, 192, 193, 196
Parsons, Louella, 180, 199
Parted Curtains, 122
Passing of the Great Race or the Racial Basis of European History, The (Grant), 170
Peck, Gregory, 141, 203
PeeWee Quartet, 20
Phantom of the Opera, The, 215
Piccadilly Theatre, 126
Pickford, Mary, 124, 138
Picon, Molly, 209
Pittsburgh Courier, The, 117, 118, 119, 166
Plantation Act, A, 128, 129–130, 149, 158, 159
pogroms, xiii, 3, 147
Pollard (juggler), 46
Porter, Cole, 191
Potok, Chaim, 214
Powell, Dick, 182
Presley, Elvis, 32
Private Izzy Murphy, 88, 90, 134, 137
Producers, The, 173
Protocols of the Elders of Zion, The, 140
Proust, Marcel, xiii

Rabbit's Foot Company, 104
radio shows, 185–186, 189
Radner, Gilda, 164, 173
Rainey, Ma, 42, 103–104, 115
Raleigh Hotel, 25
Raphaelson, Samson. See also *Jazz Singer, The*
  "Day of Atonement" and, 61–65, 69–72, 77–78, 134, 164
  jazz and, 145–146
  Jessel and, 77, 78–79
  Jolson and, 58–60, 66–67, 68, 96, 134
  making of *The Jazz Singer* and, 123, 137
  original storyline of, 80–81, 91, 154–155
  purchase of rights from, 140
  response to movie, 167–168
  on universal theme of story, 164
Rathbone, Basil, 186
Rathenau, Walter, xiii
Reno Divorce, A, 138
Republic Theatre, 166
Rice, Thomas Dartmouth, 116
Rich & Hoppe's Big Company of Fun Makers, 29
Richman, Harry, 107
Richmond Item, The (Indiana), 161
Rigoletto, 127
Riis, Jacob, 23, 28, 31
Rin Tin Tin, 122, 138, 143
Rise of Rosie O'Reilly, The, 177
rituals, 7, 8
Robeson, Paul, 106
Robinson, Edward G., 186
Robinson Crusoe, Jr., 66, 68, 98, 99
"Rockabye Your Baby with a Dixie Melody," 67, 128, 186, 198
Rogers, Will, 75
Rogin, Michael, 110
Romeo and Juliet (Shakespeare), 89–90
Rose, Julian, 35–36, 83–84
Rosenberg, Julius and Ethel, 204
Rosenblatt, Josef (Yossele), 68, 142, 150–151, 152, 207
Rosenthal, Herman, 21
Roth, Philip, 215
Rothschild, Baron de, xiii
Rothstein, Arnold, 21
Round Table, 16–17, 18–19
Royal Theatre, 165–166
Runyon, Damon, 175

Russian Empire, xii, xiii, 3–4, 11–12,
    121, 202, 203
Ruth, Babe, xi, 30, 55, 122

Sailor Izzy Murphy, 90–91, 137, 143
Salomon, Haym, 205
Sam'l of Posen (Curtis), 84–85
Sammond, Nic, 109–110
San Francisco Examiner, 183
Saposnik, Irving, 94, 166
Saroyan, William, 73
Sartre, Jean-Paul, 46
Saturday Night Live, 164
Say It with Songs, 184
Scandals, 101
Scarface, 132
Schubart, Jacob, 51–52
"Second Hand Rose," 133
Seinfeld, 164
Seinfeld, Jerry, 173
Seldes, Gilbert, 42–43, 56, 59
Sennett, Mack, 138
Sentinel, The, 169
Seredzius, 3–4, 9–10, 190
Seroff, Doug, 115
Shakespeare, William, 82–83
Shamekin News Dispatch, The
    (Pennsylvania), 161
Shapiro, Bernstein & Co., 48
Shapiro, Maurice, 48
Shop Around the Corner, The, 62
Shubert, J.J., 50, 52–53, 54, 55, 92,
    97–100, 107, 129
Shubert, Levi "Lee," 51–52
Shubert, Sammy, 52
Shubert Organization, 32, 41,
    52–53, 55, 57, 95, 96–100, 107,
    183
Shuffle Along, 105–106, 108
Sidewalks of New York, 177
Sieben, Pearl, 69, 176, 178, 186,
    187
Siegel, Bugsy, 18, 21

silent films, 123–124
Silverbush, Cantor, 165
Silverman, Simon J. "Sime," 32, 41,
    101–102
Silvers, Phil, 75
Simon, Neil, 164, 173
Singing Fool, The, 176–177, 178, 184
Sinton Hotel, 45
Sissle, Noble, 105–107
Sister Carrie, 184
Skolsky, Sydney, 182
Slightly Used, 138, 143
Slives (clown), 46
Smith, Bessie, 42, 58, 104
soldiers, billeting of, 10
Solomon, Isadore, 86
"Some of These Days," 104
song pluggers, 74, 124
spirituals, 113
St. Francis Hotel, 200
St. Mary's Industrial School for Boys,
    29–30
Star Is Born, A, 214
Star Tribune, 46
Stiller, Ben, 214
Stirling, Edward, 83
Stork Club, 44, 175
"Stormy Weather," 105
Story of Louis Pasteur, The, 186
Strausbaugh, John, 116
Streisand, Barbra, 214
Strelinger, Moritz Bertrand, 84–85
Sunshine Boys, The, 173
Suspicion, 62
"Swanee," 68, 186, 197
"Swanee River," 93
synchronized sound, 123–125, 126–127,
    149, 152–153, 158, 159

Talley, Marion, 127
Tannhäuser, 127
Tarantino's, 200
Taylor, Elizabeth, 217

251

Temple Israel, 217
Theatrical Syndicate, 32
Thomas, Danny, 204
Times, The (Shreveport, Louisiana), 160
Tin Pan Alley, 36, 41, 48, 93, 140
title cards, 127, 154, 158
"Toot, Toot, Tootsie," 149
Tracked by the Police, 138
Tracy, Spencer, 186
Tripler Hospital, 199
Trotsky, Leon, 202
Truman, Harry, 199
Tuck, Louis, 19
Tucker, Sophie, 19, 104, 116, 133, 145
Tunney, Gene, 144
"Two Patches from a Crazy Quilt," 75
tzitzit, 8

Umbria, S. S., 15
United Artists, 185
Universal Pictures, 137
Universal Studios, 180
Unorthodox, 214–215

vacuum tube amplification, 125
Valentino, Rudolph, 138
Valéry, Paul, 130
Vallee, Rudy, 185
Vanderbilt, William K., 52
Variety, 32, 41, 49, 54, 96, 101–102, 107, 129
vaudeville, 26, 29, 33–34, 35–36, 44–47
Vera Violetta, 55, 96
Victoria Burlesquers, 33
Victoria Palace, 75
Victoria Theatre, 47–48
Vilner Balebesl, Der, 5
Vitaphone, 126–127, 130, 139–140, 142, 143, 144, 158–159, 165–166, 177
von Sternberg, Josef, 137
Von Tilzer, Harry, 37, 41, 48–49, 117, 186

Wallace, Mike, 74
Wallis, Hal, 176
Wardell, Harry, 107
Warfield, David, 85
Warner, Albert, 120–122, 141
Warner, Harry, 120–122, 125–126, 135, 140, 141
Warner, Jack, 16, 60, 120–123, 126–128, 130, 135–136, 140, 141–142, 149
Warner, Sam, 120–123, 125–126, 127, 135, 141–142, 157
Warner Bros., 60, 90, 120–123, 126, 134–142, 181
Warner Theatre, 126, 127
Washington, D.C., 21–22
Washington Tribune, The, 37, 166
Waters, Ethel, 42, 58, 104–105, 115
Weisenfreund, Frederick Meier (Paul Muni), 131–132, 134, 155, 186
Welcome Stranger (Hoffman), 86
Western Electric, 123, 125, 126
"Where Did Robinson Crusoe Go with Friday on Saturday Night?", 66
Whirl of Society, The, 55–56
whistling, 40
White Elephant Saloon, 104
Whitman, Walt, vii
Whoopee!, 182–183
Wigwam Theatre, 46
William Morris Agency, 37, 41
Williams, Bert, 104, 115
Williams, Paul R., 218
Wilson, Woodrow, 68–69
Winchell, June, 176
Winchell, Walter, 57, 75, 124, 175–176, 180–181, 184, 217
Wings, 138
Winter Garden Theatre, 53–55, 59, 76, 92, 108, 112, 143, 157, 168–169, 177, 183
Wisconsin Jewish Chronicle, The, 81–82

Wisconsin State Journal, 80
Women's Zionist Organization of
    America, 161
Wonder Bar, 132, 134, 184–185
Wonskolaser, Benjamin, 120–121,
    142
Woollcott, Alexander, 86
World of Our Fathers (Howe), 32
World War II, 189–191, 195–196, 197

"Yaaka Hula Hickey Dula," 66, 67
Yankee Doodle Dandy, 123
Yiddish theater, 5, 131
Yoelson, Asa (birth name), xii, 3, 6.
    See also Jolson, Al
Yoelson, Etta, 6, 14
Yoelson, Hessi, 27, 30–31, 69
Yoelson, Hirsch "Harry" (brother)
    childhood of, 7–8, 10, 11–12, 176
    comedy routine and, 34–35, 37, 38,
        133
    emigration and, 13, 14–15
    on family life, 6
    on Jolson's marriage, 45–46
    in New York, 28–29

on Seredzius, 4
in Washington, D.C., 22–23,
    25–27, 33
Yoelson, Moshe (father)
    absence of at performance, 69
    Al's early career and, 33
    in America, 21–23, 27
    background of, 5, 6–7
    death of, 194
    description of, 30–31
    emigration of, 13–15
    Jolson's childhood and, 8–9
    retrieval of Al by, 30
Yoelson, Rose, 6, 14, 27
Yossi, Haym, 7, 13–14
"You Are My Sunshine," 199
Your Best Friend, 122
Your Show of Shows, 173, 210

Zanuck, Darryl, 135, 157
Ziegfeld, Florenz, 182–183
Ziegfeld Follies, 19–20, 50, 53, 75,
    104, 133
Zionism, 11
Zucker, Adolph, 16

A NOTE ABOUT THE AUTHOR

Richard Bernstein has been a reporter, foreign correspondent, and culture critic for forty years, starting at *Time* magazine, then at *The New York Times,* and currently as a freelance writer. His foreign postings for *Time* and *The New York Times* include Hong Kong, Beijing, Paris, and Berlin. He has written ten books and articles for numerous publications, including *The New York Review of Books, The Atlantic, Foreign Affairs, The Wall Street Journal,* and others. He lives in Brooklyn, New York.

A NOTE ON THE TYPE

This book was set in Adobe Garamond. Designed for the Adobe Corporation by Robert Slimbach, the fonts are based on types first cut by Claude Garamond (ca. 1480–1561). Garamond was a pupil of Geoffroy Tory and is believed to have followed the Venetian models, although he introduced a number of important differences, and it is to him that we owe the letter we now know as "old style." He gave to his letters a certain elegance and feeling of movement that won their creator an immediate reputation and the patronage of Francis I of France.

North Market Street Graphics,
Lancaster, Pennsylvania

Printed and bound by
Friesens,
Altona, Manitoba

Designed by Maria Carella